CW00515156

The
HEALING
STREAM

Laurence Catlow

MERLIN UNWIN BOOKS

First published in Great Britain by Merlin Unwin Books, 2016
Copyright © Laurence Catlow 2016

Merlin Unwin Books
Palmers House
7 Corve Street
Ludlow
Shropshire SY8 1DB
U.K.

www.merlinunwin.co.uk

Designed and set in Times New Roman by Merlin Unwin
Printed and bound by TJ International, Padstow, England

ISBN 978-1-910723-27-2

CONTENTS

To Helen
to Ron and Marion
to Andrew, Kelvin, Oliver and Richard

PART I

CHAPTER ONE

It all began on the Ribble and I was already nineteen. I had, of course, gone fishing in the earlier summers of my boyhood. I had roamed the banks of forbidden streams with one friend or another, half hoping to be spotted by the farmer or by the beck-watch and so rewarded with the excitement of a chase. I had dug worms and, with the help of a decrepit rod, I had flung them into the depths of a hidden pool, almost believing in the monstrous trout that were rumoured to live there. I had set off fishing and soon lost interest, wandering off to explore winding brooks where I had never been before, returning home in the late afterglow of a summer's evening and suddenly remembering that I had left my rod leaning against the willows up there on the corner above the ..

There was no sense of vocation in these early excursions; they were inspired by boredom or restlessness or by some sudden impulse of adventure. I did not, as a boy of twelve or thirteen, think of myself as a fisherman. I was a cricketer, with ambitions to make the sport my life and some day open the batting for England. I was a reader of books and even then I was trying to write them myself. I was a cricketer and an author, though the second of these callings was concealed from the world, hidden away in secret notebooks that have long since vanished and that no one else has ever seen. I was all sorts of other things, with a deep passion of commitment, for at least a month or a fortnight, but I was never a fisherman except for want of something better to do. And when, from time to time, I did go fishing, I had soon had enough of it and soon turned to something else.

There came a change when I was fourteen and my parents bought me a fly rod. It was a Mitre Hardy, eight and a half feet long. There were three pieces of gleaming yellow cane and although, once I had put them together, I had little idea what to do next, I immediately recognized that my new rod was beautiful, and that the suppleness of its motion was a pleasure to the hand. It was altogether different from those ancient greenheart sticks and those short stiff spinning rods of cheap fibreglass that I had taken fishing before the Mitre Hardy came along. We lived near the Ribble and I often saw fly fishers on the river. I had watched them and admired the grace of their casting; I had sometimes met them and they had seemed men haunted by pleasant visions. They had seemed quiet and contented men, and I had felt that some day I should like to become one of them myself. But it was a shallow feeling without any intensity or permanence.

It changed a little once I owned the Mitre Hardy. By now I had formed a vague conception of fly fishing as an art and a mystery: as a higher calling than the pursuit of trout by any other method. By this time I had also at least half-acknowledged that I was unlikely to achieve distinction with a cricket bat in my hands. And, whether I had acknowledged it or not, it was certainly the case that, away from books and other people, my greatest happiness was found out under the sky: watching birds, finding – and sometimes plundering – their nests, following becks to their source high in the hills, exploring woods and fields and perhaps dimly conscious that there was something in the sunlight and the water and the leaves and the grass, something too in all the life that belonged to them, that was of special and sustaining importance to me. I loved to be outdoors and the time was coming when I should need some discipline to give direction and purpose to the delight I found there. I was very slow to recognise that I had been born a fisherman; it was the Mitre Hardy that led me at last to this wonderful truth, but it was a truth that I only grasped when I had owned it for at least five years.

I had been given the Mitre Hardy because I had expressed a passing interest in fly fishing. Inspired by ownership I made some attempts to learn how to use it. I bought a few books belonging to the

How to Catch Them series. Two or three of them still sit on my shelves; one is by L. Baverstock and is called *Brook Trout: How To Catch Them.* It is not primarily about fly fishing, but there are chapters dealing with the dry and the wet fly and it contains some admirably straightforward advice on casting. I have no idea who Baverstock was, or what the L stands for, but I am grateful to him, because it was with his help that I learned how to throw a fly with at least occasional delicacy, though I did not learn how to land or hook or even to rise a single trout.

There was still no dedication in my efforts to become a fly fisher. Each summer, at some stage of its course, brought a brief attack of trout-fever, seizing me with the urge to be on the edge of running water, waving my rod to and fro in the desperate hope of somehow charming a fish from what seemed its almost impregnable security beneath the surface of the river. But it never worked and each day of failure made the prospect of success seem more and more remote until finally it seemed unattainable. Each summer, after I had tried in vain to catch a trout for a few weeks, I decided that I should never learn the trick, deciding at the same time that it was a trick of no real importance. In this mood of disillusion I would put the Mitre Hardy away for the season, suddenly convinced that what I really wanted to do was to play tennis or climb hills, write stories or study the habits of birds, or simply wander the countryside in search of things to interest me. And so the Mitre Hardy would go to sleep in a corner of my bedroom while, down in the cellar, my waders lay crumpled and forgotten, until another summer came along, bringing with it a few days, perhaps even a fortnight when trout-fever laid hold of me and my rod found employment again.

One summer I smashed the tip of the Mitre Hardy and it was almost a year before I could be bothered to get it mended. There was also a summer – I cannot remember which of these summers came first – when I agreed to sell it to a friend, together with my Kingfisher line and my box of flies. I think this was the summer when I realised that golf was all that mattered in life, and I think my heart was set on a new driver. But my parents heard of this plan and would have none of it; it made no difference how often I shouted that it was *my* rod and that I should be allowed to do whatever I wanted with my own property.

They were kind parents; perhaps they were inclined to be indulgent parents. But on this matter they stood firm, rejecting their son's loud assertion of his rights, insisting, in the face of all my arguments and all my indignation, that I could not sell the Mitre Hardy, that it was mine to use and not mine to sell and that the time would come when I would want it again.

I hated my parents for this. I ranted and raved and doubtless, between fresh outbursts of rage, I sulked for at least a week. At the time, of course, I could not recognise that this opposition was among my parents' best gifts to me, for without it fishing would almost certainly have been permanently discarded. And then I should never have caught a trout; I should never have fished my way up the Wharfe as the evening air turned cool and the water turned white and the blue wings brought great trout sliding out from under the roots; I should never, while moist shadows crept silently over the river and over the riverside fields, have lain sprawling in the grass on the banks of the Eden, gazing at nothing in particular and possessed by a deeper happiness than is reasonable for any creature aware of its own mortality; and I should never, on the last evening of two or three successive Septembers, have stood on the bridge over the Wenning at Clapham Station, staring upstream to the dim arches of the viaduct and already full of restless longing for the April morning when I should next be there with a fishing rod in my hand.

The Mitre Hardy was not sold. The Kingfisher no. 3 remained mine, along with my box of flies and a few spools of nylon and those other bits and pieces that made up my small store of tackle. They all waited patiently for their unwilling owner's next need of them. There may have been a summer when they were never used at all; but there came a September – it was the September before I went off to university in London – and I was seized again by the old urge. Towards the end of the same September there came an evening that found me by the Ribble; it was an evening of damp and cloudy stillness, with a grey, sliding light in the water and with soft sounds drifting on the grey air. The river was flowing on its way very quietly, while a few trout rose with gentle persistence to make delicate rings on the surface of the water; it was as though they were responding to some creative impulse, expressing themselves in exquisite and evanescent patterns of flowing light and shadow; they were sculptors of water and you might never have guessed that hunger had anything to do with it.

By now there was something different about my fishing. I had still to catch a trout, although I think that I had at last managed to rise a few of them. I was not as yet a fisher who had caught a fish, but I seem to remember that, by the age of nineteen, during those September excursions to the Ribble as I waited to go off to London – I seem to remember that by now I had begun deliberately to admire and to absorb some of the special beauties that are revealed to fishermen. I can still see the rings of those trout spreading and fading on the grey water; I know that I saw them as graceful and affecting forms and that I wanted them to remain a part of my life; I also wanted, and now with a real intensity of desire, to reach into them with my rod, my line and my fly, and to draw forth the wonderful creatures that left them as their brief emblems on the surface of the river.

That same September I had taken some books from the town library. I can no longer remember which books they were – there were three or four of them – but they all insisted that fishing, especially fly fishing, was the calling of a lifetime; I cannot think they were good books, for good books make sharper memories; I think they were probably books that lingered in the water meadows as the sun's golden orb sank flaming in the West, as the velvet gloaming stole over the riverside scene and the first fluttering bats began to squeak their vespers over the sliding stream; I think they were probably unimaginatively poetical books about the angler's vocation, but it was partly their influence that inspired in me the first real stirrings of a sense of dedication.

I began consistently to think of myself as a fisherman, though only as an apprentice with most of the rudiments still to learn; I began, between cigarettes, to smoke a pipe, and I began to believe that one day I should master the fly fisher's skills; I began to believe that the day would come when I should catch a trout; I knew this would bring a sense of complete fulfilment but, even without that first trout to claim my heart and bind me fast, I remember thinking that, even in London,

I should remain in essence a man of the riverbank.

Those unmemorable books affected me in another, less wholesome way; for between them they managed to turn a blundering beginner into a dry fly purist. It took me years to unlearn this thoughtless and snobbish affectation. Previously my efforts to catch a trout had been made almost exclusively with wet flies fished downstream, although there were a few dry flies in my box and occasionally I had tied one of them to the end of my line, turned myself round and tried to place my fly somewhere near a rising trout. But my new books now persuaded me that the dry fly was a style of fly fishing far above all others, a style that all fishers of true discernment recognised as the only proper way to catch a trout. And so it was that, even before I had ever caught one, I had proclaimed myself a higher sort of fisher by swearing unswerving allegiance to the floating fly.

The young fisher, watching the rings of those rising fish on that September evening more than forty years ago, had never caught a trout; but he still thought of himself as a decidedly superior sort of fisher, because he was proposing to cast into them with a fly that floated on the surface of the water. Quite possibly the pattern he chose had been dressed to sink and was only kept from achieving its purpose by generous applications of liquid Mucilin. Whatever it was meant to be, it passed for a dry fly; it was a fly of no great size and I am almost certain that its body was of peacock herl.

I have forgotten the precise details of its size and design. I cannot remember whether it was a Coachman or a Red Tag, a Treacle Parkin or a Black and Peacock Spider. The hook was probably a fourteen, but it might have been a twelve or possibly a sixteen, although it seems unlikely that in those early days I ever fished with hooks so small. Its name and its size and the details of its dressing are lost to me but, whatever sort and pattern of fly it was, it was certainly the most important fly of my fishing life; it was the fly that turned an inconstant affection into an abiding passion; it was the fly that finally confirmed my vocation, the fly that bound me in willing thrall to the deep enchantment of running water and made me a fisher for life; and this final stage of my conversion took place when, on a calm bend of the river, with the light already thickening towards darkness, I cast this greatest of flies into the rings of a rising trout.

My fly probably fell with a splash and was probably floating among half a dozen coils of nylon, but in spite of this the miracle now occurred, when the trout beneath my fly rose unhurriedly and sucked it down; in doing this he somehow managed to attach himself to the hook and, somehow or other, he also managed to remain attached while, in a frenzy of panic and exultation, I hauled him through the water, trembling in the ecstasy of a tight line and terrified by the black thought that it might suddenly go slack. But the hook held its purchase and the line stayed tight and very soon there was a trout flapping and splashing somewhere in the dim light beneath the rim of my waders.

I had no landing net and the tactic of beaching a fish was unknown to me. I could not have moved anyway, for I was bewitched by what had happened, bewitched and rooted to my station in the middle of the river. I remember thinking that, on a tight line, I might hold my victim's head out of the water until at last he choked to death; but this desperate stratagem was rejected almost as soon as it had been considered. I knew next to nothing about fishing, but one thing I did know was that fishers were kind-hearted men who killed their fish quickly. And so reaching out, in something like an agony of fear, I grabbed my trout and managed, through the intervention of the evening's second or third miracle, to secure a hold firm enough to lift him from the water. Then I stuffed him, still attached to the line and the hook, into the breast pocket of my anorak. It was only now that I dared to work the fly free of his jaw; the barb embedded itself somewhere deep inside the pocket and I cut away the cast with savage impatience. I remembered that a swift death would be a mercy and, stumbling and splashing to the bank, I beat my breast with a stone until the twitching shape inside my pocket became still. I had killed a ten inch trout.

There was no thought of fishing on. A single trout was complete and perfect fulfilment. He was drawn from the pocket and, in the soft shadows, every dim spot, every fin, every line and feature of his form was admired with reverent and gloating pride. Then he was wrapped in a butterbur leaf and returned to his pocket and it was time for home.

In the rapture of that first fish, as I scrambled onto my bicycle and pedalled home furiously through the falling darkness, with no lamp to warn motorists of my presence on the road and with a fragile rod tip waving somewhere in front of me – as I raced home so impatiently I was no longer a young man of nineteen with his schooldays already behind him, a young man who, standing on the threshold of the adult world, loved Vergil and Wagner and sometimes argued about the existence of God; I was no longer an inquisitive adolescent with an unhealthy appetite for beer and a mind filled with prurient thoughts about girls' bodies. Suddenly I was a boy again, a boy who could barely contain the sense of triumph now swelling inside him, a boy whose only concern was with the fish in his pocket and with his passionate longing to show it to his mother.

There were not many people still abroad: only a dog-walker or two and a few couples out for their late-evening stroll. They were lucky the serenity of their twilight thoughts was not suddenly shattered by wild cries from a dim form in the middle of the road; for I wanted to roar at them, I wanted to pull out my fish and wave it in their faces; I wanted to make them realise that the hurtling figure on the bicycle was no ordinary human being but rather one who had just caught a trout. I wanted, while displaying my trout for their admiration and astonishment, to tell them how it had risen and swallowed my fly, how I had fought and tamed it and brought it to the bank. But there was something that held me back from such extravagant behaviour, and it was something deeper than common prudence or the suspicion that late strollers and dog-walkers might refuse to be impressed; it was rather my small boy's conviction that the treasure in my pocket was too precious for public exhibition of this sort, that the right of first gaze properly belonged to a mother; and that, only when she had taken her fill of so marvellous a sight, would it be time for the rest of the world to lose itself in wonder and in praise.

I can no longer recall the moment of homecoming itself or my mother's response to the creature that I pulled from my pocket. I am sure she made appropriate noises and I know that she cooked the trout for my breakfast the next morning. It must have been a hurried breakfast, for I was beside myself with impatience to be down by the river again. I remember hooking two trout that morning, but they both came free when I tried to repeat the previous evening's performance and lift them from the water by hand. The age of miracles seemed to have ended, which made the necessity of a landing net very painfully clear to me. But it was not until the following April that, now properly equipped with a cheap net – which served me for something like twenty years – I stood once again on the edge of running water. For the day of those two lost trout was also the last day of my season, of that glorious season that gave me my first trout and made me a fisher for life.

CHAPTER TWO

The first trout of my fishing life came at just the right time; if I had gone off to London without the remembered glory of that cloudy September evening, I might never have picked up my rod again. The dim sense of calling that I was beginning to feel, even before its sudden confirmation by the catching of a ten inch trout, would probably have faded quickly and soon been quite forgotten. I should have spent my summers travelling abroad, like most of my friends, or reading classical texts, like just a few of them; and so, along with golf and half a dozen brief adolescent passions, fishing would have been remembered as something trivial that belonged to the past. My waders would have grown mould in a damp corner of the cellar; perhaps the Mitre Hardy would at last have been sold; perhaps it would have stayed propped in its corner of my bedroom, undisturbed and unremembered, for seasons on end; and the money that bought me my first landing net would probably have been put towards the cost of a Greek dictionary, or bought me some tobacco and a few pints of beer.

That first net fell to pieces at last; I have bought other nets since, lost some of them and been given several more. I have worn out at least a dozen pairs of waders since that first pair was finally thrown away; but my first fly rod, the old eight-and-a-half-foot Mitre Hardy, still hangs on the wall in the same tattered green slip. Beside it there are three Sharpes, an Eighty Three and a Fario and a Featherlight; there are two more by Hardy an eight foot Perfection and a nine foot Halford Knockabout. The Perfection is now my rod of choice and it is years since the Mitre Hardy emerged from its slip; perhaps some day I shall take it fishing again and bless the memory of the parents who forbade its sale and so, without knowing it, made me a fisher for life.

Among the books that I bought in my first weeks at university, mostly books on Latin and Greek grammar and editions of classical texts, were two that had no connection with the Ancient World; they were Lord Grey's *Fly Fishing* and Plunket Greene's *Where The Bright Waters Meet*. Already I owned one or two fishing books, but these were of the how to catch them sort, even if they did not, like Baverstock's *Brook Trout*, belong to the How to Catch Them series. I had read and unwillingly returned those books from the town library, but it did not take long for me to realise that their authors – I wonder if Dewar was one of them – could not hold a candle either to Grey or to Plunket Greene, who had soon come to mean just as much to me, in their own way, as did Homer and Vergil; for they helped, during that first real close season of my fishing life, and amid a welter of new experiences, to sustain my conviction that to be a fisherman was a deep and very special blessing. I had caught only one trout, which had turned me immediately into a passionate angler; but I was an angler with no hope of catching his second trout until at last next April came along. And so I fed my longing on the pages of *Fly Fishing* and *Where The Bright Waters Meet*. I would turn to them before sleep, when I found that Grey's praise of the Itchen and Plunket Greene's loving tribute to the little river Bourne both glowed more warmly in a mind mellowed by two or three pints of beer.

I read of southern rivers that I had never seen; they seemed wonderful rivers where great trout rose to suck down fishermen's flies; but very often, as I read of the Itchen and the Bourne, my mind's eye was moving along the banks of a northern trout stream, along the banks of the Ribble just above Brungerley bridge; and it was always September there; it was always a cloudy evening of soft and merging colours, an evening so quiet that the splash of a small trout seemed to shatter a reverent silence; and always, near the bank, there was an old bicycle imperfectly concealed in a decaying jungle of butterbur leaves, while out in the river, covered in a grey anorak and a pair of black waders, stood a figure with a fishing rod, casting his fly among the rising trout.

One of the few fishing books that had travelled south with me to London was a book with no literary pretensions and with no purpose of teaching its readers how to catch fish. It was a small paper-backed book, roughly the size of a pocket diary, and it was already dog-eared when I had owned it for less than a month. I bought it in Ambleside, perhaps a week before catching my first trout. I bought it because it was raining, because I had taken shelter in a bookshop and felt determined to buy something; I bought it because it was about fishing and because it was cheap and because I could not find a book that I really wanted to buy.

And yet this unassuming little book, which was bought in an idle moment and might well have been lost within a week, still occupies a position of high honour on my shelves. Somehow it survived its first days in my ownership and was soon transformed, by the self-sacrifice of a single trout on a cloudy September evening, into a possession beyond price, into a book even more marvellous than either *Fly Fishing* or *Where The Bright Waters Meet;* for I discovered that, whenever I opened its pages, I was immediately carried far from my surroundings, spirited off to strange and enticing lands of infinite content. I found that I could open it in London, in a students' hall just off the Tottenham Court Road, and within seconds the Tottenham Court Road and with it the whole sprawling mass of London, together with all its brash sounds and festering smells, had been left far behind, had lost any power to influence or to intrude; for the page before me, whichever one of them it was that I happened to be reading, had taken me away fishing – either to the bare border hills of Scotland or to the tumbling streams of the Yorkshire dales, perhaps to the Wharfe or to the Nidd or the Swale; sometimes to remote tarns in the Lake District where char and mysterious fish called gwyniad were said to swim among the trout. I was taken to these and to hundreds of other places, and in all of them I caught fish.

I would open this wonderful book for five minutes in the morning, before settling down to Plautus or to Homer. Sometimes five minutes became half an hour. I would turn to it in the afternoon when I decided that I deserved some relief from Plato or Vergil. Often

I preferred it to Plunket Greene or to Grey for reading on the edge of sleep. It was, throughout my undergraduate days, the best book I knew for soothing the guilty throb of a hangover. I fancy that its authors knew nothing of these marvellous powers. It was called *The Northern Angler's Handbook*. It had been conceived by T.K. Wilson; its thirteenth edition had been revised and edited by Ernest Merritt. The cover carries the contented image of a fisher, with a rod in his hand and a deerstalker hat on his head. I know that it was a cheap book but I cannot tell you precisely how much it cost, because the corner of the cover that once advertised the price has long since been worn away. It was most certainly a bargain, for its descriptions of fishing waters in the North of England and the Scottish Borders, with information about who controlled them and whether day or weekly tickets were available, and with comments on the sort of sport you might expect at different times of the year: all this gave me untold hours of delight whenever I was weary with work or with London.

Within a few years, moreover, *The Northern Angler's Handbook* had performed a still greater, an inestimable and lasting service by leading me to the Kilnsey water of the Wharfe. First of all it took me to the Wenning, and it was at least partly responsible for my appearance, fifteen or so years later, on the banks of the Eden round Kirkby Stephen. It is an unpretentious little handbook, but it is no exaggeration to say that, between them, T.K. Wilson and Ernest Merritt have influenced my life as decisively as any literary contact from Homer to P.G. Wodehouse. May God bless them and keep them happy to eternity in the spacious and exclusive region of paradise that he surely reserves for Yorkshiremen who have served humanity with unusual distinction.

In the January of my first year as an undergraduate, following the advice of *The Northern Angler's Handbook,* I applied for a season ticket to fish the Ingleborough Estate water of the Wenning. It cost me five pounds, for which I gained access to about five miles of fishing in one of the loveliest stretches of country to which a fishing rod has ever taken me. Even today it sometimes comes between me and my sleep to think how the Wenning was later treated by men who were supposed to look after her. But when first I came there the little river still wound unmolested through the lonely fields that spread out on either side of her banks.

There was a mile of water on the very top of the river. Beyond this were the becks that formed her: Clapham Beck, Austwick Beck, Fen Beck. The lower limit of the estate fishing was the road bridge below the railway station. About a hundred yards upstream, a tall viaduct took trains rumbling over the river. There was no walkway underneath. I used to wade through the water, which was passable in all but the biggest of floods, where, with the sound of each step echoing under the tall arches, I left behind me the thoughts and feelings of common reality and splashed my way into a better world.

It was on the Wenning that I first spent long days on a river, from mid-morning to moonrise and beyond; it was on the Wenning that I first surrendered myself completely to the strong enchantments of running water. And, ever since those two university summers on the Wenning, I have never reckoned days that are not full days as true fishing days; for, except occasionally on summer evenings, just a few hours is not enough; there is not time for the total immersion of the spirit that is needed for a river and a fishing rod to work their marvellous influence. There are still days when I rush to the Wharfe or the Eden for just a few hours; very occasionally they are wonderful, these little fragments of fishing days, sending me home enriched and restored; more often, even if I have caught good fish, I feel that just a few hours has not been long enough for me to find the way back into my fishing world and to drink in the healing power of being and belonging there.

The Wenning flowed down to the viaduct between straight banks, with birches and alders all along one side. The water was mostly shallow here, sparkling over the gravel and between the rocks. Then the trees changed sides and, beyond them, the river rushed round a double bend, with a high bank on one side, eaten away at its base by the pressure of the current; on the other side grass ran smoothly down to the pebbled margin of the water. After this came a line of short pools, with the river carrying through them the blue or the grey of the sky. A sharp corner, with deep smooth water, led round to an old plank bridge that I never trusted. Beyond the bridge there were mossy shallows, with gorse on the banks and with hawthorns leaning over the water; beyond the shallows there were two deep, rounded pools that brought me to a wooded corner, then to a much deeper, shadowed pool. The river turned again, widened out into shallow and windy flats, and then flowed briefly between high banks, until at last it reached the long, dark pool where the two becks met, where the salmon rested and reddened in autumn as they waited for high water to take them to the spawning beds.

She was a lovely river, a limestone river, and she flowed, twisting and turning, through buttercup meadows and through rushy pastures where lapwings tumbled and snipe drummed and curlews filled the air with sadness. The breeze blew with the cold purity of early spring days, with the fragrance of May blossom and the high-summer sweetness of elderflowers, with the smell of mown hay and meadowsweet and with the sharpness of wild mint; and over the whole landscape rose the bold profile of Ingleborough.

It was on the Wenning that I learned to fish and it was there that I became a dedicated spirit. I never caught many trout, for the river swarmed with parr and my skills were still rudimentary and fragile. I was often reduced to frenzied incompetence by the challenge of a difficult fish or by the sting of repeated failure. I never caught many trout and I suspect there were not many of them there for catching; but I saw the water alive with hatching olives and sometimes, as night was settling over the river, a huge silver or scarlet salmon would erupt out of the white stillness of a small pool. I remember hooking a sea trout one September morning and the irresistible force of his dash for freedom. It was on the Wenning that I first recognised a mayfly, and it was the Wenning that taught me the difference between an iron blue and a blue winged olive, between a sedge and a stone fly. I never caught many trout on the Wenning, but it was there that I learned to absorb myself into the life of running water and to relish long days with just myself and a fishing rod and a river for company.

I spent two university springs and two long university summers on the Wenning, fishing the river for a month in April and then as often as possible between the middle of June and the end of September. They were dry fly summers, full of wind knots and blank days, and each of the few trout that found their way into my net was more precious to me than a dozen much bigger fish from later seasons. They were not always, in fact, just as big as they should have been, those Wenning troutlings, for I confess that my eagerness to make something like a bag occasionally interpreted eight inches as nine. A ten inch trout was a monster and, on the rare occasions when I killed one, the sense of triumph lingered for days.

From the handful of larger trout that the Wenning gave me I can remember two with particular sharpness. The first came on a windy morning in April, with choppy water in the pools and a hatch of olives such as I have rarely since witnessed. It was a cold, disconsolate sort of morning, much nearer to winter than to spring, and there were still rags of snow on the flanks of Ingleborough. Cursing the wind and its rough treatment of my line I had fished my way without a rise to the junction pool. I was almost ready to call it a day; I was cold and I was bored; but then the hatch started, and not, as so often, with a preliminary trickle to announce that more is on its way, but with an explosion of olives so huge and so sudden that within seconds the river was littered from bank to bank with their dark and bobbing forms, while all round me they were flying through the wild air in helpless profusion.

I do not remember that this enormous hatch brought on a great rise of trout, but I can still see my Greenwell, skating along the river's surface in the company of countless spring olives, until suddenly it was swallowed by a trout that fought for eternity and weighed a pound. It was much the biggest fish that I had ever caught. I knelt and gazed at it, as it lay dead on the bank, in something like an ecstasy of possessive love. And, though I caught nothing else before the hatch petered out after perhaps an hour, there could be no thought of failure; for that trout, that single trout, had made the whole day glorious. I ate it the next morning with sacramental reverence, wondering between mouthfuls whether I should perhaps have put it in the freezer before sending it away to be stuffed.

The same season brought a late afternoon in September, a warm and windless afternoon of golden light beneath a blue sky, with the river falling back from a brown spate and beginning to shine. It was almost the end of my day and it should have been time for the emergence of those quiet thoughts that belong so naturally to the end of fishing days; but I was angry with myself because I had bungled things all day long; even the parr, fish that I sometimes pretended were trout before shaking then free, even the parr had mocked and defeated me; until at last, in the run immediately above the viaduct, and while a train rumbled slowly over the track above me, at last I hooked a trout and knew immediately that he was big. He shook his head and dived and slapped his broad tail on the surface of the water, and my heart beat wildly with the terror of losing him; he was slow to surrender, but the hook held and he stayed for the net and weighed over the pound; and, all by himself, he chased away the discontent of a whole day's incompetence. I drove home in the belief that I was a mighty fisherman.

Failure was too commonplace to be memorable, but there was a fish I held briefly, certain that he was huge, until he dived into the roots and broke me. And, though the sun was shining and the hawthorns were white and the air was full of their sweetness, in spite of all this, and for all my twenty summers, I was very close to tears; for I had guessed, from the feel of him, that he was a trout of at least two pounds.

There was another lost fish that I shall never forget; he belonged to the day late in August when I learned my examination results, which were better than I had dared hope and sent me off to the Wenning in a mood of festival. I fished right up the river and way up Clapham Beck, much further than I had ever been before. The fish I was catching were small, mostly parr, but the afternoon was warm and, as I moved through the bright air, I was full of comfortable and complacent thoughts, telling myself that I was a scholar as well as a fisherman, a man of letters as much as a man of the river bank; and it was delightful, anyway, to be exploring water that I had never fished before, miniature water with a new feature every second footstep.

Some time late in the afternoon the blue wings came drifting thickly down the tiny pools, clustering on every corner and trapped in untidy lines against each trailing willow branch. It was a big hatch and, in those days, I always greeted the appearance of blue wings with special pleasure, partly because I had read so much about them in chalkstream literature, which made them seem flies with distinctly aristocratic connections; but also because, with their three tails, they were among the few olives that I could identify with real confidence.

It was a big hatch and the fish fed greedily. I caught nothing of any note, though I persuaded myself that one or two were long enough to kill – they may well have been – until, under a straggling willow bush on a sharp corner, I turned my wrist and found that I had hooked a monster. Perhaps he was a brooding cannibal, tempted from his lair by the profusion of fly. I am still convinced that he was a very big fish. He was on for something like a minute, but it was a hopeless struggle and he smashed the nylon with savage contempt, leaving me standing there on the bank, standing there and shaking with excitement and with the anguished frustration of loss. Three or four times I pulled slack line through the rod-rings, hoping against hope that my trout had not really gone, that, if only I pulled long enough, I should feel his angry presence again as my rod sprang back to life. But there was nothing, nothing but a dangling length of limp and hookless nylon. And suddenly all the pleasure of a soft afternoon in August had disappeared, taking with it all my pride in those high examination marks. I was no longer a scholar-fisherman, but only a defeated young angler, oppressed by the misery of his failure and emptiness.

Losing a big fish, especially for an inexperienced fisher, is a bitter and wounding experience; it leaves scars. The sudden collapse of tension, the giddy descent from wild exhilaration to that aching sense of separation, all this is too much to come to terms with in a few hours or even in the course of a whole day. It is, I imagine, rather like falling off a mountain, like being jilted in love. Whatever it is like, it hurts abominably. I was haunted for weeks by the grim memory of my brief contact with the monster of Clapham Beck. Throughout September, if the becks were flowing full, I fished quickly up the Wenning and went in search of him. But, even though the blue wings came thickly again a time or two, I found nothing rising beneath his willow bush, and I never caught a fish longer than nine or ten inches from his pool or from any of the little pools that belonged to his winding beck.

It was on the Wenning that I learned to fish. When, after a couple of seasons, I began to grow out of her and began to spend most of my fishing days elsewhere, I was still no expert – I have yet to become one – but I had mastered the elements of my sport and could expect to catch at least a few trout when there was no excuse for an empty bag. I still fished nothing but the dry fly, and this peculiar affectation, partly a lingering inheritance from those dimly remembered library books, but also deriving from a sort of fear of the unfamiliar and from my unwillingness to devote time by the river to the labour of learning new and difficult skills – this foolish devotion to the dry fly must have cost me scores of trout. The story of my conversion to the upstream wet belongs to a later chapter. When I drifted away from the Wenning I was still, or so I thought myself, a dry fly purist: a higher breed of angler than your run-of-the-mill fisherman with his sunk and dragging flies. It was all ignorance and self-deception but, beyond doubt, I was a much better dry fly purist than I had been on the April morning when I first cast a floating Greenwell onto the bright waters above the viaduct at Clapham Station.

For two long summers the Wenning was almost the only river that saw me on its banks; and then, in my last year as an undergraduate, I discovered a river where the trout were so much more plentiful, and so much bigger, that a day spent in the shadow of Ingleborough began to seem a second-best sort of fishing day. I still fished on the Wenning more often than elsewhere, but this only lasted for a single season; when I left London and moved to Cambridge, although I renewed my permit for the river, I did not spend more than two or three days there, which in time persuaded me that even five pounds was too great a price to pay for a privilege so rarely exercised. And then, for more than twenty years, I left the Wenning alone, except for one visit made on an impulse and without a fishing rod. It was an unhappy experience and soon I shall describe it, but first there is just a little more to be said about those two summers when a day's fishing meant a day spent on the Wenning and her becks.

It has been easy for me to recall a few of the more memorable incidents from my association with the Wenning. I find it much more difficult to recapture the spirit of all those ordinary days that brought perhaps a single trout of nine inches, or no trout at all, and were passed chiefly among the river's teeming parr; for the Wenning, when I first fished her, was a fine sea trout river, and there was also a back-end run of salmon. It is, I suppose, odd that I never made any serious attempts with the sea trout, for the sight of them excited me and the mystery of them appealed to my imagination. I fancy that if ever my dry fly had caught me one, the course of my fishing life would have been transformed. But it was the hope of brown trout that drew me to the Wenning; later years and other rivers have brought me a few sea trout and an odd salmon, but it is brown trout that have filled and inspired my fishing life. I have not followed the same fisher's progress that I have observed in so many of my friends: a progression from brown trout to sea trout, from sea trout to salmon, a progression that does not necessarily lose contact with its beginnings, one which very often continues to cherish the fish that were its first passion, but which enlarges itself to find new skills and new emotions in pursuit of fish from the sea.

I am not sure why I have remained almost exclusively faithful to the brown trout, unless it had been the conviction that learning how to catch them is more that a lifetime's study. Perhaps I should look into this in some later chapter; perhaps I shall never get round to it; what I want to do now, anyway, is to rediscover the feelings of the young man who wandered the banks of the Wenning more than forty years ago, not in those great moments of fulfilment or failure, but in the normal course of his fishing days as he caught a few unmemorable trout and scores of shining parr.

I know, to begin with, that I loved my fishing; I know that I pined for it in London; I know that one weekend in the May of my second year as a student, after re-reading that wonderful passage in *Fly Fishing* where Grey describes the intolerable oppression of confinement in the Capital during the cream of the trout season, I was so deeply affected that I got on a train and went straight home in order to spend the weekend on the Wenning.

I know lots of things about myself as a young student and fisher. I know that I went to Mass every Sunday and that, in between churchgoing, I drank lots of beer, feeling occasionally that I was inclined to drink too much of it; I know that I enjoyed my Latin and my Greek and worked fairly hard at them. I also devoured novels and fishing books; for I had soon moved on from Grey and Plunket Greene and *The Northern Angler's Handbook,* although I often returned to all three of them; but in between *War and Peace* and *Anna Karenina* I now began to delve into Skues. I discovered not only Turgenev but also the fishing articles of Arthur Ransome. I thought that George Eliot's *Middlemarch* was very fine indeed; but I also thought that Negley Farson's *Going Fishing* was every bit as fine in its own way.

I remember lots of things about the young fisher who spent long days on the Wenning and came home from each one of them hoping that he could fish there tomorrow. But beyond being certain that I loved the little river and the days that I spent on its banks, I find it difficult to uncover my fisherman's soul in those early years of its growth. I am not quite certain what it was that bound me to a river where I knew the quality of the brown trout fishing was second-rate; I could have bought cheap day tickets for at least twenty waters within easy reach of my home, waters where I would have found much better fishing than I found on the Wenning. I knew this well enough, and occasionally I did fish elsewhere, but it was still on the Wenning that I chose to spend almost all my fishing days.

I think the sense of freedom that I found there was very precious to me. I did not want to fish rivers where trout were numerous but where the men in search of them, being restricted to a single bank or to a few fields, were forced to rub shoulders with each other throughout the day; I did not want to feel crowded, confined or restricted; I wanted to start at Clapham Station, knowing that the river ahead of me, the river and its tributary becks, were all mine almost to their beginnings, knowing that I could fish my way to the top of the Wenning and then wander as far as I chose up Clapham Beck, unless perhaps I preferred to try my luck on Austwick Beck, or in the sluggish pools of Fen Beck where I always felt that a few monsters must be lurking but where I never managed to find one.

I am sure this sense of freedom formed a large measure of the Wenning's power over me. And with the freedom went the delight of loneliness: the virtual certainty that I should meet no other fisher at any moment of the day. I wanted my fishing days to be days of withdrawal, days apart from human contact, days given over to water and flies and fish, to these and to the beauty of the lonely fields through which the Wenning flowed. There was doubtless something instinctive in this craving to be alone; perhaps there was also a conscious acknowledgement that my days in the quiet company of running water were a necessary balance to the noisy and self-indulgent conviviality that made up so large a part of my life as a student. I do not think there was much sense of guilt in this; the loneliness was complementary to the beer and the laughter and the loud voices; the student and the fisher needed each other and most of the time they thought of each other as friends.

I went to the Wenning in search of freedom and beauty and loneliness. But there was something else that sent me back, again and again, to the same undistinguished little trout stream; and – though I am now interpreting my early years as a fisher in the light of later experience – I still feel certain that it was my desire to know the Wenning as intimately as possible, my longing, through constant association, to make it all my own. I yearned to establish some special communion with the river to which I devoted so many of my fishing days. And it has always been like this. My attitude to rivers has always been possessive, not because I want other fishers excluded from the Wharfe or the Eden or from whatever river it is that draws me to itself, but rather that I need to fish it into my heart and think of it as a part of me. The Wenning was the beginning of this feeling and, even though I no longer spend time along its banks, it is most certainly still a living part of me. I only regret that I cannot reach into the past properly to find the young man who, at the age of twenty, fell in love with a river for the first time.

I wanted to make the Wenning mine; I think that I also went there again and again because I believed that I had found just the place for my apprenticeship as a fisher, convinced that this river, with its eight and nine inch trout and its teeming shoals of parr, was the right river on which to learn the fisher's skills; for only when the lessons of the Wenning had been fully absorbed and the fisher's skills properly mastered, only then would it be time to migrate to the banks of more famous rivers. I am not sure, looking back, that, in practical terms, this was a wise choice. The Wenning's trout were not numerous; there were too many parr for that and the parr rose all day and they rose at anything, which must often have misled me in my choice of fly. It was a difficult river to interpret and doubtless I got it wrong time and again; probably I would have made quicker progress on a river where the parr were not always getting in the way. But although, in purely practical terms, the Wenning was perhaps the wrong river for a novice fisher, she was perfect in most other ways. She was the right size; she was very beautiful; she offered the variety of her becks; she offered the freedom of loneliness, and she helped me to absorb into myself something of the deeper blessings of the fisher's calling. She never gave me many trout but I am profoundly grateful for her many other gifts. She taught me much of what it means to be a fisherman.

I abandoned the Wenning soon after I started fishing the Wharfe; for, with its splashing hordes of parr and its few trout, the Wenning could not stand comparison with a river where the trout swarmed in every pool: a river moreover where they grew big and where skilful anglers caught them in twenties and thirties on the same day. I had left the Wenning within two years of my first visit to the Wharfe. I left because I had fallen in love with another river, but it never seemed like a rejection. I felt rather that, by a natural and inevitable process, I had grown out of the Wenning; I fancied that the Wenning was herself telling me that it was time to leave – it may sound odd but I really did think like this – and, though I no longer went to the Wenning, always I thought with warm affection of the little river where I had learned to fish; my memories of those two summers in the shadow of Ingleborough were a continuing delight to me. I thought of the Wenning as the nursery of my fishing life; I thought of her bright parr and her six and seven inch trout as the playthings of a novice, believing that I was now ready for the challenge of bigger things, although I can remember thinking that perhaps one day, when I was an old man, I should revisit her and fish her once more and find that she was still just the same.

It happened sooner than I expected and I did not find what I was looking for. In the meantime my way occasionally took me over Wenning bridge and, each time I passed, I left the car where I had always left it in the days when I had come there to fish; each time too I leaned over the parapet of the bridge and, after looking at the water beneath me, looked upstream to the arches of the viaduct and to the river that flowed under them; I looked for the splashing rise of a parr; I looked for an olive fluttering from the water's surface; I made sure that everything seemed as it had always seemed and then drove away happily, telling myself that one day I would bring a rod to the Wenning and cast a fly among her parr and her troutlings, telling myself at the same time that it would not be for many years, that I was still too young to go searching for the past, and that I wanted to be making memories on the Wharfe rather than following them back to the little river which I had now outgrown.

I cannot remember how often I stopped by the bridge and gazed at the Wenning for a few minutes; but I remember the last time very clearly; it was a summer of savage drought and, though I was now a member of the Kilnsey Club on the Wharfe, it was a summer when I spent as much time climbing hills as trying to catch fish; it was early September and I think I was returning from a day spent on Ingleborough; I know that the currents of the river were feeble and very thin and that their edges were all clotted with slime. Doubtless I stood there praying for rain, so that I should be able to take my rod to the Wharfe and find its trout eager for my dry flies.

As I stood there on the bridge all those years ago, looking at the weary trickle of water creeping on its way beneath me, there came no sudden longing to fish the Wenning; but all at once I was seized by an impulse to revisit the nursery of my fishing life, not in search of sport and only partly in sentimental homage to times past; it was mainly because I felt curious; I wanted to see if the river beyond the viaduct looked as I remembered her; I wanted to discover whether the pools that had once filled my dreams would now seem unalluring places; and, anyway, the sun was shining and it would be pleasant to wander up the fields for half an hour before driving home; in half an hour, too, the pubs would be open and it would be good to stop somewhere for a pint and to drink a silent toast in honour of the little river that had taught me so much.

I had no waders with me but the river was very low. Taking off my boots I carried them with me and paddled under the viaduct through an inch or two of tepid water. Then, wandering up the rough pasture along the edges of the river, I watched the parr dimpling in all the little runs and in all the shadowed glides beneath the alders. Nothing that I saw made me regret for a moment that I was there without a fishing rod; for the sun was so warm, and the river was so thin, and the rising fish were so obviously midgets, that it was not a scene to stir predatory urges in the heart of a fisher; even a full water would probably have failed to stir them.

I felt no immediate desire to fish the Wenning again; I had stopped there in passing and decided to walk up the fields to take another look at the little river on which I had spent so many days; I went there to make sure that things were still much the same, to check my memories and perhaps to readjust them, and also to confirm that the Wenning, though indeed a happy memory, was not a trout stream to bother a fisher who was now a member of an exclusive fishing club on the upper waters of the river Wharfe.

I had, I suppose, turned into something of an angling snob but, in spite of this, I was more affected by my return to the Wenning than I had been expecting just a few minutes earlier while splashing under the arches of the viaduct. I was beginning to sink into a pleasant haze of recollection; but at the same time there came some twinges of longing for those days on the Wenning three and four years ago, not for the sport they had given me, but rather for the strong and simple feelings that I had brought to them. I was a much better fisherman now, and the Wharfe gave me many more and much better trout than the Wenning had ever done; but I was beginning to discover that life was more difficult to manage than I had once thought it: I was beginning to find that the world beyond the riverbank could push its way into my fishing world and tarnish the deep and necessary pleasures that I found there. I was not always as comfortable by rivers as I knew that I had once been; and the sight of the Wenning on this sunny afternoon, trickling into the little pools where formerly I had found such uncomplicated contentment, this confrontation with the past stirred up some feelings of the nervous disquiet to which I was now increasingly prone.

So it was that I walked up the rough pasture, to the sharp double corner at its top, with some sense that I was walking through a land of lost innocence and simplicity. They were not anguished thoughts; rather they were faintly nagging ones, gnawing away along the edges of my contentment, for I was undoubtedly in a sunny mood, being filled with that feeling of simultaneous well-being and weariness that comes to those who spend days walking up and down steep hills. I suppose that, in part, I was simply acknowledging that, in leaving the Wenning, I had also left the last remains of boyhood there behind me. But it was delightful, as well as mildly disturbing, to find that I was back on the little river, and I was determined to suppress every unpleasant thought, abandoning myself to recollection and roaming for a time in the remembered sunshine of the past.

I wandered up the rough pasture, then round the sharp double bend and then on to the line of limestone pools beyond. I found exactly what I was hoping to find; for I found that everything was just the same; the set of every current into every pool seemed just as I remembered it; the monkey flowers along the fringes of the water seemed to be spreading their patches of yellow in just the same places; the straggling line of alders still ran down the far bank just as it had used to, and still the same branches stretched themselves out over the same pools. I did not bother to look, but I remember thinking that, if I searched those branches carefully enough, I should probably find, embedded in their bark, one or two rusty hooks that I had left in them three or four summers ago.

Everything seemed the same and, although this unsettled me with those twinges of anxiety, it spoke a much stronger message of comfort and reassurance; and each step that I took made me feel closer to my old self; the differences seemed trifling, for the heart, I told myself, was still the same fisher's heart and the love of fishing now beat there even more strongly than before. I sat down by a pool to smoke and to watch the parr and to remember, if I could, whether the little basin of water before me had ever brought to my net any trout worth killing.

It was then, all at once and inexplicably, that there came to me an experience of unexpected and piercing intensity, one of those moments of sudden insight or revelation that take possession of us when we are in search of something quite unlike them, in search of some shallow comfort or some trivial pleasure. I had stopped my car on Wenning bridge to gaze at the river for a few minutes; I had decided to splash under the viaduct and walk up the fields to see if my memories were still telling me the truth; it was a diversion for a late afternoon at the end of a day in the hills; it was wholly unpremeditated and it was undertaken in a spirit of half-sentimental curiosity; there was certainly no expectation of strong or difficult emotions.

And yet, something like ten or twenty minutes after it began, you could have seen a man of twenty five sitting on the banks of the Wenning, sitting there and wiping the tears from his eyes, while at the same time telling himself in a whisper that as long as he remained a fisher he would never go too far wrong, because the fisher's calling would preserve him from excess and strengthen the better part of him, because the fisher's calling brought with it those long hours of loneliness which became bitter and tormenting hours whenever the mind exposed to them was unhappy with itself and unsuited to its own company.

They were tears of dedication; they were the tears of an idealist who, with a sudden and startling clarity, had seen a vision of fishing as a vocation for the temperate and the pure, a vocation which brought endless enrichment but at the same time insisted that its followers should keep themselves untainted, should make themselves worthy of the blessings that were so generously poured out upon them. It was a peculiar and very personal vision and it is still very much alive in me. Those sudden tears on the banks of the Wenning, as I sat there in the sunshine without a fishing rod in my hand, marked the moment when this conviction first took hold of me. It has been with me ever since and, as a later chapter will perhaps show, it may just have made me a better man.

I went no further that September afternoon; I had found the little river unchanged and took away with me the confirmation of my memories and a new vision of fishing, to which I wish I had remained true. It was several years before I came to the Wenning again, unless I drove over the bridge below the station without bothering to stop or bothering to remember. Anyway, some years later there came a day in August when I climbed Ingleborough instead of going fishing and, of course, I stopped to look at the Wenning on my way back. As once before I decided to take another look at the pools and runs that I had fished all those years ago as a novice angler; and so very soon I was splashing my way under the arches of the railway bridge to the rough pasture beyond.

I walked slowly along the river, then round the sharp double bend to the line of limestone pools that lay half in late-summer sunshine, half in the shadow of the alders and the steep ground rising above the far bank. I passed the spot where, on my last visit, I had experienced that strange vision of my fisher's vocation; it was an experience for which I now felt profoundly grateful and as I stood there, my gratitude was extended to the river that had inspired it. I felt grateful, I felt happy; I was walking by the Wenning without any of the disquiet that had troubled me when I had last been there. I lit my pipe and walked on round the next bend.

I was expecting a rickety plank bridge, with mossy shallows and with untidy hawthorns leaning berried branches over the water; I was hoping to wander up to the cupped pools beyond them and then on to the deep junction pool, all the way drinking in warm memories of the past. But there were no mossy shallows and there was no rickety bridge and there were no thorns with reddening haws along their branches. There were no pools splashing into each other. There was almost nothing that I remembered, except for an old birch tree still standing on the bank where the bridge had once crossed the water. I was no longer looking at the little river that I had once fished; I was not looking at a proper river at all, with those eccentric features that flowing water always produces when left to express itself in its own way. Instead of this I was looking at a featureless channel of water creeping in the shadow of steep and regularly shelving banks. I was looking at a canal; I was looking at a ditch; I was looking at the latest achievement of the men of the River Board and I was sickened by what I saw. All round me I was gazing at the ruin of my dreams and suddenly I was full of anger.

I was angry with myself for revisiting the Wenning, for destroying the past by so foolishly trying to repossess it. But I was much angrier with the men who had planned and executed so monstrous a sacrilege. I have always talked to myself on riverbanks, usually in a whisper; but that afternoon, as I walked back to the car without going on to look at the becks because I was frightened of what I might find, as I walked back down the fields I roared and cursed and ranted, praying that the despoilers of the Wenning would be punished, would be tortured by guilt, would be visited by sleepless nights with waking nightmares and black visions of despair, would be stricken with premature senility and with public incontinence.

I fished the whole of the next season without a licence, which was a cowardly and feeble gesture, but it was better than no gesture at all, and at least it meant that the men of the River Board had three or four pounds less to spend on their schemes of destruction. It was not my last visit to the nursery of my fishing life; when next I came to the little river it was once again with a fishing rod in my hands, but it was a whole twenty years after the day that poisoned my memories of the Wenning and, during those two intervening decades, made me think of her as a despoiled and deeply wounded stream.

Postscript: The story of how I came to fish the Wenning again is told in an earlier book: *Confessions of a Shooting Fishing Man.* In preparing this book for publication I have asked myself whether my initial response to the work on the Wenning all those years ago was an overreaction. The length of river affected was fairly short but, as I discovered when I returned to fish the Wenning, Clapham Beck had been very shabbily treated. I do not regret my intemperate words.

Chapter Three

One April morning – it was during the Easter vacation of my second year in London – I drove off for Buckden, a village at the head of Wharfedale where, according to the *Northern Angler's Handbook,* tickets for a stretch of interesting water could be bought from the village pub. I found Buckden and its pub (appropriately enough called *The Buck)* and I bought my ticket, although the landlord insisted that I was wasting my money by spending it so early in April to fish water so high up the dale. He was not far wrong. My memories are of a biting wind blowing straight down the river, of pools that reflected a leaden sky, of cold and tedious hours spent casting against the wind, with nowhere any sign of a rising fish or a hatching fly, until all hope of a trout was long since dead and I fished on with frozen fingers and no pretence of pleasure, fishing on merely because I had come there to fish and because I had told myself that I would not give up before five o'clock.

In the end I did catch a fish. It was an enormous grayling and it cost me a bitter struggle to return it to the river. It was the first grayling of my life and it was much bigger than any trout that I had ever killed. It must have been close to two pounds; it might even have been a genuine two-pounder; anyway it looked like a whale to my eyes, which had not often been able to feast themselves on the sight of a great fish lying beaten on the bank. I remember thinking that I should have preferred not to catch so big a fish, since to gain such a prize, only to gaze for a few seconds at those silver flanks, at that shining blue back with its huge, spiked fin, at that small, pouting mouth so unlike the mouth of a trout – to gain such a prize and then, after so short a possession, to slide it back into the pool from which it had come, all this was almost more than I could bear. It was an inauspicious beginning to my long association with the river Wharfe.

The grayling, anyway, went back and not long afterwards I decided that enough was enough. But the same evening, on my way home, I stopped for a pint at the *Tennant Arms* in Kilnsey, where I knew that the Kilnsey Angling Club had its headquarters. I wanted to know more about the Kilnsey Angling Club, for what the *Northern Angler's Handbook* had already told me had stirred both curiosity and desire:

> *'The K.A.C., founded 1840, takes over the fishing on both banks at Kettlewell and save for an odd short break or two has practically the whole of the fishing down to Netherside. Upstream from Kettlewell to beyond Starbotton, where trout to 14lb. have been taken, other good stretches are also in the hands of the club. They also have two miles of fishing on the tributary Skirfare. This is excellent trout fishing and grayling are now more numerous than before. Members pay £26 5s. and the entrance fee is £15. The hon. Secretary is Mr. D.E. Riddiough, 'The Brow', Lothersdale, near Keighley.*
>
> *'A limited number of day tickets at 25s., which allow fly fishing only, are issued. Application for tickets (not available on Sundays or on Bank Holidays) must be made to the head keeper, Mr. J. Ingleby, Kilnsey.'*

On my way to Buckden I had glimpsed stretches of Kilnsey water from the car, some of them shining in brief bursts of pale April sunshine, and the landlord of *The Buck* had told me that my best chance of meeting Mr. Ingleby (though he preferred to call him old Jerry) would be in the bar of the *Tennant Arms*. Old Jerry was not there. I was too early for him, but I learned that Kilnsey members rang him at the pub between nine and ten in the morning in order to book their beats; non-members could ring just before ten and, if the river was not too busy, and as long as Jerry had not drunk too much beer the night before, there was every chance of a day ticket for one of the unoccupied beats. So much I was told, but the barman also showed me the room reserved for members of the Kilnsey Angling Club. It made an immediate and very deep impression.

Hanging round the walls there were three of four stuffed trout, confined in bow-fronted cases with, on each of them, a plaque recording the weight of the fish and the name of the fisher who had caught it. In a rack against one wall there were some old rods pointing at splayed angles towards the ceiling, long rods of greenheart and heavy cane. In the middle of the room stood a solid, square table of polished oak; in the middle of the table there was an old pair of scales, shining bright, with a set of brass weights stacked beside it. Along the mantle piece stretched the backbone of the 14lb. trout mentioned in the handbook, which, as I later learned, had not been caught by a member or his guest, but found dead or dying on the edge of the water by a farmer years and years ago.

On the walls of the clubroom, between the cased trout, hung maps of the Kilnsey beats and pictures of Kilnsey trout. Near the door there was another table, smaller and lower, which supported a huge glass case; inside it two otters were frozen in combat over the carcass of a fish. Hanging in this corner by the telephone was a framed list of the Kilnsey members, forty in all, and beneath the list was a slate, also surrounded by a wooden frame, on which were chalked the names of the fishers who had been on the river that day and of the beats they had been fishing. I remember that the date was also written on the top of the slate and, at its bottom, the two words 'fly water': clearly old Jerry's morning verdict on the state of the river.

Round the hearth was a wide brass fender, next to it a coal box with an ornamental brass sheet over the lid. No fire was burning and it was cool. There was only one window, looking out over the road and the fields beyond in the direction of the river, and the room was full of the grey light of a cloudy evening. The soft gleam of metal and glass and of polished wood was gentle to the eye. There was something subdued and soothing about it all.

The clubroom of the Kilnsey Anglers seemed a very quiet room. Its cool air breathed out tranquillity and the lingering smell of twist. It was a room that spoke of the past, a room belonging to the turn of the century rather than to the nineteen-seventies, so that the telephone on the wall seemed almost an anachronism. It was a room that spoke of a long tradition stretching back more than a hundred years to the time of the club's foundation. It was a room that spoke to me with silent insistence: of its dignified past and its honourable customs, of the trout that had been weighed on its scales, of the fishers who had brought them in for weighing and then sat in the leather arm chairs, drinking pints of beer or glasses of whisky and water. I seemed to hear the talk that had passed between them as they rested there, talk of flies and fish and the river Wharfe, of the cost of labour, the price of yarn and the many problems of trade. It was a haunted room, but its spirits were all kind. When they came in they took off tall hats and put long rods in the rack or propped them against the wall. Their casts were fine strands of horsehair; their flies were tied on eyeless hooks whipped to the casts. And some of them talked of the creeper as well as the fly, others of the upstream worm.

I spent perhaps five minutes in the clubroom of the Kilnsey Anglers. When I walked out it was already my ambition to sit there by right, with my own name printed on the list of members and chalked, as often as possible, on the old slate that hung next to it. There were no living fishers in the clubroom or at the bar. The barman said that Jerry could not be expected for at least another hour and so, unable to wait so long, I set off for home; but before I lost sight of the Wharfe I stopped the car to gaze at the grey line of the river flowing down through the open fields to Grass Woods. I wanted it to become a part of my life.

Since that evening, when I carried away with me haunting visions of the Wharfe and a profound yearning to feel that I belonged there on her banks, since that evening few days have passed without there rising before my mind's eye some picture of the river that I most love. It may be where I hope to fish tomorrow; it may be where I long to fish next spring; often it is Spout Dub or Black Keld or one of the deep and nameless pools way up the river towards Yockenthwaite. Sometimes, when sleep refuses to come, I lie in my bed and wander the Kilnsey water with closed eyes; sometimes I get to Kettlewell, sometimes to Starbotton; there are times when I get right up to Beckermonds and am forced to acknowledge that I can go no further. There are times when the fly comes down thickly and the trout are rising eagerly in every pool; there are times when the strap of my bag bites into my shoulder; there are remembered and imagined times on every beat of the river and there are times when I am enjoying myself so much that sleep turns into my enemy.

Other rivers have wound their way into my heart: the little Wenning, with Ingleborough looking down over her, the graceful Eden with its wealth of fly and its pink-fleshed trout, the wilder beauty of the highland Truim, the waving weed and the splashing weirs and the shining chalk of the Driffield and the Foston beck. These and a dozen other rivers flow through my memory and my imagination, but it is not every day that I hear their voices and remember them. It is different with the Wharfe, which is never forgotten and never forgets me; she speaks to me constantly.

There are times, of course, when I am not listening. I may be sitting in a pub, swilling beer and laughing among friends; but then, all at once, I catch the calling voice and fall silent for a few seconds. I may be teaching Latin to twenty yawning boys, lecturing then on the strange attributes of the gerundive, when suddenly I hear the sound of flowing water, telling me that the trout are rising under the trees above Watersmeet; and then, although my mouth still opens in praise of passive verbal adjectives, my heart has abandoned grammar and flown off to the Wharfe. Sometimes I can follow my heart in a Land Rover and be fishing by two o'clock.

My memories of the first day I fished at Kilnsey, which was in the summer of the same year, are filled with a scorching impression of bright light and dazzling water. It was July. The river was very low and the sun was relentless. Jerry had told me over the phone that I could not expect any worthwhile sport, but I was very eager to fish at Kilnsey and determined to waste the price of a day-ticket. I took the beat above Conistone bridge. I caught one trout and convinced myself that it was big enough to kill. By six o'clock I was drenched with sweat. My head was aching from the constant assault of the sun and its reflected light. My skin was burned; and my throat was desperate for the slaking comfort of bitter beer.

I had caught one trout that I perhaps ought not to have killed; but I had seen hundreds of them: resting in the shadows beneath trees or poised as dim shapes deep down in the pools. I had also frightened scores of fish, sending them shooting for cover, alarmed by my blundering approach or startled by the heavy falling of my line. I had killed one trout that might just have been ten inches long, but I was drunk with the sight of them. At the end of that long day of fierce heat and savage brightness I was already dreaming of the day when I should come to Kilnsey under cloud, to find the river running with a touch of colour and with, in every pool, its trout on the fin.

I fished four or five more days at Kilnsey that season, and perhaps half a dozen the next. I never found ideal conditions and never managed more than a brace of trout, but with each visit I loved the river more, with its clear water and its white gravel, with its little falls and its deep pools delved beneath them, with its carved shelves of yellow rock, with its long trout-filled runs. There was open water and there were shadowed stretches where the river flowed beneath trees. There were great pools where the current seemed to lose its way and where the trout always seemed to rise beyond the reach of my flies. There were long stretches where the water bounced from boulder to boulder; there were little mossy glides under leaning willows; there were shallows where the gravel shone through. There was water of endless variety and everywhere there were trout.

I loved the river more with every visit but, as much as anything, I loved drinking beer in the bar of the *Tennant Arms* at the end of the day. There was often a member or two, talking together over a drink, and they were always ready to welcome me into their conversation and tell me of the river and of the club, of the river's fish and the flies you needed to catch them.

It was my first real experience of fishing talk, for I was the only fisher in my family and, except for very infrequent bankside encounters, there had been no social element to my sport on the Wenning. It was a new and delightful pleasure: to leave the river feeling thirsty and tired, to sit leaning on the bar or sitting round a table, swallowing beer and talking between gulps with men who shared my opinion of what men should talk about. At about eight o'clock – never before and rarely much after – Jerry would arrive, and he always stayed until closing time;

except, I seem to remember, on Wednesdays, when he left after a single pint of Guinness and bitter, abandoning the *Tennants* for an evening's dominoes at the *Devonshire Arms* a few miles down the valley in a little village called Cracoe.

Jerry was my hero. In London I was taught by eminent scholars, men who had written books on Vergil and Homer and half a dozen other Greek and Roman authors, men who composed Latin or Greek hexameters in the bath and who emended classical texts while chewing their breakfast sausages, men who spoke at least seven languages and dreamed in six of them; but I held none of them in such high reverence as I held Jerry Ingleby, who spoke nothing but slow Yorkshire English and blinked between the end of each sentence and the start of the next. Jerry was the servant – for me he was at the same time the mouthpiece and the embodiment – of the institution I most admired, of an institution which was to my mind almost as venerable as the papacy; he was the keeper of the Kilnsey Angling Club and I hung upon every slow word that fell from his lips.

Jerry was a short man. He generally wore a dark, threadbare suit and a flat cap. He smoked twist and coughed a lot. His face was deeply lined, looking almost as though it had been roughly shaped from the weathered limestone of his native fells. It was a face slow to express emotion; it shaped itself very gradually into a smile or a rare scowl. There was indeed something almost geological about the changing features of Jerry Ingleby's face; they took time. When first I met him Jerry was about seventy and had been the Kilnsey keeper for at least forty years. He pronounced, often and very solemnly, that he had entered the club's service as a means of avoiding proper work; it was not, on the face of it, an absurd claim.

He lived no more than a few minute's walk from the *Tennant Arms* but, showing a true countryman's disdain for unnecessary exercise, he always drove there, arriving each morning at roughly nine o'clock. Before his breakfast he had already driven to Conistone bridge, to look at the river and declare it a 'full water', a 'fly water', a 'low water' or occasionally, in time of summer drought, even 'a worm water'. But, if on the previous night he had been trapped at the bar for longer than usual, this was a part of his daily round that could be abandoned; on such mornings he guessed the state of the river, or learned it second-hand; on such mornings the ritual of the telephone became his first duty.

Between nine and ten, although there was some flexibility in his interpretation of when to arrive and when to leave, Jerry sat in the clubroom, smoking his pipe and coughing down the phone, advising members where to fish, chalking their names onto the slate and, between mouthfuls of smoke, dispensing slow wisdom to those members who appeared in person to book their beats. At some time around ten o'clock Jerry decided that his continued presence in the clubroom was unnecessary and, climbing back into his van, he then drove up to the rearing ponds to feed the stock-fish. Next came a leisurely tour of the beats, with pauses to survey the water from all the best places. If the day was warm, Jerry would park on the high bank above Wash Dub, which caught the morning sun, and then settle down to read his newspaper for half an hour in a thick fog of smoke.

Jerry's tour of the river was partly intended to discourage poachers, or to detect any that remained doggedly undeterred. It seemed to achieve its purpose, for very few fishers ventured onto the club's preserves without permission, and not many fished there without being spotted by old Jerry. His binoculars were soon focussed on any suspicious presence along the banks, and he was willing, if he thought it advisable, to delay or to bring forward the time of his setting out; he was even prepared to tamper with his immemorial route; and there were days, he often assured me, when he had already driven the water before he came into the clubroom to deal with the phone.

There was also a social purpose to Jerry's unhurried progress along the roads of upper Wharfedale. Many of the older members of the club had known him for thirty years or more and they looked forward to the appearance of his van at some predictable time. Jerry knew perfectly well that, when Mr. So-And-So fished a particular beat, he always came to the road bridge at eleven o'clock and rested there smoking for a while. Jerry's van would appear five minutes after eleven and, when Jerry had wound down his window and relit his pipe, he would talk with Mr. So-And-So about old times and speak disrespectfully of the few members he did not like. Then he would continue on his way to Kettlewell or Starbotton and find out what had happened there since yesterday. He knew everybody in the dale and everybody was happy to interrupt his work for an exchange of news with Jerry. He was a feature of the place, he was himself an institution; he might easily have become a tourist attraction. Certainly he was a potent element of the spell that drew me to Kilnsey.

Jerry learned much that was useful in the course of his morning round. He also learned much that had nothing to do with the club or the river, for he was interested in everything that happened under the Wharfedale sun and not in very much that happened elsewhere. But this leisurely progress from place to place possessed a value far beyond the importance of the information Jerry gathered from it; for his van and his presence inside it and the words he passed with the people he met in the course of each morning: all this meant that the inhabitants of Conistone and Kilnsey, of Hawkswick and Kettlewell and Starbotton, looked upon the club as a familiar and welcome part of the life of the dale. The affection they felt for old Jerry diffused itself over the institution that he served, and so they thought of the Kilnsey Angling Club, as they thought of Jerry himself, as something which had always been there, as something that would surely continue to be there for years and years to come, and as something of which, on the whole, they rather approved.

Jerry never drank at lunchtime, except, I believe, on the day of Kilnsey Show. His afternoons were quieter than his mornings. Sometimes he made a second and shorter round. He fed the trout in the ponds again before making his tea and then resting at home until it was time for the pub. He supplemented his income by castrating and slaughtering pigs. In winter he joined the beating teams on local shoots. He was an expert flanker on the moors. His position, as keeper of the Kilnsey Angling Club, was know in Wharfedale as 'best job i'North'. And Jerry himself was, I think, inclined to agree. More than once, after we had drunk a pint or two together, he took the pipe from his mouth and, blinking solemnly, revealed the great secret of his success as a river-keeper:

'To do my job properly, sir,' – there was a pause here, followed by a few more blinks, before he continued with a slow emphasis on the assonance of the vowels – 'you have to be born idle and bone idle.'

He was proud of it.

The easy rhythm of Jerry's life only became clear to me once I had joined the Kilnsey Angling Club. In the early days, when I bought day tickets for the water, I knew little more about him than was revealed by his pub talk. But it was this pub talk that so enthralled me, even though Jerry was no expert in the way that some river keepers are practical entomologists of distinction or innovative flydressers or themselves master anglers. There was nothing of William Lunn or of Frank Sawyer about Jerry Ingleby; I am not at all certain that he was much interested in fishing and I would not swear that he had ever caught a trout on the fly.

It was not Jerry's expertise that held me spellbound; it was the sense of tradition that emerged from his recollections of dead members and times gone by; it was his talk of men who had been happy to fish the fly if the fly was what the trout wanted, but who had always fished the upstream worm for preference, fishing it with long rods and silk lines and Stewart tackles whipped onto casts of gut; it was his memories of seasons forty years ago when the creeper had been so numerous, and the trout so wild for the creeper that, in the month of May, those members who still practised the old skills had regularly filled their creels to overflowing with dozens and dozens of trout.

I would say to Jerry that I had caught or missed a couple of nice fish in the runs on either side of Black Keld; he would remember a September afternoon a few seasons before the war when he had been there with the secretary, who had taken thirty trout before lunchtime and then slept through most of the afternoon in the shade of the old sycamore, waking in time to kill a further dozen before he drove off to his dinner in the clubroom. I would mention that there had been a big hatch of iron blues once the wind had got up in the afternoon; Jerry would compare it with the hatches there had been twenty years ago and dismiss it as no more than a trickle.

I loved this talk of the past between mouthfuls of beer, especially since Jerry, with his old pipe and his battered suit, with the deep furrows and the slow features of his face and with those blinking eyes, seemed himself a remnant from an earlier time. And every word that he uttered, while the smoke of his twist hung round his head in pungent and swaying layers, every word Jerry spoke made me long more passionately to become a part of the tradition that was his favourite theme. By the time I refilled his glass and left him at the bar I was not always as clear-headed as I should have been for the journey home. I went slowly, driving with fuddled caution, and as my car glided through the long shadows of the folded landscape, I dreamed of the next day when I should fish at Kilnsey and of the next evening I should spend in Jerry's company at the bar of the *Tennant Arms.*

I returned from those early trips to the Wharfe with a belly full of beer but always with a light or an empty bag. Sometimes I brought home a single trout, sometimes a brace, as often as not no trout at all, until at last there came a day in September when, after Jerry had confirmed that a day ticket was available, I set off to Kilnsey for my final visit of the year. In those days I fished with breathless speed, rushing from pool to pool in the belief that I was bound to find rising trout round the next corner. When I rang Jerry I always asked him if the water above my beat was free and, if it was, I would sometimes fish through two or three beats before I sat down for my lunchtime sandwich. Sometimes Jerry would announce in the pub that he had seen me at noon, already two miles above the top of my beat; he would probably add that one of the members had stuck to a hundred yards of water and killed a dozen trout. But beats are not for the young; young fishers want the freedom of mile upon mile of water; they want to know that, if the mood takes them, they can follow their river way up into the hills and fish on right to the source.

I started that September morning at Watersmeet, the big pool where the Skirfare flows into the Wharfe. My own beat was already known to me but, beyond it, stretching all the way to Kettlewell, there were three beats I had never fished before, and none of them were taken. I knew already, as I stood at Watersmeet ready to make my first cast, that, before I made my last one I should have leaned over Kettlewell bridge, wondering whether to fish on towards Starbotton. In fact I had reached Kettlewell before three o'clock, in time to drink a pint at *The Bluebell* and savour the taste of triumph. I sat outside with my beer and was thinking of a second pint when Jerry's van appeared and stopped right in front of me in the middle of the road. Very slowly the driver's window came down. Then Jerry, deaf to the sound of the horns behind him, lit his pipe unhurriedly and coughed a few times and blinked once or twice before, between a few more coughs and a few more blinks, he told me that, while I was sitting on a bench drinking beer, the trout were feasting on the sort of hatch that had been a daily event forty years ago. He almost ordered me back to the river.

It was a warm and cloudy day and there had been some fly from the start. They were blue wings and, through the morning, they had come in a trickle with trout rising here and there; but as the day wore on the hatch became ever thicker. When eventually I staggered from the river at seven o'clock, the blue wings were streaming off the river in countless thousands.

I killed my first trout some time round midday, from a shallow glide beneath the ashes and sycamores that line the river upstream from Watersmeet. I seem to remember fish feeding in the little pools and runs towards the top of my beat, and in Mile House Dub itself; but none was added to my bag until I clambered over a stile and came for the first time to Spout Dub; where a small spring spills into the Wharfe over a natural wall of yellow limestone, spilling into the broad pool that lies in the damp shadow of this little cliff; where the river rushes into the pool through a narrow neck and then hurries down the stony line of the bank, hurrying under the dank overhang of the yellow rock; where water drips into the river from clinging ferns and creeping mosses, while the current slowly surrenders its dash and sparkle to the calm pressure of the spreading pool; where, since I first stumbled upon it more than thirty years ago, I have caught more trout than from any other pool, any glide or run or corner of that wonderful length of the Wharfe which it is my best blessing to fish.

Spout Dub, secluded between its cliff on one side and a plantation of larches across the water, is a secret and special place. It is a prince among pools and I recognised something of its distinction as soon as I saw it; for I saw at once that it was very beautiful and that there were trout rising down the edges of the fast water, not one or two trout but at least a dozen of them. The wind was gusting inconsiderately downstream, but there were holes in the wind and I managed, every fourth or fifth cast, to coax my line through one of them. Drag was never more than a second away and I frightened most of the fish that I covered. More than once, just as my fly was uncurling over the water, the wind remembered that it was meant to be blowing and slapped both cast and fly onto the nose of a rising trout. But some of these trout, refusing to be put off their food by the clumsy efforts of a young fisherman, rose to gulp down my fly. I missed some of them clean; others I pricked. But I hooked and fought and tamed, I netted and killed and bagged a whole brace of them; and that brace from Spout Dub meant that there were now three fish in my bag with at least half a day's fishing still ahead of me.

Already there were three trout in my bag and, between them, they convinced me that every fish in the river was now at my mercy; I could fish on for six hours or more and I might finish with whole dozens of trout, with a bag such as the old members that Jerry talked of had so often made with the creeper or the upstream worm. I was light-headed with the excitement of it all, with the wildness of the wind, with the skating of the olives, with the greedy pouncing of the trout. On my shoulder I could feel the weight of the fish in my bag. There was the memory of a bending rod and the certainty that it would soon be bent again. There was the feeling that, as far as catching fish was concerned, the day had scarcely begun. I have, I suppose, known profounder happiness by the banks of a river; but never again have I felt so careless an exuberance or so sure a conviction that the world is a wonderful place.

In fact I caught no more trout between Spout Dub and Kettlewell. I did not cast over more than a few of them. The sudden belief in my ability to catch trout all day long, merely by waving my rod somewhere in the direction of a rising fish, was such a warm and comforting assurance that I fancy I was anxious to avoid the risk of immediate disillusionment. And there was also something intoxicating about the changing features of the river: water slipping over smooth shelves of yellow rock: shaded runs beneath high banks or leaning trees: shallow and windy flats: sheltered, unruffled pools: cascading water, gliding water, tumbling and turbulent water, shining and shadowed water: all glimpsed briefly as I raced along the banks and clambered over dry-stone walls, heading for Kettlewell and a pint of bitter beer at *The Bluebell*.

My meeting with Jerry decided me against a second pint and sent me back downstream rather than upriver towards Starbotton. By six o'clock I was at Spout Dub again. All afternoon the blue wings had been hatching and, in spite of missed rises and lost fish, I had managed to catch and kill a fourth fish. I was feeling very pleased with myself. My earlier fantasies of trout in tens and twenties had not come true, but this did not bother me at all. Four trout was more than I had ever killed before and, although I was eager for a fifth or even a sixth, four trout was already enough; it seemed no longer enough once I had returned to Spout Dub and entered a scene of unashamed and frantic gluttony.

The wind had risen through the afternoon and now it was tearing down the pool, whipping the water into flying foam and little white-topped waves. In the wild air the larches streamed; and, driven on by the wind, the blue wings were fleeing down the river like a routed army. Every eddy was filled with jostling crowds of them; every seam of the current carried them in clustering scores; they were packed tight against the sides of every rock; the bobbing foam was thickly speckled with them; the whole pool was littered with them and the sky was alive with their flying shapes.

The trout were beside themselves, splashing and rolling at the fly, sipping and gulping and snatching them down. The run at the top of Spout Dub was a riot of pouncing snouts and smacking tails. But there were blue wings all over the pool and, wherever there were blue wings, there were feasting trout. It was a wonderful spectacle: the teeming fly and the scores of trout; it was a marvellous demonstration of the richness of limestone water, and I see it all the more vividly because it is so rarely witnessed now.

For the next hour I battled unequally against the wind, struggling to cast my fly over those gorging trout. I cannot remember how many of them I put down, how many I hooked and lost, how many ignored my fly. I cannot even remember what fly I was using, though it was, of course, a dry fly. But I do remember very clearly that I killed three more fish and that I left the river with seven dead trout in my bag. I did not keep a diary in those days and so I cannot tell you how big they were, although some of them were certainly good fish, three-quarter pounders or even genuine pounders; but it was not their size that mattered; it was rather that there were so many of them. Until then I had caught trout in ones and twos and threes. A brace of trout had been a memorable achievement; three had made a red-letter day. But now a single outing had brought me seven trout. It was almost beyond belief and I could barely wait to tell Jerry, in response to the question that was certain to follow his first mouthful of beer – I could barely wait to announce, in a matter-of-fact tone of voice, as though it was the sort of thing that happened every week, that in the course of a single day I had caught and killed seven trout.

I did tell Jerry this, once he had walked into the pub and taken his first swallow and asked me the usual question. He blinked a few times, lit his pipe and lifted his pint to his lips again; then, in a dry and matter-of-fact tone of voice, he said that a member called Bill Stockdale had been out in the afternoon and had killed twenty trout in two hours.

I did not make another good bag at Kilnsey for a year or two. I still fished there on day tickets and, at the end of each day, I still drank beer in the *Tennant Arms* with Jerry Ingleby. But then, one evening in January – it was during the second of my three years in Cambridge – my mother rang to tell me that a man called Mr Riddiough had been in touch with her, wondering if I might be interested in joining the Kilnsey Angling Club.

Chapter Four

The Kilnsey Angling Club, when at the age of twenty three I became its youngest member, was an institution with thirty nine other members, most of whom never bothered to fish. This was an ideal state of affairs for those who did, and one of them was called Bill Stockdale. He was already an old man when I first got to know him, but he was still on the river three or four days a week, and I suspect that he caught more trout than the rest of us put together. In those days at Kilnsey there was no such thing as a limit. There was no need of one. The river swarmed with trout and a Kilnsey fisher killed as many of them as his skill permitted and his conscience allowed.

Bill Stockdale was a superb fisherman and killing trout never seemed to trouble his conscience. In fact he revelled in it and his baskets were often huge. A day that brought him fewer than half a dozen trout was a poor day indeed; and he not only caught more fish, he consistently caught bigger fish than anyone else. I remember meeting him from time to time on the riverbank and how, if I was feeling rather pleased with my bag of two or three eleven inch trout, any sense of pride or satisfaction would immediately be driven away by the trout Bill pulled from his pocket; for always there were so many of them, and they were never the pale stock fish that sucked down my flies: they were trout with a dense pattern of black spots, trout with amber fins and with yellow bellies: they were the wild trout of Wharfedale and the best of them was always well over the pound.

Bill Stockdale declared that my dry flies were ridiculous; they were, he said, exactly the sort of stuff and nonsense you should expect from down South; they were not Yorkshire flies and they were no good for Yorkshire trout, which ate flies with sensible names like Orange Partridge and Waterhen Bloa; and sensible fishers did not drag these exemplary patterns through the bright waters of Yorkshire's rivers; they flicked them upstream on a short line, drifting them over the lies of hungry trout, and in this way they often filled bulging creels.

I had, of course, already heard of the upstream wet. I had also read of it in Stewart and was familiar, through Skues and Sawyer, with its metamorphosis into chalkstream nymph-fishing. But now, in the person of Bill Stockdale, and in the yellow-bellied trout that he pulled from his pocket, I met the blunt and beautiful proof of its effectiveness. Once or twice I watched Bill fishing his slow way up the river, casting his flies no more than a few yards ahead of him, then suddenly lifting his rod and hooking another trout as though by some process of magic or some rare gift of second sight; for I had seen no splash, no pull on the line, no movement of any sort that would have told me to turn my wrist and set the hook. It was a marvellous performance and it filled me with an immediate and intense desire to master Bill's method and start catching trout on the upstream wet.

But whenever I tied a leash of wet flies to my cast and threw them upstream into the currents of the Wharfe they seemed altogether different from the flies Bill Stockdale used, even though they looked more or less the same and undoubtedly had sound Yorkshire names like Orange Partridge and Waterhen Bloa; some of them, in fact, were Bill's own flies, for he had given me half a dozen of his spiders one afternoon when we met on the river at Black Keld; they may have been Bill's flies but, as soon as they were attached to my nylon, all power seemed to have gone out of them, for they could no longer charm trout onto the hook and bring them splashing into the net. All that happened, except on the frequent occasions when they embraced each other in a knotted tangle of nylon, was that they drifted back to me, with no indication that they had roused the slightest interest from a single trout, until at last I grew weary of the hopeless tedium of it all and reverted to the dry fly.

Sometimes, especially if the river was full, instead of turning back to the dry fly I turned myself round and fished the same sunk patterns downstream. This caught me a fish or two, but I pricked half a dozen trout for every one firmly hooked; anyway, I was so deeply imbued with Stewart's contempt for downstream fishermen, and so profoundly impressed by Bill Stockdale's wonderful achievements, that I gained little satisfaction from the few trout that attached themselves to my sunk and dragging flies. It was a tactic I continued to use from time to time, but it was no more than an occasional stratagem for a high and coloured river when there was little prospect of success with the floating fly.

I more or less abandoned my efforts to catch trout by the method of W.C. Stewart and Bill Stockdale, becoming once again, except for brief periods of downstream aberration, a disciple of Halford; but it was a calling no longer followed through conviction; rather it was forced upon me by my incompetence in the style of angling that I now regarded as the highest of the fishing arts. I had once thought of myself with pride as a dry fly purist; but the fisher I now most admired, a fisher steeped in the tradition of the river I so loved, was a fisher who dismissed the dry fly with scorn as a southern affectation. And he justified his contempt by catching trout after trout with delicate little wet flies cast towards the river's source. Bill Stockdale converted me, but unfortunately, at the time of my conversion, I lacked the skill to follow my change of heart by changing my style of fishing. For a couple more seasons I continued to fish almost exclusively with floating flies; but I now fished them in the belief that they were second best, and I knew that I should never find fulfilment as a fisher of flies until I had met and finally mastered the challenge of the upstream wet.

Meanwhile I got to know the Kilnsey length of the Wharfe. I left Cambridge for a week in April and for a week when the iron blues were hatching in May, for a few days in August and for almost a fortnight at the end of September. I left Cambridge to go fishing on the Wharfe and, when I could afford it, I did not drive home in the evening but fished right through the day and spent the night, or as many as two or three of them, at the *Tennant Arms*: where I would lounge in the clubroom after breakfast, chatting and smoking with Jerry and drinking in that delicious sense of belonging there among the old rods and the stuffed trout and the smell of twist. The day, from ten until six, belonged to the river. In May and August there was usually more fishing in the evening; but beer and fishing talk were the chief pleasures of the evening, and both the beer and the talk often continued deep into the night.

During the first season of my membership I fished every beat of the Kilnsey water, except for a long stretch way up Langstrothdale that the club had held for years but which Jerry had more than once dismissed to me as not worth a visit. He thought so little of it that it was not included in his daily round of the water. I had never heard any of the members talking of days spent up at Yockenthwaite and Beckermonds and, when I asked Bill Stockdale about our fishing right at the top of the river, he said that he had tried it once twenty years ago, had caught nothing that weighed more than two or three ounces and most certainly had no intention of ever going there again. In fact I doubt whether, when I joined the Club, its highest beats above Buckden and Hubberholme had been fished at all since Bill Stockdale's single visit all those years past, except perhaps by worming farmers and a few poachers in time of flood.

Once or twice I had driven along the first miles of the Wharfe, but this had been after weeks of settled summer weather when even the main beats below Kettlewell were crying out for rain; up there at Deepdale and Yockenthwaite the river had seemed more rock than water, with no more than a thin trickle of wetness, half-choked with slime and flannel weed, oozing over the gravel or creeping very wearily between great glaring slabs of limestone. I could not believe that any trout worth catching lived in this apology for a river; and so it was with receptive ears that I absorbed Jerry's contempt for the neglected runs and the disregarded pools that were waiting for me to discover their wonderful secrets in a few years' time.

But in the course of that first Kilnsey summer I fished all the other beats of the club water and already I was beginning to look upon some of them with special affection, particularly those above Watersmeet. I think I have already mentioned that Watersmeet is the large pool where the Skirfare flows into the Wharfe. In those days a derelict fishing hut was still standing there in the angle of the confluence, its door jammed permanently half open, its single window-frame long since rotted away. It had become a summer home for swallows rather than a retreat for fishermen. The green paint had almost gone, its few remains blistered and peeling. The corrugated roof was warped and rusty and gaping along every join. There was a metal plate hanging loosely on the door from a single screw, on which you could still just make out the three letters – KAC – that had once more clearly proclaimed its owners and its purpose.

The first time I came to the hut as a member of the Kilnsey Angling Club I squeezed through the stubborn door and sat smoking for a while on the rickety bench beneath the remains of the window. I felt proud to be exercising my member's privilege by sitting there among piles of bird droppings, sitting there surrounded by dust and cobwebs and by the musty smell of decay.

The old hut disappeared long ago, ousted by a much smarter and more serviceable hut in which you can stay dry during a cloudburst. It is a much more efficient hut, with a door that both opens and closes and with glass in all of its windows. It is without doubt a bigger and better hut and has every right to be there. But I cannot sit in it and smell the past, as I could in the rusty old ruin that stood there before it, and it offers no welcome to the swallows that hunt the river all summer long.

Above Watersmeet the river is known in the club as Kettlewell Beck. It is, in fact, still very much a river, but smaller and more secretive than the river it becomes once it has gathered the waters of the Skirfare and spread itself to accommodate them. From Kettlewell to Watersmeet the Wharfe flows with endless variety and, in the first summer of my membership, most of my fishing days were spent there, exploring the water I had glimpsed so fleetingly on that day in September when I discovered Spout Dub and first caught enough trout to call a bagful.

I found loud runs and silent pools, all of them teeming with trout. I found little falls, where the river tumbled over water-carved shelves of yellowed and mossy limestone, where the trout lay all along the edges of the turbulence. I found great boulders with water-delved lairs beneath them, lairs in which the river's best trout rested and grew fat. There were lines of trailing willows with fine trout down among the water-washed roots; there were places that looked unexceptional, but the subtleties of water's movement made them the haunts of heavy fish: little glides where water slid enticingly, or tiny pockets between stones where water rested on its journey, inviting the trout to join it there and share its repose.

There were narrow channels where the current flowed smoothly over the ridged and fluted rock, places where the alchemy of water and sunlight turned the poised trout into golden shadows. There were sharp corners and shadowed flats, there were long deeps and there were shining banks of gravel. There were pools that mirrored bare branches on cold April days; but when next I came to them in May they would be flowing with waving reflections of green; there were pools from whose surface the sky stared back at the sky. There were high and stony banks, there were steep banks and walled banks and there were banks that brought grass smoothly down to the edge of running water. There were long runs of boisterous, boulder-strewn water. There were trout everywhere.

I fished for them with my dry flies, while Bill Stockdale fished his sensible patterns and filled his creel – or pocket – to overflowing. The spring olives hatched, the iron blues came thickly down the pools; hawthorn flies trailed their long legs in the sunshine and swarms of black gnats coupled over the river and then fell onto the water in passionate surrender. Summer brought blue wings and pale wateries; September brought golden light and sharp evening air, with dewy mornings and huge mixed hatches on warm afternoons; and often there were early falls of spinner before the chill spread down from the pale sky and the river fell quiet.

Those early Kilnsey days were very precious to me. They were, in one sense, an escape and a delusion; but I fished through them with a vision of peace and beauty that grew out of truth and was soon to work upon me with changing power. At Cambridge I was often miserable; I was unsettled and frightened by my immoderate appetite for beer, which made me feel that I was no longer my own master; and this feeling of impotence filled me with anxiety and with guilt. I knew that I was not working as I should, which hurt all the more because I loved my work whenever I got down to it properly; it was a delight to sit and to read, to think and to write, whereas to spend long nights drinking beer and gin, then to squander whole days lying in bed with a hangover and an overwhelming sense of self-loathing, this was a feeble surrender; it was a waste and a misery. I had come to Cambridge to make myself a scholar, but all that I had managed to do was to make myself a drunk. It did not bother me that I was spending public funds to pay for bouts of squalid intemperance; but it filled me with shame to think that I was using my parents' money for the same purpose. There were whole weeks when I could barely bring myself to open a book; these would be followed by weeks of hard labour when I stayed sober and began to feel happy again, began to feel that I deserved a drink or two at the end of another virtuous day in the library.

My life at Cambridge was a rickety compromise between the pursuit of learning and the satisfaction of cruder appetites. But the pleasure of a pint of bitter beer was often tainted by my secret acknowledgement that it was a pleasure that had now turned into a vice. It was this that made my return to the Wenning, on that summer afternoon when I suddenly sat down and burst into tears, more complicated than I had been expecting; it was this knowledge that, in Cambridge at least, drink was turning into my master that inspired my vision of fishing as a pursuit for the temperate and the pure. And somehow at Kilnsey I felt almost true to this vision.

For at Kilnsey things were different. At Kilnsey there was no fear or guilt. There were long days on the river and, when I had put away my rod for the night, leaving it among the old rods in the rack against the wall in the clubroom, then it was time for pints of Kilnsey beer, swallowed with innocent delight as I listened to Jerry's talk of the past. They were slow pints, with long gulps at long intervals, and they were drunk in happy thanksgiving for all the pleasures of the past day. And somehow, at Kilnsey, I knew when to say no to another pint. I never woke up the next morning with that sickening feeling of shame, and if sometimes I did wake up with a headache, I could still remember the end of the night that had caused it; and it was soon chased away by the clear air that I drew into my lungs as I walked to my fishing. And there was, of course, never any question of staying in bed, for there were important things to be done; there were trout to be risen and hooked and drawn over the net. Whenever I was at Kilnsey for a few days, I began to feel that I was in charge of myself again; began to feel confident that the partial restraint I practised there would soon impose itself on my life in Cambridge. Kilnsey and the river Wharfe made me feel whole again.

In those early Kilnsey days I was much younger than my years. I was a boy of eighteen rather than a young man of twenty three. I was filled with a passionate love of fishing and, on the banks of the Wharfe, I forgot almost entirely about everything else. While playing a trout that looked or felt worth keeping, I held my rod in something like an ecstasy of tension. If the trout threw the hook or broke the line, then my world turned black; if it stayed for the net, then all the excitement of the fight softened into a deep and glowing contentment; I would lie on the bank and light my pipe; I would stare at the sky or follow the patterns of light flowing down the currents of the river. At such times I drank in the beauty of my surroundings with an intense physical delight. I can remember, more than once, weeping for love of it all, weeping and praying that Kilnsey and its river and its trout would be with me for a lifetime, not just for a few years; I remember hoping that I should be able to sit by the river as an old man, to sit in the grass by Black Keld or Spout Dub, watching the water and the flies and the rising trout and at the same time thinking to myself, with thankfulness rather than with any feelings of pride, that I had been worthy of all the blessings that the river Wharfe had poured out upon me.

After catching a good trout I would lie on the bank smoking and feeling happy until it was time to start fishing again. At the end of a Kilnsey day, as long as I had caught trout, the feeling of peace I carried back with me to the car was almost palpable. I suppose it was the contrast that affected me so powerfully – between the sense of happy fulfilment that had now taken possession of me, between this and the listless discontent that was so often my burden away from the river.

I remember a late September day on the Skirfare. It was a day of unbroken autumn sunshine, with golden light lying over Littondale and its enclosing fells; the river was full and clear and shone yellow beneath the changing leaves; the breeze was no more than a slight movement of warm air, drifting upstream and helping my flies to fall softly on the water. All day there were clouds of smut swarming over the river, and all day the trout rose to gorge themselves. It was, I think, the first time I had encountered, or at least clearly recognised, a rise to smut. Fortunately my fly-box held a few small black flies – they were probably knotted midges – and some of the feasting fish were willing to eat them. I killed six or seven trout and a grayling well over the pound. They came at intervals through the day, so that the flavour of success never turned sour, while the thrill of expectation never faded away. And through it all the sun shone and the river flowed and the fish sipped away on its surface while the gathering swallows chattered round the barns and cottages of Hawkswick. I fished for half an hour, then I lay in the grass and smoked for five minutes, then fished again and wanted it never to end, wanted to live in this peace and this beauty, in this excitement and this serenity for the rest of my life.

Before I acknowledged that it could not be so and drove off for the *Tennant Arms,* I lay for a time sprawling in the grass by the pool at the bottom of my beat. I can remember how, as I gazed up into the sky, blowing smoke into the evening air and sniffing the sharp smell of the riverside mint – I can remember how both the rising line of the fells and the blue expanse beyond it seemed to my eyes to be moving with the ripple of running water. Turning to look at the fields and the trees all round me I found that they had learned the same trick; it was as though the miracle had occurred and I was now looking at the whole world through a fisherman's eyes. It was a wonderful illusion.

The trout were still sipping among the drifts of smut, but by now I was happy with my catch; I did not want to fish any more, only to lie on the edge of the river, to lie there thankfully with this feeling of perfect contentment and of perfect health. My happiness was so intense, and my conviction of well-being was in such contrast to the jaded creature I so often felt myself to be, that I suddenly began to examine my hands and my arms; and then, rousing myself, I went down to the edge of the river, where I knelt and stared, Narcissus-like, at my reflection in the water of the pool. But I was not hoping to lose myself in wonder at the beauty of the image staring back at me; I was not looking for beauty, but for the tokens of debauchery, for lines and blotches, for bloated flesh and baggy eyes.

There were no such signs, unless I refused to see them. I saw a pair of hands that seemed unmarked by any evidence of excess; I saw a face as yet unravaged by an immoderate life, a long and thin face, a quiet and rather serious face with searching eyes, a face that smiled and smoothed itself into serenity even as I looked at it; for the force of my happiness was much too strong for the anxiety that lay beneath it. And, anyway, the face that I was examining was only twenty three years old.

A few minutes later, when I began to stroll back along the banks to Hawkswick, watching the trout and the swallows, I think I had almost forgotten ever feeling different from how I felt now: completely in tune with myself, and with the quiet fells and the shining river and the slanting light.

I did not bother Jerry with any of this; but I told him that I had killed seven fish. And he told me that he had seen Mr. Wood and Mr. Watson at lunchtime, that they had both been fishing the upstream worm and had each caught upwards of a dozen fish before they stopped to eat their sandwiches and to drink a glass of whisky in his company. And this information, filtering through thick drifts of pipe-smoke, brought with it the birth of a new ambition that would bind me even closer to the tradition of the Kilnsey Angling Club; it was an ambition that had to wait for its fulfilment for almost twenty years.

As I became familiar with the Kilnsey beats, especially those above Watersmeet, so I began to associate particular places with those interludes of rest that formed an important part of a day spent at Kilnsey. They were places where I loved to lie and smoke after eating my sandwiches, or in the late afternoon before returning to the car, or while waiting until the sun sank lower and the light changed and it was time to fish the evening rise. They were places to savour success, places where, on those days when things went well, I would lay my catch on the grass and gaze at the shining and spotted beauty of a leash or more of brown trout.

They were also places that possessed some mysterious power to soften the bitterness of failure. I would come to them when the fish had risen short all day, or when I had lost a succession of apparently well-hooked trout, or on days when they had fed greedily for hours on end and I had failed to interest a single one of them. I would lie there smoking gloomily, oppressed by the burden of my incompetence, but slowly my mood would soften from despair to resignation; memories of better days would begin to mingle themselves with present experience; under their influence the sun would find its way back to me, and before long I was happy again to be a fisherman, and looking forward eagerly to the evening's or the next day's sport.

They are places where I still love to begin or to end a day on the Wharfe, or to rest for a time in the middle of one. I am sure that every fisher has his own such places on the river that he loves best, places where its spirit is distilled to a special and addictive potency. They are places that draw him irresistibly whenever he is fishing somewhere near them, and, even in winter, while his rods hang idle until the arrival of another spring, even in winter he still thinks of them on the edge of sleep or visits them in his dreams.

About a mile below Kettlewell there is a large pool called Knipe Dub. A few feet from the water rises a tall, triple-trunked sycamore, stretching out long branches half way over the water. Behind it a high bank, covered with an untidy scrub of hawthorns and sheep-chewed saplings, climbs steeply perhaps thirty yards to the Kettlewell road. It is a peaceful and sheltered spot and it is always in shadow. There is the quiet expanse of the pool, with the murmur of water from the stepping stones a short way upstream; there is the faint stirring of the leaves and the drone of a myriad insects swarming among them. There are shafts of dusty sunshine cutting through the shadows. Often, tucked away in a hollow of the trunk, or half-hidden in a pile of stones right on the edge of the bank, there is a battered metal flask and a sandwich box. There may be a rod there too, propped against the sycamore; and, whenever the rod is there it almost certainly means that I am there too, sitting on a flat stone beneath the sycamore, or leaning my back against the trunk, or sprawling on the grass in a patch of sunshine: smoking or drinking tea or eating sandwiches or perhaps even asleep.

In summer it is a cool refuge; you can sit there, watching the trout swallow the drifting smut and planning how to catch them when you are ready to fish again. There will be swallows dipping onto the water; there will be wagtails fluttering between the rocks; sometimes too you will hear the squeak of a kingfisher and then, low over the water, catch for a second the passing flash of his gaudy feathers. Inevitably there will also be the continual whine of engines from the road above, punctuated by the crash of grinding gears and the impatient blaring of horns. But these discordant intrusions do not shatter the peace; in fact they deepen it because, coming from outside the world of the river, they possess no real power to penetrate. They are peripheral noises, telling you that hundreds of sweating motorists are heading for Kettlewell and its pubs and shops and cafes, telling you to lie back for relief that you are not one of them and to feel even happier than before that you are a fisherman.

I have been beneath the sycamore at other times of the year. I have been there in bare and early spring, with the rooks cawing, with the branches swaying and creaking in the wind. I have sat there shivering while hail lashes across the grey surface of the river, chewing a sandwich, gulping mouthfuls of tea and still hoping for a hatch of olives in the afternoon. I have been there with the river in thick spate, with the pool transformed into a restless confusion of foam and flotsam and rushing brown water. I have sat there watching the river on September afternoons, with yellow leaves drifting down the river and floating down onto my cap, with no breath of wind beneath the cloud and with the melancholy of the season gathered all round me like a vapour on the quiet air.

It is a special and precious place and I think of it possessively as my place, as a place stored with the memories of more than thirty summers on the Wharfe; there are memories of raw April mornings and of soft summer afternoons; there are memories of still August evenings when the spinners fell only on the edge of darkness. Sometimes I sit under the sycamore and think of the huge hatches of iron blues that once came from the river at the end of May. Sometimes I remember dead friends who once sat with me there beneath the shelter of the leaves. I can remember sitting there so full of contentment that there was no room left in me for any bitter thoughts; but I have wept there and I have grieved there; I have felt guilty and unclean. And sometimes, as I sit there now, especially in September, sometimes my memories cluster so thickly round me that I seem like a man looking back with little reason left to look forward; it is at such times that the weight of the past becomes oppressive; it is then that, resting beneath the yellow leaves, I feel a sharp and sudden longing for the days when I came there unencumbered by anything but the pull of the strap on my shoulder and the burden of immediate experience.

But there is a particular period from the past that, though it is full of memories of Knipe Dub, I cannot recall with nostalgic yearning, because it was the time when, in the course of a whole season, I never rested serenely in the shade of the sycamore. I was there often enough, but the mood I brought with me beneath the leaves came from beyond the river, filling me with brooding and restless discontent; it was the mood of a man who was at last unhappily and, I suppose, healthily aware that he could find no easy escape from the confusion of a disordered life; a man most deeply out of love with himself, a man who had betrayed his own vision of himself and could no longer find consolation or peace from his contact with a great trout stream; for the touch of bright sunshine and the sight of pure water, mingling with the recollection of departed innocence and lost delight, bred such a feeling of guilt and so strong a conviction of unworthiness that he now felt most hopelessly wretched where once he had been most easily content.

I cannot remember the day when I first felt miserable on the banks of the Wharfe; but it was certainly in the year when I had left Cambridge and discovered that I had not left behind me the appetites formed there, that I was unable to resign to the past what I most disliked in myself. I came home for a year, to study for a teaching qualification in Lancaster, which was only a journey of forty minutes from my parents' house; the course was a fatuous waste of time and demanded very little of me beyond attendance. I could have done it in Cambridge, where it would have been no more worthwhile but would certainly have been much more expensive; and anyway I wanted to finish with the sort of life I had been leading there. I wanted to spend a year at home, learning moderation and fishing the Wharfe at least three days a week during the season. The second of these ambitions came true.

Perhaps, in looking back, I exaggerate the excesses of that year and the guilt that grew out of them; but certainly it was a year of countless pints. And because I loved my parents and wanted to spare them the certain knowledge that their youngest son was a drunk, and because I preferred to spend long nights in the pub rather than quiet nights at home, I took more and more to staying with friends in Lancaster, where there was usually whisky once the pubs had at last closed and where, if a bottle was opened between two or three of us, it was rarely put away while there was anything left in it. It was a wretched year, during which the force of habit, growing insidiously towards compulsion, persuaded me to live in a way that I hated. There were no longer bouts of gloom; depression and a sort of restless feeling of impotence composed the settled condition of my spirit. There were spasms of determination to change, but they came to nothing. They were more like twitches than spasms.

April brought fishing and false hope, and doubtless there were days when, shrugging off my burden, I felt briefly at peace again by the river. But, even on the Wharfe, it was a dark year; even on the Wharfe depression was always waiting in the shadows. I went there in flight from myself and found the attempt futile. And I also found, whenever I was staying at Kilnsey, that it was much more difficult now to drink in only moderate excess. And no one but me seemed to disapprove of large whiskies after midnight; and, though I disapproved, I still drank them and felt only half-fit for fishing the next morning. Jerry clearly thought that I was a much better man than he had first thought me. I thought nothing of the sort. It was a wretched season and, towards its end, there came a September night at Kilnsey when I drank much longer and much later than ever before.

The next morning I stumbled from my bed without knowing how I had got there, unrested and red-eyed and sick with shame. I knew at once that I did not want to fish, only to creep away somewhere and hide in the shadows until it was time to go home. The thought of fishing the places I loved, Spout Dub or Black Keld or the little pools below Kettlewell, seemed a monstrous sacrilege. I knew anyway that it would be torture, and that the stirring of any happy association would immediately be strangled by guilt and misery. But, in spite of this, I did go fishing in the end; at least I went through the motions of it. There was no resolve left in me; I could do nothing but helplessly follow the forms of an empty ritual, telling myself, while knowing that I was telling myself a lie, that I might feel better after a few hours on the river.

Breakfast was an agony; every mouthful of food turned into a crushing moral rebuke for the man who could barely swallow it without vomiting. The clubroom was a sort of hell, for I sat there with a heaving stomach and saw everything round me as a vision of the past. And Jerry's commentary on the previous night's carousel, his coughing good humour as he reminded me of events I could not recall and of my squalid involvement in them, his recollection of still wilder drinking bouts in earlier years, his admiring references to dead members who had been able to revel the whole night away and then fish all the following day without even the ghost of a headache: all this was almost beyond my endurance; for I was no longer, like Jerry, someone for whom a hangover was a passing physical discomfort, the unpleasant but inevitable and acceptable burden of previous pleasure; my hangover was something different and something terrible; it was the proof of an unpardonable and incurable moral failure that had now made me unworthy of everything and of everybody that I loved. I was beyond hope and beyond redemption.

I left the clubroom and, going to the river, I walked the banks in mocking sunshine, scarcely bothering to fish. I stood by Spout Dub as blue wings hatched and the trout rose to eat them. I sat smoking at Black Keld and, with every inhalation of tobacco, I sucked into myself a deeper hopelessness. I was weary almost to the point of collapse; I was taunted by the rending memories that rose to greet me round every corner. There was no escape, no momentary release from the contemplation of my depravity. I was very, very unhappy and, in the course of that day, as I wandered from pool to pool and waved my rod over a few of them, I came to feel that I was walking by the Wharfe for the last time, since, through this latest act of excess, I was already an effective exile from the river and the landscape that I most loved. It was a day that ended in terrible gloom under the sycamore by Knipe Dub.

I cannot remember how long I sat there, but I know that, when at last I rose to leave and dragged myself up the steep path that led to the road, I began to whisper very slow and very solemn words of farewell: to the river and to the fields and to all the ruined happiness that I was leaving with them. And then suddenly I sat down again and burst into tears and wept like a child, for I had remembered those tears of dedication on the Wenning two years past. I have never, never before and never since, been closer to despair.

I suppose that briefly, perhaps for a week, or more likely for half of one, I imagined that I had really said goodbye to the Wharfe, really believing that my life as a fisherman was already over. It was the best conviction that has ever come to me, for it forced the almost immediate acknowledgement that it could not be so, that I could not abandon Spout Dub and Black Keld and all those half-secret places with names that I alone knew; and this perception brought with it an urgent determination to win back my sense of belonging to the paradise that I had lost. And how could this come about, except through the imposition of some order, some discipline, some restraint upon the chaos that was threatening to swallow me up?

Many students drink recklessly. Early in my university days I had already begun to drink more than most of them. I was a student for twice as long as is usual, and this gave my taste for excess twice as long in which to put down deep roots. Perhaps, on the day when I crept away from the Wharfe with the dreadful conviction that I could never return, perhaps I was not quite the moral ruin that I thought myself; perhaps I was a very foolish and weak-willed young man at last facing up to the truth that he drank far more than was good for him; perhaps that agony of shame and renunciation was itself a form of emotional self-indulgence, an unnecessary extravagance given the fact that the routine of employment, and the simple process of growing up, would have helped me to grow out of my student ways, would themselves soon have taught me moderation and regular habits.

Perhaps, on the other hand, I was already tottering on the edge of alcoholism, only a few steps away from complete enslavement or total abstinence. I no longer know the truth of it, but I remember years of gathering unease and growing evasion, and I remember a black day of revelation when every attempt at false assurance was suddenly at an end as I surveyed what I had made of myself and concluded that, even at the age of twenty five, I was no better than the wreckage of a man.

It was the River Wharfe that saved me, because I knew that I could not break our association and at the same time I knew just as surely that I should never again find peace or pleasure or fulfilment by her banks until I found that I could sit there without shame and self-loathing. There were, of course, other pressures at work on me which, even without the help of the River Wharfe, might by themselves have managed reform. But, at the time, it was not the desire to spare my parents pain that strengthened my determination to change. It was not my Catholic faith, even though it told me unambiguously that I had fallen into sin. It was not the fact that in a week or so I should be changing from a student into a schoolmaster. It was none of these, although I suppose they were all active at the back of my mind. At the time it was the prospect of fishing Spout Dub with all the old delight, it was the hope of lying under the old sycamore with no thoughts but fishing thoughts, it was my passionate longing to be alone by a river and happy with my own company: it was these hopes and visions springing from my life as a fisher that became to me a strength and an inspiration.

I did not renounce strong drink; perhaps I should have done, but the thought of a few drinks with Jerry, to wash away the dust of a hot day by the river, to celebrate a basket of fish or in consolation for an empty creel, was a prospect that I could not deny myself. And I suppose I knew anyway that I should never manage to abandon pubs for the rest of my life, or sit in them drinking nothing but bitter lemon or ginger beer. I did not forswear alcohol, but I made rules and learned gradually to keep them, so that slowly a pint of bitter beer turned back into an object of genuine pleasure rather than a symbol of shame and failure.

There were lapses, plunging me back into darkness and forcing me to wonder whether I should ever be able to respect myself again. And then, one Sunday morning after such a lapse, one Sunday morning after Mass I knelt before a statue of the Blessed Virgin and promised her, for love of her son, that I would never again swallow more than five pints of beer, or their equivalent in spirits or wine, during the course of a single day; and that I would not cheat the Queen of Heaven by guzzling five pints between ten and midnight, then a second five between midnight and two o' clock.

I spelt out the terms of the promise precisely, knowing how necessary it was for me to have a clear picture of what I was binding myself to. I thought of it as a sort of contract, with me making the promise and with Mary promising in return that she would help me to keep it. It seemed at the time that I was committing myself to a regime of almost impossible asceticism and I knew that I should need the intercession of God's mother if I was to remain faithful to such a resolve. She did not let me down.

Towards the ending of convivial evenings, when it seemed to me that just one more pint, or perhaps a stiff whisky, could scarcely be reprehensible, she was there to remind me that, in my case, it would. She was there every Sunday after Mass, thanking me for remembering her and offering me her help for the coming week. Slowly she taught me to look upon my five pints as a rare indulgence rather than a regular dose; and slowly too she helped me to be more content with myself. She has never left me since. She goes to the pub with me and knows just when to interfere. She calls late at night, when I am alone with a bottle of scotch, and tells me that two drams is quite enough. She gatecrashes receptions and keeps a motherly eye on my behaviour. And, should you ever have the misfortune to sit next to me at a dinner party, and if you notice that I am doing furtive sums on my fingers, you will know that she is whispering to me from under the table, telling me to reckon up my units before I help myself to another port.

Occasionally I have let her down, but even then she has refused to abandon me, ordering me to pull myself together and to forget all about fishing until I have sought penance and absolution in the confessional.

She is the patroness of my life as a fisherman because it was she who preserved it. On the last Sunday of every season I kneel in the little Catholic church in Grassington and thank her for everything that she has done for me. And whenever April brings me back again to the sycamore by Knipe Dub, always I rest my rod against the wall; then I settle myself with my back against the trunk, looking out over the quiet water of the pool, and, before I light my pipe, I whisper the words of the Hail Mary in solemn thanksgiving and supplication.

It is a tradition that began when I returned to the Wharfe on a bright and chilly April day six months after that terrible September farewell. I had fished through the morning and caught a brace of trout during a trickle of spring olives. I had fished with more than my old fervour, with a new intensity of delight; I had walked by the river, flowing clear and full and with that shining purity that belongs to April, and I had felt that the Wharfe was running down from the hills to greet my return, to welcome me back and invite me to be happy again by her banks. Sitting under the sycamore, as it rubbed its bare branches across the cold sky, and as I swallowed scalding mouthfuls of tea to keep me warm, I suddenly prayed the Hail Mary in spontaneous gratitude for the day and the river and for my presence beside it. I prayed it for Jerry as well; for he had died during the winter and no one had told me and things would never be quite the same again.

CHAPTER FIVE

I have already mentioned that, in the first year of my membership, I fished all the main Kilnsey beats from Grass Woods to Kettlewell. When I came back to the Wharfe, having left her one late September afternoon in the belief that I could never return, I fished them all again, though this time I added the water above Kettlewell bridge and was delighted by what I found. I started this process with the beat that stretched from Black Keld to the Stepping Stones; I started there because it was the beat where briefly it all seemed to have ended. But my next Kilnsey day was spent on the club's lowest water and, as far as was possible, each successive visit took me just one beat higher than the last. It turned into an imperfect sequence, because sometimes the stretch I wanted had already been taken by another member; sometimes I had to skip a beat and come back to it on my next fishing day. But the symbolism of my upstream progress retained much of its force; it was an act of repossession and it was a very deep joy.

I fished from Netherside to the Falls, from the Falls to Conistone bridge; I fished from Conistone bridge to Byrom and from Byrom to Watersmeet. Then it was on to Mile House Dub and Spout Dub and up past Knipe Dub to the Stepping Stones. And it was these beats that I reclaimed most passionately, because it was these beats that I loved best, the four of them that stretched from Watersmeet to Kettlewell, the four where, to my mind, the Wharfe became in turns everything a trout fisher could want of a river and where, at least to my eyes, it seemed just the right size. There was the Skirfare too. I came to it when I had fished up the Wharfe almost to Buckden. It was back down to Watersmeet and up the little river to Skirfare bridge, to Sleats Gill, to Hawkswick bridge and so to the last mile of water winding under the fell through flat and open fields.

As I became better acquainted with the Kilnsey Angling Club, getting to know more of its members and absorbing just a little of its history, I realised that Bill Stockdale belonged to a great tradition stretching back to the days of Pritt, who had himself been a Kilnsey angler, and to the fishers of still earlier times. While fishing the river or resting and smoking on its banks I often imagined Pritt and his friends, with their tall hats and long rods and mutton-chop whiskers, flicking their flies over Spout Dub or Watersmeet or Black Keld, flicking out their flies and then suddenly turning their wrists to hook yet another trout, which would be swiftly tamed – all five ounces of it – and then laid in a battered wickerwork creel on top of the twenty or even thirty trout that were already there. And always these fishers from the past put their faith in spare Yorkshire flies, in the Orange Partridge and the Waterhen Bloa and the Purple Snipe; always, of course, they fished them wet and they fished them unfailingly upstream.

In this way Bill Stockdale's method, which I had seen to be a wonderfully effective way of catching trout for a man with the skill to fish it efficiently, now shone before my eyes still more brightly as the method of history: as the traditional as well as the best way to catch a Kilnsey trout. Its appeal was now virtually irresistible, for I felt that, by learning at last to fish the upstream wet, I should bring myself closer to the past and establish a warmer contact with those dead anglers who still fished their way through my imagination. So it was that I turned again to Bill Stockdale's way with the trout of upper Wharfedale, determined to master its challenge and to achieve my final metamorphosis into a true Kilnsey fisherman.

Many of the members talked reverently of the upstream wet: as the truest test of a fisher's skill and as the surest tactic, when fished by practised hands in the right conditions, of filling a basket. Most of Jerry's heroes had made their monstrous catches with wet flies fished upstream or with the creeper or the upstream worm. But, although members talked of the upstream wet and were loud in its praise and had all fished it when they were young, it soon became clear to me that very few of them still fished in this way. Many fished downstream and had never fished differently; but I am not thinking of these; I am thinking of the experts – there were perhaps half a dozen of them apart from Bill – and I think I am right in saying that, in the early years of my membership, these half or dozen experts now fished dry as I did, although unlike me they fished with lethal delicacy, throwing long or short lines exactly where they wanted to throw them and dropping their floating flies a yard or a foot or a few inches above the noses of feeding trout.

They were certainly fine fishermen, even if their skill was perhaps less refined and precise than it seemed to me forty years ago; they caught many more trout than I did, but they had abandoned tradition in favour of more obvious delights; they were not the men to pass on to me the secrets of the upstream wet. In looking back I am almost certain that Bill Stockdale would have been proud to make me his disciple and pass on to me the mysteries of a dying art; at the time I was unwilling to approach him and to ask his help; I thought that he was too busy catching trout to concern himself with a young and clumsy fisher; I did not realise that he could have taught me the theory of his method in half an hour before dismissing me to the river to spend whole seasons learning its efficient practice.

With no riverside tutor to guide me I went back to my books. By now I had read Stewart several times, loving his vigorous prose and his delight in huge catches and his lawyer's taste for argument. He was the great champion of the upstream wet and he had very clearly been a master angler, but his explanation of the method was out of date and imprecise, or so it struck me at the time. Apart from *The Practical Angler,* my fishing books were mainly chalkstream classics (it would be years before I got my own copies of Pritt and of Edmonds and Lee); but Plunket Greene and Grey had been joined by Sawyer and Hills and Skues; it was Skues who proved the decisive influence, for by reading and rereading *The Way of a Trout with a Fly* I drank in his advocacy of the nymph; and he wrote so persuasively, with such cogent logic and such caustic wit, and he caught so many enormous trout, that I came to regard his nymphs as improved versions of the spider patterns of the North, which is, I suppose, how he regarded them himself.

I began to imagine how, by introducing the nymph to the Kilnsey length of the Wharfe, I should remain faithful to the past, by fishing a sunk fly toward the source of the river, while at the same time winning for myself the status of an innovator: as the man who had introduced Hampshire wisdom to the streams of the North Country. I dreamt up this ridiculous fantasy long before I had acquired anything but the most rudimentary knowledge of traditional upstream fishing, long before I had realised the difference between a nymph of the Sawyer-school and one after the fashion of Skues. I think that I had still to hear of Oliver Kite or the induced take, and I certainly had no idea that northern fishermen – notably, of course, W.H. Lawrie – had been experimenting with nymphs thirty or forty years before I decided to become their champion on the banks of the Wharfe.

So it was, anyway, that, as a fisher inspired by the long tradition of a Yorkshire river, my first determined efforts with wet flies fished upstream were made, not with Bill Stockdale's sensible patterns but with strange immigrants from the South, flies with stunted hackles and swollen thoraxes and bulging wing-cases, or still stranger creations put together from turns of copper wire and a few fibres from a pheasant's tail; for I searched out a few nymphs in the trays of the local tackle-shop and, in defiance of the shopkeeper's contempt – he said that they were useless, that he had forgotten where they came from and that I would do much better with spider patterns or with dry flies – in defiance of Ken's scorn I bought half a dozen of them. I think there was a Pheasant Tail among them; there was something called an Olive Nymph and something called an Iron Blue. What the others were called I have long since forgotten, but I was convinced they would all prove equally deadly and I looked forward very eagerly to the underwater wink with which the trout would greet them: a sign to the progressive angler to turn his wrist and drive home the hook.

These nymphs were bought out of season – it may have been November, it may have been at the beginning of March – but there came a day in April and it was not the raw sort, with a biting wind that still belongs to winter and blows rain and hail and driving sheets of snow down from the fells; nor was it the mild, damp sort with that sense of quiet expectancy, with a low cover of cloud and a mist of drizzle on the air, with wet stones and soaked grass and water dripping slowly into the pools from buds and branches; it was neither of these. It was the vibrant sort, the warm and sunny sort with a lively upstream breeze, with singing birds and sailing clouds and a pulse of excitement running through everything. It was the April day when I saw the year's first swallows. It was that rare sort of April day: the sort that is unequivocally spring.

I had fished dry in the morning and, although a trickle of olives had brought a few trout onto the rise, the dry fly had been a flop. Coming to Knipe Dub I rested, as always, under my sycamore and chewed a sandwich thoughtfully. There were fish feeding and they did not want a Grey Duster or a dry Greenwell or a Blue Quill; it could be that some other dry fly would do the trick; but perhaps they were feeding just under the surface on the hatching nymph; perhaps the time had come for those peculiar creatures that had recently come to live in one of the compartments of my fly-box; perhaps, in other words, it was time to become a practising rather than a theoretical disciple of Skues by tying a nymph to the end of my cast and proving its virtue on a river hundreds of miles from the very different rivers for which he had devised them.

I still have quite a clear picture of the Olive Nymph that was chosen for the beginning of the great experiment; I am quite certain that it was weighted – though probably only slightly – and that, without knowing it, I was therefore about to become a disciple of Sawyer rather than of Skues. I knew very little about artificial nymphs; I had never fished one before; the only patterns I had seen – apart from pictures in books – were those in the local tackle dealer's tray from which I had chosen the half-dozen in my fly-box; but I was suddenly convinced that, with my Olive Nymph now ready to swim seductively down the currents of the river Wharfe, I was about to catch a sackful of trout.

Half an hour later I was less certain; for just as soon as the Olive Nymph had touched the water and disappeared things were no different from my earlier efforts with the traditional upstream wet (I cannot think why I had fancied that they might be); immediately I felt cut off from all contact with my nymph, which seemed to have escaped into a secret and independent existence somewhere beneath the surface of the river, somewhere beyond my knowledge or my control. I watched the water for gleams and winks and bulges, but I had little idea what I was looking for and it seemed to me that the whole river was full of bulges and winks and gleams. I watched the end of my line for slides and pulls and tell-tale deviations; they seemed to happen all the time and I could not tell whether they were caused by the current or by a taking trout. I pulled in line with my left hand, but with no idea whether it was too little or too much, and with no obvious sign to suggest to me that I had risen a trout or frightened one or made them all shake with silent laughter at my clumsy efforts to catch them on the nymph.

It was very dispiriting and the confidence that had only recently been brimful within me had soon almost drained away. I did not tell myself that nymph-fishing was beyond my limited skills and should be abandoned; I said that I had made a start and would come back to it soon; I argued that conditions were probably more favourable for the floating fly and that it was time to have another go with the Grey Duster or the Ginger Quill. But then, as I lifted the line for another cast, thinking that very soon the Olive Nymph would be returning to its compartment in my fly-box, I suddenly realised that I had hooked a fish, acknowledging almost at the same moment that he had also been lost.

There had been an electric tightness to the line; there had been a tug and a splash and the briefest vision of a struggling fish, and then the struggle was over and the line was loose, leaving a fisherman caught somewhere between exultation and despair, but a fisherman with no intention of retying his trust to a Grey Duster, but determined to persevere with the Olive Nymph until he rose and caught a trout with it, fishing on, if needs must, for hours and hours on end; for that pricked fish, although it had pricked itself without any wilful intervention on my part, had taught me that it was really possible, that I could, if only I fished hard enough and long enough, catch a trout on the nymph. Already I was dreaming of the day when I should kill more trout than

Bill Stockdale and be acknowledged as the man who had introduced the deadly refinements of the chalkstream to the rougher waters of the Yorkshire dales.

In those days I still fished with a silk line, dismissing the new plastic lines, just as I dismissed glass-fibre rods, as unpleasant and unlovely modernisms. I had, of course, tried neither the new lines nor the new rods; but I knew that split-cane and silk were what I needed. I still have the old double-tapered Kingfisher number three; it is supple and slender and altogether more beautiful than any of the lines that have supplanted it. Even after my conversion I used now and then, as a sort of homage to times past, to take it fishing and tell myself how smoothly it uncurled over the water. My conversion, in fact, belonged to that first afternoon's nymph-fishing, when I found that suddenly I was longing for a line that my eyes could follow more easily in rough water; I had soon determined that, on my next day's nymph-fishing, I would be equipped with a white fly-line, a white and plastic one of exactly the type that I had so recently thought repellent. For the time being I had to make do with outmoded silk.

I was fishing the little pools and runs above Knipe Dub, gazing into the water, gazing at my sliding line, waiting for the moment to strike. I fancy that, in my fisherman's eyes, there was something of the probing lust of a heron's gaze; but my fisher's lust was unsupported by instinct or experience or by a murderous beak. I must have missed fish. Certainly, thinking that I had seen a twitch or pull on the line that owed nothing to the current, I struck at least a dozen times and half-expected to feel the solid resistance of a trout. Perhaps hope was beginning to wither again, perhaps the inspiration of that pricked trout was beginning to fade; but then I turned my wrist without knowing why – I was fishing the broken water along the edges of a pool that I now call Deepwater Dub – and found that I was connected to a trout. He fought and he splashed and just once he leapt into the sunshine. I think he weighed ten ounces.

He was no monster – though, in those days, a ten inch trout was perfectly respectable – but he brought me as much joy as any trout that I have ever caught. He was a momentous and memorable trout, one of the most important trout of my fishing life. I can remember thinking, as I admired him on the bank before slipping him almost unwillingly into my bag, that the blackbirds were singing in celebration of my achievement and that the swallows had flown all the way from Africa just to watch me hooking trout on the nymph. Guessing that they had not made the journey for a single demonstration I was very eager to give them more and was soon fishing again, casting upstream with bright hope and with deep faith in the irresistible attractions of the Olive Nymph on the end of my line.

It was one of those wonderful times by a river when expectations are raised and then fulfilled. There are other times when one trout seems certain to be the first of many but it turns out not to be so; for the hatch fails or the fish turn awkward or trout after trout drops from the hook or the river rises in sudden spate or some unaccountable whimsy puts the fish down. This was not one of those occasions when hope leaps up and shines as brightly and as briefly as a rainbow in the sky. It was an afternoon in spring when a young fisher found new eyes, or found a new way of looking with those that he already had, for he found that he was beginning to see the signs, beginning to mark the indications, beginning to understand the messages that tell an upstream angler when to strike. He was very happy, because he was beginning to hook fish on an unseen fly drifting towards him; and every bird along the riverbank seemed aware of his performance and seemed to be competing with his neighbour to produce the loudest acclaim.

There was not a big hatch, but there were olives fluttering from the water and the wagtails were waiting and ready to pounce. There was no great rise of trout to this trickle of fly, but here and there a fish was making rings and, beneath the surface, they were willing to grab my nymph. They were spring fish and I suppose they were hungry fish, seizing what they took for food with an eagerness that perhaps helped a novice to interpret the signs they sent to him and to turn his wrist at the hooking time; it may have been this, though I rather doubt it. I no longer believe that the signs of spring are necessarily more obvious than the summer and autumn signs. More likely it was one of those moments of revelation and discovery, those wonderful and exciting moments when, after long periods of search and doubt and confusion, hidden things begin at last to become clear, when secrets finally begin to uncover themselves, when strange languages suddenly start to make sense.

The two hours that followed were marvellous. I could not have been happier, not even if I had stumbled upon the hidden key to alchemy or if, after years of laborious and unpromising research, I had suddenly, and when least expecting it, discovered the secret of eternal youth. I had, in fact, made a much more precious discovery: one that brought a pleasure with no threat of eventual satiety or despair; I had discovered that I could catch trout fishing a sunk fly upstream and my only desire was to fish today, tomorrow and every other day, always fishing upstream and always fishing an Olive Nymph; for the excitement of that electric twitch on the line, the thrilling fulfilment of lifting my rod to feel the sudden weight of an unglimpsed trout: this was all a delight so marvellous that it could never pall, could never breed boredom or disenchantment or disgust; it was a refined delight, connected to a fragile length of nylon, but it brought a thumping elation that subsided only slowly, as I gazed at the fish I had just killed, into a deep and glowing contentment.

The sun shone down and, from time to time, I stood still in the river for a few moments, enjoying the warm touch of the breeze on my cheek and following the patterns of light in the water and over the carved bedrock beneath, or looking at the buds on leaning branches and feeling that they were unfolding even as I stared at them. I remember that, in one such interlude, a pair of mallard flew upstream, high over my head, and that I took off my cap and waved it at them in some sort of spring greeting. I was light-headed with the joy of it all and my heart was so full that it went out to everything around me. There was something close to rapture in my response to the events of that afternoon; it was one of those times when to be a fisherman is the best blessing in the world.

I may have caught four fish; it may have been five, but I was already an expert when at last I finished, and already I despised the dry fly, pitying the poor fishers that knew no better than to think it best. Bill Stockdale was spared my pity and contempt, receiving instead a mixture of gratitude and condescension: gratitude because it was he who had inspired me to fish wet flies in the direction God had always intended them to be fished: condescension because he had not progressed beyond those primitive northern spiders that had now been supplanted by the nymph. I never had the chance of drawing his attention to the patterns of Skues and Sawyer and so earning his derision. I never saw him again. On the day I caught my first trout on the nymph he was already dying of cancer. At the time I knew nothing of this. He lingered on for perhaps a year and, although he was driven over to the Wharfe once or twice to look at the river that had given him so many trout, I do not think that he ever fished again.

Away from the river I had turned into a schoolmaster and my home, at least during term, was now in Bristol. It surprises me, when I look back, that I never thought of leaving the school for a day and setting out fishing on Sundays, taking my rods to Blagdon or to Wales or to the rivers of the West Country; but at this time fishing for me meant Kilnsey and Kilnsey alone and, even during the holidays, with the Ribble and the Ure and the Eden within easy reach, even then I thought of nowhere but Wharfedale and the Wharfe, and of no length of the Wharfe except for those gracious miles between Grass Woods and Kettlewell.

I was besotted with the Kilnsey water and it was here, during the first summer holidays of my life as a schoolmaster, that I spent days on end fishing nymphs, only to find that there were long mornings and hot afternoons and glowing evenings when the trout would have none of them; when, if they wanted anything at all, it was the Grey Duster that I had thought never to use again and which I tied to the end of my cast with some feeling of failure and defeat.

My knowledge of natural flies was superficial, going little beyond the ability to identify spring olives, iron blues and blue wings, to tell spinners apart from duns, sedges from stone-flies and to see clouds of small black or blackish flies swarming over the water and lump them all together, whether they were bred from land or water, whether they were just small or very small indeed, as black gnats and an infernal nuisance.

I fished three or four patterns of nymph. They were, I think, all weighted, all dressed on fourteen hooks and, whenever they failed, I went back to the Grey Duster, which I possessed in various sizes, although when the iron blues hatched I used a fly designed with the iron blue in mind, because I had learned several years earlier that trout eating iron blues were selective and sometimes very difficult. The Grey Duster was also abandoned when the trout were clearly gorging themselves on little black things; it was abandoned in favour of a knotted midge or something similar. I cannot remember that these small black flies often caught me trout, with the exception of that day on the Skirfare which I have already mentioned. I was able to tie very simple flies but I rarely bothered, fishing with shop-bought flies or flies given to me by friends.

The point of all this is to show how limited were the options I chose to exercise, which now explains to me why, in settled summer conditions, I found it so difficult to catch more than the occasional trout. The nymph, in particular, was a bitter disappointment; it brought me a fish now and then but it never repeated the triumph of that glorious afternoon in April when I had first used it. More and more I reverted to the dry fly, but I still longed for that wonderful twitch on the line, that slide or twitch or jerk that suddenly turned into the throbbing pressure of a hooked trout.

I cannot imagine why it never occurred to me to try spiders again, flies designed for Yorkshire rivers, flies with soft hackles sensitive to the rough embrace of tumbling water. But it never did, not at least until a Sunday in August when, coming to the Wharfe after Mass in Clitheroe, I found, looking down on the river from the road above, that it was big and brown and not at all, it seemed to me, a river in the mood to surrender a bagful of trout to the nymph or the dry fly.

When I got down to the water it was in fact neither as big nor as brown as I had thought. It was certainly full and fast and coloured, but it was already fining down, already beginning to glow. It was, in short, a wet-fly water and, unless there was more rain, it would become a better water by the hour. It turned my thoughts to spiders and for some reason I decided to fish them downstream.

The day was typical of a sort that often comes in August. There was thick cloud hanging low, with damp air beneath it and barely a breath of wind. The leaves were unstirring in the heavy stillness, dark and limp and tired. There were no birds singing and the loudest noises were the impatient sound of the river and the swish of my line beneath the trees. Clumps of seeding thistles spiked the fields, sticking out of the sodden grass like broken and tufted arrows, while the sheep, covered in half-grown coats of soggy wool, browsed with a dishevelled and dejected air.

There was that feeling that belongs to still and cloudy days in August: the feeling that summer has lost its bloom, grown old before its time and sunk into a senile torpor from which it will never be roused. There was something almost oppressive in the calm, something that bred the beginnings of autumn sadness and told me to take slow steps along the bank; and the smoke from my pipe had no energy to rise and curl; it sank down wearily, spreading and then dissolving along the surface of the water.

Only the river was out of tune with the brooding stillness of the day, for it was running with lively purpose, raised and impatient and shot with the dark lustre of peat. It was a river full of restless energy and its fish seemed to have caught the mood; for they were poised on the fin and eager to grab every fly that came their way. I discovered this with my first few casts, for they all brought fish snatching at the flies, although none was firmly hooked. And then I paused and looked round and realised that there was a trout busy in every eddy, every pocket of resting water, and in all those quieter margins beneath the banks. The fly were, of course, blue wings and it was already a big hatch; the greed of the trout had soon stirred my own fisher's appetite, sweeping away the slowness of August thoughts with the sudden urge to turn the hunger of the fish to my advantage by catching at least a score of them.

I had started at Knipe Dub, with a Greenwell on the point, a Partridge and Orange above it and, for some reason, a Butcher – indisputably no member of the spider tribe – on the top dropper. With so much surface activity, and with the river less full and less coloured than I had first thought, I was already considering a change to the dry fly, but I decided to give my team of wet flies a few more casts to prove itself. Within five minutes this had brought me a trout; I think he took the Greenwell, but frustration soon set in; with almost every cast I rose another fish, but time and again they shook themselves free with a wiggle or a splash. An expert with downstream flies would very quickly have filled his bag; but I was no expert and I never fished downstream flies with any confidence or conviction; I never managed or mended the line, which was swept round by the current while I waited for trout to grab my flies. I did not expect to hook them, except by chance, and at the same time I knew that chance brought very few trout to the net.

It was now that on a sudden impulse, one of those happy impulses that change men's lives, I turned myself round and did not change to a dry fly; instead of this I started fishing the same three wet flies upstream, casting them to the edges of turbulence and to the quieter flow under the bank. I had been fishing for no more than a few minutes, fishing water that I had already fished with my downstream flies, when the line slid forward and I hooked a trout. The next pool produced three or four, all taken from the edges of the stream; they were small even by the standards of twenty years ago and only one of them was killed. Deepwater Dub brought me a genuine pounder and from the next run, a long run where the river flows along a steep wooded bank; here from the sides of the current I caught so many trout that even the next day I could no longer remember whether it had been ten or a dozen or even more. But years later I can still remember the excitement of every cast, I can remember those sudden twitches on the line and I remember the yellow gleam of turning trout shining through the darker stain of the river's flow.

The leaves were still and dark. The banks were a weary tangle of matted and sodden decay. It was a dank and gloomy sort of day, sunk into melancholy, and the clouds, too heavy to support themselves in the sky, were sagging down over the fells. It was a day for quiet reflection on the passing year, it was a day for pensive thoughts and there was I, exultant in the middle of it all, catching and killing trout and impatient for the next cast and for the next fish.

The rise went on for hours, right through the morning and deep into the afternoon, but it was one of those days when fishing the water is just as productive as fishing the rise. They are wonderful days for the upstream wet: days when every cast is made in the hope of another fish. I caught trout from quiet pockets behind stones, I caught them from the tail of every pool, from the sides of every run; I caught them from foam-filled eddies and from glowing peaty glides where I could see them rising and turning as they seized my fly. The line twitched and darted, it paused and slid and jerked; once or twice it seemed almost to leap forwards in its eagerness to catch me another trout. I do not think that I have ever experienced another such day; I have known trout similarly greedy for most of a morning, for part of an afternoon or for a couple of hours; but this frenzy of greed, which seemed to have infected every trout in the river, this orgy of feeding had already started when I came to the river at ten in the morning and it was not quite over when I left some time after six.

I fished almost to Kettlewell, catching trout all the way. Then I staggered back to my sycamore on the edge of Knipe Dub and lay beneath the leaves, smoking and drinking tea and munching sandwiches that had long been forgotten for more important things. I have no idea how many trout I had caught; it cannot have been fewer than fifty and it may have been many more. It was my first successful day with the upstream wet and most certainly it brought more fish to net than any of the innumerable days that have come since. It was the day of a lifetime, given to me at this new beginning to confirm me as a fisher of upstream flies.

It seemed almost beyond belief as I lay beneath the sycamore with a feeling of perfect and weary and bemused contentment. The wonder of it all is still alive in me. As I sprawled on the edge of the river, trying to blow smoke rings and not much bothered that, except by accident, I could not manage it, not much bothered because I was so happy that I had at last learned to do something much more important; as I lay there smoking, anyway, I realised how the cloud had lifted from the hills and how there were shadings of blue across the sky; the daytime heaviness was softening into early evening calm. I thought of

Bill Stockdale, the Kilnsey master of the upstream wet, and prayed for him. Then, to finish the day, I went down to the lower of the two little falls beneath Knipe Dub and killed a trout of one and a half pounds; it made ten in my bag, which was more than had ever been there before, and so I trudged back happily to the car and left the Wharfe until the next day brought me back. Of course I fished upstream wet and I caught some trout, but it was something like half a dozen rather than fifty or more. It was enough.

Ever since that Sunday I have been, first and foremost, a fisher of upstream flies that sink an inch or two, soft-hackled flies that wake to life and movement in the rough currents of a northern trout stream. There are those who, as I did myself for a short time, fish these rivers with nymphs, and there are certain circumstances when a weighted nymph is likely to be more successful than traditional spiders: when, for example, fish are deep in the pools and especially in the first weeks of the season, on cold April mornings with no hatching fly when any heavy nymph, but best of all a Killer Bug, will sometimes produce sport from an apparently lifeless river; but I am convinced that, in most northern streams, in swift and knotted and tumbling currents, the Partridge and Orange, the Waterhen Bloa and the Purple Snipe are, on most occasions, far more effective than anything from the mind of Skues or Sawyer. There are times, by the way, when chalkstream trout find them irresistible.

The experience of a gloomy Sunday in August almost banished the nymph from my fly-boxes; within a season I had virtually abandoned the dry fly as well, embracing the great tradition of Stewart and Pritt and Bill Stockdale. For something like ten years I fished almost exclusively with soft-hackled spiders and almost always I fished them upstream, searching likely water with a short line, casting over rising fish, moving slowly on my way, trying different patterns and different sizes, enlarging my knowledge and my experience, enthralled by the subtleties, the excitements and the deep satisfactions to be found in this beautiful style of angling.

It was foolish, of course, to swear allegiance to a single method and it must have cost me scores of trout. My fishing approach is much more varied now; it is even broad-minded enough, or perhaps vulgar enough, to include something called the upstream worm. How my practice as an angler became less narrow – in particular how I relearned the virtues of the floating fly and then began to dabble with worms – will be explained in later chapters. But nothing has changed my belief that, although the wet-fly fished upstream is not the only way, it is the best single way of fishing the troubled rivers of the North. And when these same rivers have been lifted by rain and are running full and glowing from the peat, then it is that we fishers of the upstream wet head forth in the morning with high hopes and easy hearts; and the evening often finds us resting and smoking beneath the branches of some favourite tree, lying there with thankful hearts, with hope fulfilled and with a bulging creel lying somewhere beside us in the grass: a creel that has been filled with trout put there by the Partridge and Orange, the Waterhen Bloa and the Purple Snipe.

CHAPTER SIX

I spent three years in Bristol; they were three happy years which taught me, among much else, that I wanted to remain a schoolmaster; at the same time I realised that, although I enjoyed living in Bristol, I should never feel truly settled there; I knew that sooner or later, finding the pull of the North irresistible, I should search out some place in which to put down deep roots. And so it was that I came to Sedbergh and decided, almost as soon as I had arrived, that I wanted to stay; for I found that I liked the school and at the same time I realised that, surrounded by its hills, watered by its own rivers and less than an hour's drive from the only river that really mattered to me, Sedbergh was without doubt the place that I had been waiting to find and to recognise as the place where I belonged.

The best way to the Wharfe from Sedbergh is to drive up Garsdale to Hawes, where you turn left and head up through Gayle and over Cam Houses; then it is down to Oughtershaw and Beckermonds before following the beginnings of the river through Yockenthwaite, Hubberholme and Buckden, through Starbotton and Kettlewell and so, after the rough poetry of these northern names, down to the main beats of the Kilnsey club. I made this journey once or twice in the September of my first term in Sedbergh, but then the season finished and it was a road untravelled except in the imagination for almost six months.

It was not until the following spring that I realised just how wonderful it was that fishing now belonged to the free hours of my working life and not only to the holidays. Most weekends I followed the road up Garsdale to Hawes, then over Cam Houses and down to Kettlewell; it took me past the club's neglected water on either side of Yockenthwaite, which was often so thin that it seemed to deserve its neglect, although there were times after rain when the water seemed almost to be imploring me to investigate; but I was always eager to get down to Watersmeet or Black Keld and so always I drove on, arguing that I should surely catch nothing but midgets so high up the river; always I drove on but my curiosity was beginning to stir and more than once I told myself that, some day soon but not just yet, some day before too long I should pry into the secrets of the Yockenthwaite water with a rod and a team of wet flies, if only to confirm that Bill Stockdale had been right in insisting that it grew nothing but troutlings.

Perhaps I drove down the beginnings of the Wharfe a dozen or more times in the course of the spring; and then there came a Sunday when I set off for Kilnsey after midday Mass, impatient to be on the river below Kettlewell and happy that I had spent the morning working at my books, so that I should be able to fish just as long as I chose, perhaps even staying deep into the spring evening. It was a glorious prospect, for the sun was shining; there had been showers overnight and I could see, as I drove up Garsdale, that the Clough, which is Garsdale's river, was raised and shot with peaty light; it was a perfect water for the upstream wet and the Wharfe would almost certainly be just the same, full and flowing with the dark radiance that it brings down from the moors.

There are little waterfalls all the way up Garsdale; that Sunday was probably the day when I first properly noticed them, with the water spilling and foaming over their limestone shelves. Ever since I have always looked out for them on my way to the Wharfe, because nine times out of ten they tell me what sort of sport to expect when I get there. Sometimes they are a weary trickle, sometimes they are almost bare slabs, asking me whether I have remembered to collect my worms from their moss-filled jar in the potting shed. There are times when the yellow rock is engulfed by a rushing torrent of brown water, confirming what our keeper has already told me on the phone: that it has rained all night, that the river is in full spate and unfishable. Sometimes I refuse to believe what I have been told on the phone; sometimes the urge to fish is so strong that I set off in spite of what the keeper has told me, and always it takes at least two waterfalls to convince me that I have been told the truth, that I am wasting my time and should do better to get back to Sedbergh, to put my rods away and get out my gun in order to make war on rabbits rather than on trout; sometimes two waterfalls are not enough; sometimes it takes a third or even a fourth vision of surging water to drive home the message and put my car in reverse. And then, as I return down the valley, I glance at the waterfalls again, but now resentfully, as though it is all their fault, as though they have turned into wild cascades on purpose: just in order to ruin my day's sport.

Once or twice I have ignored the message of Garsdale's waterfalls; I have told myself that some of the rain might have missed Wharfedale or that the Wharfe might already be falling. I have driven on and then driven back an hour later cursing myself for a fool; but, whatever the state of Garsdale's waterfalls and whether or not I pay attention to what they are telling me, I know that fishermen should never be allowed to drive along roads with rivers flowing beside them. We are a menace in such places, because our eyes are never looking where they should be and at any moment we are likely to drive straight into an approaching bus or tractor, or to leave the road altogether and join our thoughts in the middle of running water.

On that Sunday in the first summer of my life at Sedbergh, I managed to avoid contact with passing traffic and to keep my car out of the river Clough. Soon I was heading down into Wharfedale from Cam Houses, down through Oughtershaw, with its old hall half hidden by the trees, past Beckermonds, with its little cluster of cottages in the narrow angle of the two becks that come together to make the Wharfe, over the green-painted iron bridge at Deepdale and then along the river to Yockenthwaite. And it was somewhere between Deepdale and the old pack-horse bridge at Yockenthwaite that a sudden inspiration came to me. I had never seen the high river quite like this before, so full and bright and crying out for a fisher with a team of wet flies. I fancied I had seen trout rising in some of the roadside pools; I was convinced that, if only I cast to them, they would rise to my flies and that some of

them would be worth catching; and this was, after all, Kilnsey water
and there was nothing to stop me fishing it. I had not booked a beat
but merely told the keeper on the phone that I might well drive over in
the afternoon and find a deserted stretch of the river for a few hours'
amusement.

I parked the car opposite the farm at Yockenthwaite and was
soon putting up my tackle and thanking God for an upstream breeze;
I was intending to fish my way up to the pools and the rising trout
that I had so recently glimpsed through the windscreen of my car, but
when everything was ready I found that this intention had just been
abandoned because I had been seized by a second inspiration, by a
sudden urge to find out what happened to the river below Yockenthwaite
bridge, once it had turned its first corner and flowed out of view. Hidden
water, secret water, water with something of mystery in its flow has
always drawn me, although at the same time I have always loved the
familiarity of water stored with the memories of many years. So it was,
anyway, that I crossed the bridge and turned downstream, where the
river left the road and was hidden away by the steeply folded land. I
wandered off downstream and wandered straight into what must be one
of the loveliest miles of fishing in the whole of England.

I was eager to make a start, very eager to catch my first
Yockenthwaite trout, but I was drawn irresistibly by the beauty of the
river and the fields on its either side, which seemed to be telling me
to find out what happened round the next corner or over the next stile
and beyond the next wall. There were great smooth slabs of limestone
where the water flowed yellow; it shone like amber down swift runs
and rock-channels; it splashed and foamed in the sunlight over little
shelves and miniature waterfalls, and there were deep pools delved in
the rock where the water was as dark as Guinness and full of mystery.
I thought there might be two and three pounders down there in holes
and crevices. I could not believe that this stretch of the river was a home
only for troutlings.

There were places where the river was open to the sky and
carried its colour and brightness through a rapid succession of small
pools; in many places there were willows leaning over the water and

trailing their branches in the stream. In other places flowering sycamores and knobbled ashes, now at last bursting into leaf, brought rocking shadows dappled with sunlight, with the drone of insects up there in the leaves and the sweet smell of blossom thick on the air. Here and there the floor of the valley spread itself almost to a field's width. In one spot the steep sides closed in and the river went singing on its way down a little gorge, arched over by birches and ashes and elms.

There was a blackbird or a thrush in every tree; there were larks and curlews floating above them in the blue sky. There were bluebells and primroses under the branches and down the shaded banks, and the narrow walled meadows were so full of buttercups that it was difficult to remember that fields are meant to be green; and up there on the rocky crest of the hill the may blossom was already whitening on the thorns while, somewhere up among them, a woodpecker was laughing himself silly in wild outbursts of manic glee. But the best thing of all was that the river was the heart of the whole landscape, was cradled and sheltered by the steep fields that it had shaped for its passage, and it went on its way, shining and singing and more beautiful than any of the countless beauties that surrounded it, beauties that themselves celebrated its central and surpassing beauty by singing back their greeting to its unending song of joy.

It seemed so close to perfection that I was almost unwilling to start fishing, afraid that failure might darken the wonder of it all. But there were trout rising and they did not all look like midgets; and swallows and martins and screaming swifts were feasting over the river, while wagtails fluttered from stone to stone and seized their prey from air or water. Perhaps I spent twenty minutes, walking and watching and marvelling; it may have been half an hour and I think I sat down to smoke for at least five minutes in the middle of it all.

At last, anyway, I had walked far enough and it was time to start fishing. I got into the water and I made my first cast, which did not catch a fish; not did the next one or the next forty that came after it; and they were not all speculative casts; some were over rising trout and none of these fish paid the slightest attention to my flies, one of which, I seem to remember, was a little Greenwell spider. Then I realised that there were, in fact, few duns hatching; but although there were not many olives coming off the water, there were hawthorn flies trailing their legs in the sunshine above the stream and there were clouds of black gnats swarming over the river and swimming in unwilling drifts down every current and glide.

Off went the Greenwell in favour of a small William's Favourite or something similar. It was a change that brought almost immediate results, catching me a trout that was most certainly not a troutling, a trout that would have been thought a worthy trout five miles downstream at Spout Dub or Black Keld. He was a trout three or four ounces below the pound, he was my first Yockenthwaite trout; he was as beautiful as the water from which he came; he was a glory and a triumph and an omen of things to come; he was also an omen that did not have long to wait to be proved truthful. He was briefly admired and knocked on the head and stuffed in my bag; perhaps two minutes later the rough water at the top of the pool had brought me a fish at least a whole ounce heavier.

There now followed a most glorious hour, when every pool and run brought fish grabbing at the fly and splashing in the sunlight as I dragged them over the net. And there was much more, in the joy these fish brought, than the exhilaration of sport and the savour of success. There was, of course, the thrill of discovery, the sense of revelation and wonder that came with each new feature of the river, where every trout that it surrendered was a secret revealed, a treasure uncovered. But there was something deeper than this; it was an afternoon when I was walking through a new and better and more beautiful world; and it was somehow an even better and more beautiful world because others had declared it a world not worth bothering with. I walked through it with shining eyes and with a heart full of easy rapture. It was one of those times that I think come to all fishermen: when we win back something of the vision of our angling boyhood but at the same time experience it with the deeper gratitude of a grown man.

I was so happy that I was also merciful. I must have caught at least twenty trout in the hour or two that followed the catching and killing of the first. But there were still only three trout in my bag when I came back in sight of the single arch of Yockenthwaite bridge; and it was almost in the shadow of the arch, in the twisting neck of water that connects the bridge pool with the pool below, it was here that a much bigger trout took hold; he fought hard; he weighed one pound and a half and, as I gazed at him in the grass, I thought of Jerry Ingleby and Bill Stockdale and wondered why they had dismissed the water that had just given me so fine a trout as a water where only six-inchers swam. At last the slander had been exposed.

As I drove home that evening, unbothered by a rumbling gear-box, I knew that I was in the grip of a new obsession: that, as far as I was concerned, the finest stretch of water controlled by the Kilnsey Angling Club now started somewhere above Hubberholme and extended indefinitely upstream. I determined to find out precisely where the high water began and ended, so that I might explore every inch of it and catch trout from every pool. I wondered impatiently when I should next be able to get over to Wharfedale and thought that I might be able to manage it on Thursday afternoon.

Above Oughtershaw the road climbs steeply up the fell side before going over the tops and down into Wensleydale; as I drove up the long slope I looked down on the silver windings of Oughtershaw Beck, very bright and enticing way below me in the sunshine, sinuous and shining and full of distant allure; as I looked at this bright vision of water, I was gripped by such a longing to take my rod and follow the water to its source that, if I had been certain that I should not have been poaching – which, by the way, I should have been – then I might well have surrendered to the sudden impulse; I might have turned the car and driven back to Oughtershaw and then put on my waders and gone fishing all over again. Instead of this I drove home to Sedbergh, which was now twice as marvellous as when I had left it a few hours ago, because I had not then realised what it meant to be no more than forty minutes from Yockenthwaite.

Such was the beginning of my happy obsession with the top of the river Wharfe, the long-neglected stretch of water that, as I established before long, ran down from the first pool of the river at Beckermonds, through Deepdale and Yockenthwaite, to a small barn, perhaps three quarters of a mile above Hubberholme, a barn where the inflow of a small beck marked the downstream limit of this most wonderful beat. During the rest of the season I fished there as often as possible, but I discovered that I could only indulge my obsession with restraint; it turned into an obsession that was almost temperate, a temperance imposed, not by the force of my character, but by the nature of the river itself, which had soon taught me that its beginnings were only worth fishing after rain; for the water fell away so quickly that, in summer at least, it was hopeless for sport with the fly only a day or two after conditions had been perfect. This meant that I could never get enough of it, could never feel sated with the beginnings of the river Wharfe; it also meant that I did not neglect the main beats of the club water; I still fished at Watersmeet and Spout Dub and Black Keld and still found contentment there. But whenever the rain came, whenever the river rose and began to fall and clear and shine, then I was up there on the high water, proving to myself all over again that Bill and Jerry had both been wrong.

CHAPTER SEVEN

I was a member of the Kirkby Stephen Angling Association for two years before I ever got round to fishing any of its water. I kept meaning to go, especially as Kirkby was so much nearer to Sedbergh than Kilnsey, which was the main reason why I had joined the Association in the first place. I kept meaning to go; I kept insisting to myself that the next time I went fishing it would be on the Eden at Kirkby Stephen, but always, when the next time came, I found some compelling reason for heading off up Garsdale on my way to the Wharfe. My discovery of the wonderful fishing at Yockenthwaite was at least partly to blame, for whenever I knew that conditions would be just right at Yockenthwaite, whenever my mind's eye could see the water flowing bright and full under Yockenthwaite bridge, then there was not even the pretence that I might choose to fish anywhere else. I was captivated by Yockenthwaite and its little river and its not so little trout. In fact conditions were rarely ideal for Yockenthwaite; they were more often hopeless but still, in spite of telling myself that it was time for the Eden, I would set off towards Kirkby Stephen and end up at Watersmeet or Spout Dub or Black Keld.

Fishing for me had come to mean the Wharfe, a river that I held in something like sacramental reverence as a river that had flowed through my life with moral force and healing power. My attitude to the Wharfe was that of a worshipper, which explains, I suppose, why

I found it impossible to go fishing anywhere else. And so for two whole years the Eden, barely twenty minutes drive from Sedbergh, was denied the honour of my presence on its banks and had to wait patiently for the day when at last I would get in its water and try to catch some of its trout.

I cannot remember what finally persuaded me that to fish the Eden would not be an act of infidelity or apostasy; perhaps it was a sudden attack of common sense but, whatever it was, I can remember my first Eden day very clearly. It was a morning in mid-April, a morning of yellow spring sunshine with a cold breeze blowing through the bright air. I went to the beat between Blandswath and Musgrave, where the river flows in a long and erratic half circle between two bridges and is joined by the Belah towards the top of its wandering journey through the fields.

Walking downstream from Blandswath bridge I was immediately struck by the colour of the water, by the red stain it carried from its crumbling banks of red clay, by the red glow of sandstone down the runs and glides. The pools seemed longer, less turbulent features than the deep dubs of the Wharfe at Kilnsey, the runs less rocky and broken; undoubtedly there was a more leisurely air to the river's passage than to the impatient progress of the Wharfe above Kilnsey. I was high up the Eden, little more than ten miles from the source, but it was a softer and wider landscape than the steep-sided valley that hems in the upper Wharfe. The hills were a prospect rather than a presence, with the blue shapes of the Pennines sweeping up to Cross Fell somewhere above Appleby, with the bold outline of Wild Boar Fell sharp in the sky five or six miles to the south. Compared with the Wharfe at Kilnsey there was almost a lowland feel to the river and its landscape. There were long lines of willows, flushing orange and brown in the spring sunshine; there were tall trees in the broad pastures, spreading chestnuts and noble elms, and already there were lambs everywhere.

I fished until four o'clock; at some stage of the day a bailiff appeared to ask me for my licence, which was, of course, back in Sedbergh. He seemed to believe my assurance that I had one; he did not threaten me with prosecution or drive me from the river and we chatted about the Eden and its trout for five minutes. He told me that fly-life was plentiful, that the trout were mainly wild, that some of them were big, that there was a healthy stock and that, although there were days in early spring when big hatches brought on a general rise, I would probably have to wait until May for the river to reveal its riches. He also told me that in future I should always carry my licence with me – advice which I have generally ignored – and then he left me to my sport. There was a trickle of olives on either side of noon and I caught a fish from the long and gentle run above the junction with the Belah; but it was a grayling, a big one well over the pound; it was also limp and lustreless, a spawning fish that I returned to the river as tenderly as possible.

I spent most of my time walking the banks, looking for rising trout and marking down promising places for future visits. Already I had sensed that I should soon feel at home on the Eden, with its red and crumbling banks and with its long pools and glides; I realised that there was room for two rivers in my fishing life and I was pleased that at last I had made the effort, forcing myself to abandon the Wharfe for a day and try my luck somewhere new.

This first excursion to the Eden, although I did not drive home with a bagful of trout, was undoubtedly a success, simply because I left the river wanting to return. My second visit came about a week later. This time I fished further upstream on either side of Eastfield bridge. There was a dusting of new snow on Mallerstang Edge; often there were dark clouds over the hills, with sheets of hail or snow streaming beneath them, but down on the river it was mainly sunshine with a squally wind gusting upstream. In the morning I fished from Beckfoot up to the bridge and I was delighted by what I found: a river now roughly on the scale of the Wharfe at Yockenthwaite, perhaps slightly larger and evidently less prone to shrink away to a trickle, a river where limestone and sandstone mingled their influence, so that it flowed with merging impressions of red and yellow. There were deep pools, but they were neither so deep nor so mysterious as the rocky dubs of the Wharfe; there were long flats with streamy runs flowing into them and on either side of the river there were level fields, wide fields full of the sounds of curlews and oyster-catchers.

At lunchtime I fled back to the car with a storm racing up behind me, ripping catkins from the alders and tossing them onto the water with little splashes of spray. It was a wild dash beneath the menace of rushing cloud, with hail rattling against my old Barbour and with my cap blown onto the shingle. But I made it without a soaking and the storm failed its promise; in ten minutes spring had returned and it was suddenly spring of the warm and windless sort. As soon as I had listened to the Archers, while drinking tea and chewing a sandwich and then smoking for a few minutes – as soon, anyway, as events in Ambridge had run their course for another day, I went fishing again and found that a few trout were rising on the flats above the bridge. The water was low and very clear; they were difficult to approach, but one stayed for me to cast to him and I caught him on a wet Greenwell. I killed him too; he was my first Eden trout and he was also the last of the day, for the trickle of olives had soon petered out altogether. He was the only trout of the day but he was a beginning and, not knowing at the time that he would remain a single presence in my creel, while fishing on and searching likely water in the hope of a brace, I suddenly realised that I was enjoying myself enormously and liked the look of everything that I saw.

I found too that it was a relief to be fishing a stretch of water where there were no memories, where there was only this present and the prospect of future intimacy. Memories are a delight and an enrichment, but they can also become oppressive and there are times on the Wharfe, especially in September, when the weight of long association seems so heavy that it almost stifles the immediate sensations of a fishing day. There come autumn days at Kilnsey when I spend more time thinking about the past than working out what the fish are up to and putting a few of them in my creel.

On the banks of the Eden, on that afternoon in April thirty years ago, there were no memories waiting for me and I found it exhilarating. It was a pure delight to round a corner for the first time and see the river spilling over a yellow shelf of rock before spreading into a pool full of promise and bright water; then to pass on under the trees and out again into the sunlight, following the wandering path of the water and discovering something new round every turn. I saw the river as it was, sparkling under alders and birches with their tips all purple, and I saw it as it would be when the leaf had burst and the blossom was blowing, with iron blues scattered like black petals across the water. I saw it in fact and foresight and, because I had never been there before, there were none of the tawdry associations that we leave behind us like footprints wherever we go; there was none of the sadness that I had brought to other places and that could never quite be separated from them. There was only the unsullied brightness of the river, the inviting seclusion of its banks and the sudden conviction that one summer evening, here on the Eden, I should fill my bag with shining trout and feel absurdly happy.

That first summer on the Eden turned into a summer of savage drought and the river was slow to reveal the wonderful fishing with which she rewards those who give time to her. It was, in fact, a season or two before I realised just how special a river the Eden is, but I saw at once that she was most definitely worth fishing and I had soon learned that she bred dayflies and sedges in teeming profusion, that there were much bigger and more dependable hatches of spring olives and iron blues, of blue wings and pale wateries than the general run of my experience on the Wharfe, while the trout that fed on them were often large and always wary and, with few exceptions, as red-fleshed as a sea trout.

I am not going to bore you with the fly life of the Eden, although I shall find it difficult to leave this chapter without telling you a little more about the richness of the river. Before this happens, if it happens at all, there are one or two other things to mention. I shall touch briefly upon experiments with fishing the worm in low water; I shall mention one or two more beats of the Kirkby Stephen fishing; above all I shall try to describe a particular evening when, although I caught only two trout, the glory of the river came to me in sudden revelation.

It was a Saturday evening and the Eden was desperately low, no more than creeping on its way and choked with clotted slime. There was not much of it left and what there was stank of sewage from the inflow of Winton beck. It was not the sort of evening on which you would expect to acknowledge at last that you have fallen in love with another river. It was the beginning of June and I had come to the Eden with all my usual tackle: nets with holes in the mesh, fly-boxes that had not been sorted for years, so that Greenwells kept company with Grey Dusters and Orange Partridges rubbed hackles with Poult Bloas. There were two or three cane rods with bent tips, there was a fishing bag that smelt of dead fish, there was a pair of waders that let in water through at least half a dozen tears and patches; inside them was a clammy pair of stockings that had probably been there since the end of March. There was all this and there might well have been, also relics from some earlier fishing trip, a mouldy sandwich or a decaying sausage roll or a few black bananas. There was all the customary paraphernalia in all its habitual disorder; and the reason for mentioning this is that there was also something else. It was separated from all the usual clobber, set apart from it in a position of honour on the front seat; it was a new addition to my fishing gear; it was a white cotton peg-bag and there were living things inside it, reddish and wriggling and lurking in damp moss. They were, of course, worms and I had come to the river that evening in a mood of high enterprise, resolved to take my first steps towards mastery of a method that Stewart had reckoned second only to the fly. I was determined to fish low water as it is meant to be fished and catch my first trout on the upstream worm.

For about a week I had been gathering worms from the compost heap at the bottom of the garden, digging them up and then housing them in a moss-filled pot and hiding them away in the cool gloom of the potting shed. In between these worm hunts I read what Stewart and Nelson had to tell me about the upstream worm and even bought a book devoted exclusively to the principles and practice of summer worming. Now I proposed to apply my new knowledge and empty the river for, although there seemed to be differences of opinion about how best to cast a worm, and about what size and colour and sort of worm was most ideally suited to low water fishing, there was complete agreement that, if thrown and managed by competent hands, the upstream or clear water worm, the running or the summer worm, was a most deadly way of filling a creel. Had not Nelson, fishing a shrunken Eden one day in 1889, and eager to catch as many trout as possible to feed the sheriff and his retinue at lunch during the next day's assizes, caught nineteen and a half pounds of trout from trickles of water beneath a burning sun? And Stewart, fishing his border streams at a time of extreme low water in July, had caught no less than seventy eight and a half pounds of trout in three consecutive fishing days. There was no controversy about the effectiveness of the worm, but it was also praised as a high and subtle art, and for years I had been telling myself that it belonged, just as surely as the Orange Partridge and the Waterhen Bloa, to the great tradition of North Country angling.

For at least five seasons I had also been telling myself that I should begin to master the wormer's art, drawn by its proclaimed effectiveness and by the challenge of doing it properly and by the same feeling for the past that, ten years earlier, had made me a fisher of upstream flies. I had been keen to make myself a wormer for at least five seasons; at the same time I had been unwilling to sacrifice fishing days to the business of acquiring new skills. The same reticence had long held me back from learning the ways of the upstream wet, but it had been done at last and now a summer of savage drought had finally brought me to the edge of a river – what was left of it – with a bag of worms.

I started at half past six, not with a fifteen foot rod as recommended by Stewart but with a nine foot fly rod, closer to Nelson's practice. And Nelson insisted that he cast his worm, well-scoured and tough, almost as he cast his flies but somewhat slower and a shade more gently. With his much longer rod Stewart swung his worm underarm and urged it forward over the water. Anyway, I proposed to do what Nelson did, I intended to cast my worm slowly and delicately, as soon, that is, as I had baited my hook: a single size 12 hook rather than a tackle with multiple hooks, since I felt that the choice of a 4-hook Stewart tackle or the 2-hook Pennell tackle could wait until I was throwing my worm with something like confidence and catching a trout or two.

As to the worm itself, the authorities recommended a small and lively worm, but I could not remember how many inches meant small and I could not recall their advice on colour. My bag held a baffling selection of worms. There were short thick worms like trunks for bonsai elephants, there were longer, limper creatures like twitching threads, there were passive and apparently belligerent worms, there were pink and brown and almost white ones and there were worms as red as the dawn. I decided eventually that two inches and not too thick made a small and attractive worm and I was fairly sure that the old masters had proclaimed their universal preference for a red worm. Without as much as a prick of guilt I impaled on my hook a worm as nearly as possible matching these criteria and prepared to make my first cast.

It was not a success. The worm flew behind me, promptly flew off the hook and was never seen again. The next worm did the same and the one after that as well. I had soon acknowledged that, however slowly and gently I tried to cast, the movement was still far too brutal to preserve contact between the worm and the hook. Perhaps my rod was too stiff? Perhaps the worms had not been in moss long enough? Perhaps I was too clumsy? Whatever the reason, I could not fish the upstream worm in the manner of Nelson and so I turned to the Stewart style of propelling the worm, swinging it out behind me and then swinging it forward with something of a lover's tenderness.

I tried this several times and then recognized that my nine foot rod was far too short for Stewart's method; for my worm, although it managed to remain attached to the hook, sailed through the sunshine and came to ground repeatedly somewhere on the gravel just a yard or two in front of me. Once or twice it managed to reach water, tepid and very shallow water on the very edge of the stream, slime-clotted water where no trout other than a trout with dementia would ever have thought of stationing himself. My worm, moreover, not only refused to travel any distance; it also refused to go where it was pointed, swerving to one side or the other, catching in moss or stones and finally departing from the hook. It was a difficult business and I remember that, in spite of the frustration of it all, I managed to be amused by the comedy of my incompetence.

I never got as far as a take, which was just as well, for there was bitter controversy among the experts about when to strike. Some upheld the necessity of an immediate response, others insisted that a fisher must wait until his trout had taken a firm hold of the worm and was heading back to his lair to enjoy his meal.

I do not suppose that I persevered in my attempts to fish the upstream worm for much more than half an hour and, for a season or two, that was more or less the end of my efforts to master a method of fishing praised by the old masters as the best way to fill a basket in time of drought. I shall return to the absorbing business of the upstream worm; it is a subject that deserves a chapter to itself; those of you who disapprove will be able to leave it unread. That Saturday evening, anyway, it was back to the fly beneath a changing heaven.

The sun had been fierce all day, with just the suggestion of a breeze: no more than a faint stirring of hot and dusty air. I was waiting for the glowing serenity that the sun spreads with its sinking on still summer evenings, the serenity and the delicious coming of cool air. But suddenly there were two skies: great storm clouds – swollen, still swelling and ominously black – sweeping darkness down from Mallerstang, the hills already streaming grey beneath them, while by the river I was still walking through the languorous calm of windless sunshine under a blue sky. But already I could feel a steely menace creeping into the light and I knew that the quietness all round me must soon be blown away. There was a feeling of tense fragility to the stillness and, as the storm spread into the sunlight, the air was dark and shining at the same time, shining with a dusky metallic glare, shining with a dull pewter gleam and broodingly still. It was the stillness that awaits a cataclysm.

Then the wind came, tearing elm blossom from the branches, whipping up dust from the parched fields, and briefly, with opaque shafts of sunlight still piercing the western clouds, with growling thunder and streaming trees and a rainbow rearing over the meadows, briefly it was like the beginning of the world's end.

With the wind came rain. In less than a minute I was soaked, caught by the bursting storm as I charged back to the car. It was a wild torrent of water and looked certain to last. I sat there smoking, steaming and sweaty, for a time, while the rain battered the roof and the windscreen. I was half angry with the storm for ruining my evening's sport, half grateful because the river was in such desperate need of rain. But the storm had soon spent itself. There was a rim of light over Mallerstang Edge and before long the whole sky was clear again, the air cool and marvellously damp, the river unmoved by the brief downpour and now filling with the whiteness of fading day, its surface scattered with leaves and blossom and broken by the rings of rising trout.

I resumed fishing above Eastfield bridge and returned a few small trout. I came to a waterfall and kept one of eleven inches from the wide pool below it. The fury of the storm made the moist calm that had replaced it twice as delectable; the soft shadows of the deep evening were doubly welcome after the fierce light and glaring colours of the day. Beyond the waterfall, which is, in fact, no more than a shelf of mossy limestone, I came to a long rock pool, where the river flows over ridged and fluted rock, a pool that leads up to a shallow and slightly curving run. I call the place Quiet Corner. The pool hides beneath a canopy of trees and it was now full of shadows and strewn with fallen blossom that caught my flies every second cast. And water was dripping into the river from every leaf, so that in the deep gloom it was difficult to distinguish between the rising fish and those splashing drops.

This was the evening on which Quiet Corner, and the run that belongs to it, became a special place. It may even have been the evening when it was given its name. It is not really a corner at all; there is no more than a slight deviation from true straightness, an insignificant turn to the left of an upstream fisher. It happens where the run, which is beyond the trees, surrenders to the calming force of the pool. The high bank on the right and the move from canopy to open sky somehow exaggerate the impression of a turn. Anyway, I call it a corner and it is most certainly a quiet and lovely place.

I caught nothing from the pool and came to the run where, although you have left the trees, they are still close behind you and waiting for your back cast. It is much better to roll or switch out the line here, a truth I relearned that evening with the loss of a fly. The water was sliding whitely under a dimming sky of palest blue; there were dark rings in the white velvet and there were sipping sounds coming out of them; there were splashes in the faster water towards the head of the run.

The fly I had given to the trees was a wet Pheasant Tail, which had failed to impress two or three rising fish back in the shadows of the pool. There was, I think, an Orange Partridge on the dropper. I cursed, of course, but it was, in fact, a fortunate loss because it forced a change of pattern at a time when, aware that night was falling fast and that I was short of time and had clumsy fingers in the near dark, I should almost certainly have persevered with the fly on the end of my cast. The trees behind me had made this impossible by claiming my Pheasant Tail. Somehow I managed to knot on a wet Greenwell and, almost as soon as he touched the water, there was a boil and then the glorious pull of a heavy fish heading back under the trees, a powerful and determined fish, bending the rod with a throbbing pressure and unglimpsed, invisible in the failing light.

The near darkness, the angry protests of the fish you cannot see, the sound of his struggle in the shadows as he beats his tail somewhere on the surface of the pool, your wild uncertainty whether he weighs a pound or at least twice as much: all this brings a special intensity of excitement to the fight of a late-evening trout. And even when it is all over and you lift him splashing from the river, even then, as the relief of victory floods over you, your heart refuses to beat to a slower rhythm because you can just make out a dim and lashing form, writhing in the mesh of your net, so that, deceived by the falling darkness and led on by hope, you think for a few moments that you have caught the fish of a lifetime.

I thought just that but, when I had stumbled to the bank and stilled the wild movement in my net, I saw at once that he was a good fish rather than a monster. I reckoned him a few ounces short of two pounds. The spring balance seemed to be telling me that he weighed one and three quarter pounds but it was almost impossible to read the scale. I knew, anyway, that he was not a two pounder – I had yet to catch one – but, if there was brief disappointment, it was brief indeed and had soon softened into deep and serene contentment. I sat there in the grass on the edge of the river, not caring that it was wet. I lit my pipe and looked at the dim forms of my two trout, thanking God, as I so often do, that he had chosen to make me a fisherman.

It was time to finish now. Night had come and *The Red Lion* was calling me back to Sedbergh. There was a short walk to the car, with a yellow moon rising over the fields and with, across them, the still and gracious shapes of two tall elms, rising into the moonlight like ghosts of trees rather than substantial things. The river was shining and there were bats squeaking over the waterfall with the beginnings of mist now curling up from the pools. It was very cool and very peaceful after the heat of the day and the brief frenzy of the storm. It was cool and peaceful and there were two trout in my bag. There were days when I wanted ten of them but this evening two was enough and the thought of them, with the prospect of beer at the end of a short road, filled me with deep happiness and confirmed my resolution to catch more trout and still deeper happiness from this river that flowed less than half an hour from my front door.

There were heavy showers overnight and next afternoon the grateful Eden was flowing cleaner and fuller, not in spate but in lively abundance and with that amber glow that we fishers of the upstream wet so love. I fished for about four hours. I fished the same beat as the evening before and killed three trout from a dozen caught. The best of them was another big fish and the turning gleam of his flank brought my heart leaping into my mouth like a sea trout. For some seasons my fisher's heart had been longing for a trout of two pounds, for a trout that would make the most experienced and expert angler feel proud. I had felt sure that the trout of the previous evening was the fulfilment of my dreams and now I was certain again: convinced that if the trout on the end of my line stayed for the net I should at last have fought and tamed a trout weighing two pounds. He was, in fact, exactly the same weight as the trout from Quiet Corner; he was so beautiful that disappointment was impossible and, anyway, within two or three casts I had killed another trout well over the pound. That same afternoon my pipe set my jacket on fire; the water of the Eden helped me to limit the damage and then I fell into the river at Quiet Corner. I came home besotted with the Eden and it has been like that ever since.

I am besotted with the Eden but it is a gentle sort of infatuation. There are two rivers in my life now, but they mean very different things to me. The Wharfe flows through the heart of my life; it is a river that has brought me the joy of a lover and a river where I have felt an outcast's despair; it has bred in me thoughts far beyond laughter or tears and it is a place where fishing sometimes turns into worship. It is, in truth, not as fine a trout stream as the Eden and very soon I shall tell you why, but I bring to fishing the Wharfe an intensity of feeling that I shall never find on the Eden and it is good that this is so. We do not want all our friendships touched with passion; we want, with some, an easy association and, with others, binding love. And so it is with me and my two rivers.

A blank day on the Eden hurts me less than on the Wharfe, because I take to the Eden easier expectations. A good bag comes rather less often on the Eden, because the trout, though plentiful, are somewhat fewer and somewhat more discriminating; a good bag on the Eden brings me joy but it is a lighter joy than comes with a limit of six Kilnsey trout, even though the Eden trout are on the whole more beautiful than the wild trout of the Wharfe.

There have been times, at the end of a day on the Wharfe, when I have laid my catch in the grass and looked with reverent wonder at the spotted beauty of five or six trout, and I have felt that they are the river's reward for my devotion, for making myself worthy to come back to her and catch some of her great store of trout; and there are times, most often at the ending of September days, when I feel such a pressure of joy that it almost hurts; it is an emotion in which joy and sadness meet each other and make something profound. It is an emotion that, as a fisher, I find only on the Wharfe. The Eden has inspired careless rapture, deep contentment, sincere gratitude but on the Wharfe there are complex layers of feeling that I shall never experience fishing anywhere else.

I am not sure that so intense a relationship with a band of running water is altogether healthy; perhaps it is a sign of emotional deprivation, of stunted human relationships, but there it is and for the time being at least I have said more than enough about it. I wrote that the Eden is a finer trout stream than the Wharfe and I had better justify a claim that places the river I most love second best. There are two reasons for this superiority; the first is the quality of the Eden trout and the second is the abundance of her fly life.

The trout of the Eden are the most beautiful that I have ever seen, especially the big ones, for they are rarely big-headed or thin, even in early spring, and, even in high summer, their girth stops short of obesity. At Driffield I have caught trout so fat that it seemed a wonder they could lift themselves from the chalk bed of the stream, let alone rise to take my fly and then bend my rod double with the power of their discontent. They were fine trout; it was a privilege to catch them but they were too gross for beauty, whereas a typical two pounder from the Eden – I have now caught just a few of them – is everything that a two pounder ought to be. The belly is butter-yellow, deep but not bloated; the back is chain-mail silver and black; the flanks are densely spotted with both red and black, and the perfect fins shine with a translucent, amber glow. The head is strong but rarely malevolent and the lines of the fish from head to the broad and powerful tail, the lines along the back and under that yellow belly, speak of fitness and strength rather than emaciation or grossness. The scales shine with a pinkish sheen, a hint of the flesh they conceal, which is often as red as the flesh of a salmon and its taste is incomparable.

The trout of the Eden are very beautiful. They can be difficult to catch and at least part of the reason for this lies in the river's rich diversity of invertebrate life. I could hold forth at considerable and inexpert length on this subject, but shall try to confine myself to no more than a few paragraphs. And the first thing to say is that the Eden breeds much more abundantly all the same ephemeropterans that I find on the Wharfe. Spring olives, pale wateries, iron blues and, of course, blue wings all appear in their season, sometimes in huge numbers. There are also days early in the season when the true march brown hatches in sudden short flushes. Brook duns come in May and are generally ignored. The river swarms with freshwater shrimp, which explains the pink or red flesh of its trout. Spring brings enormous hatches of grannom; summer brings a baffling diversity of many other sedges and throughout the season there is the usual selection of stone flies, including a fair number of the huge ones that gave earlier generations of fishers such sport with the creeper. Land-bred hawthorn flies and black gnats abound, as do the river-bred smut.

I may have forgotten some important insects. This is because I want to sing the praises of a particular dayfly that I did not know at all until I came to the Eden, not even its name. Since making its acquaintance I have come across a few specimens on the Wharfe, but the Eden produces hatches in vast quantities throughout May and early June; I owe this fly a deep debt of gratitude and will briefly tell you why.

It is a cousin to the march brown and proclaims its kinship with the clan device, with that distinctive femoral blotch. It does not occur in any numbers, if at all, on the chalkstreams; it is a child of the rocky and broken waters of the North and West and it has lived and bred and died through centuries of obscurity. Its relative is uncommon yet famous and we all carry March Browns in our fly-boxes, fishing them on waters where the natural has never been seen or disappeared whole decades ago. But there are fishers who haunt rivers where the march brown's cousin hatches in countless thousands and who cannot tell it apart from a spring olive or a B.W.O.

It is a handsome creature, with smoky blue wings and an olive green body; the male has big black eyes and both sexes, though not as large as a march brown, are noticeably larger than the common run of upwinged flies. Courtney Williams knows about it and suggests a few patterns that I have found wholly ineffective. More recent northern writers, notably Malcolm Greenhalgh, have recognized its local importance, but it deserves much more than this. There should be poems to greet its first appearance each year, panegyrics and fanfares and bottles of whisky poured out in libation to the river gods, for when the olive upright hatches in numbers, as it most certainly does on the Eden, then big fish join in the feast and fishers have only themselves to blame if they do not catch them in sackfuls.

The olive upright, for so it is called, is a very important fly on rivers where it abounds. It has been particularly important to me, because it was the fly that finally turned me into something like an all-round fly fisher. I remember the afternoon on the Eden when I first encountered it, suddenly aware that the river was alive with hatching flies and rising trout. I thought they must be unusually late spring olives and tried to catch them with a Waterhen and Orange Partridge. When this failed I thought of blue wings but realized almost immediately that the flies so thick on the surface of the river were too big for blue wings. There were too big for spring olives as well and when I bothered to pick a few flies from the water I saw at once that they were beyond my previous experience. I tried at least half a dozen patterns in my attempt to interest fish, but the trout did not even touch one of them, sending me home fishless and frustrated.

A search through Harris taught me that my new flies were olive uprights and I went straight to Courtney Williams, where eventually I found his entry under the name of the spinner, the yellow upright. Williams confirmed what I seemed to have learned that afternoon, namely that imitations designed for hatches of spring olives were ineffective when trout were eating olive uprights. He gave details of a dry fly, called the Hedgepig's Belly, which I ignored because I was a fisher of the upstream wet, tying instead a few of the simple nymphal pattern which he recommended for service on rough streams. With these in my box I waited to catch a limit of big trout when next I came to the Eden and found fish feasting on olive uprights. I did not have long to wait but I did not catch a limit, in fact I did not catch anything at all and I was beginning to feel a distinct coldness towards the new fly in my life.

Our third meeting saw olive uprights hatching in prodigious abundance and saw me incapable of interesting a single trout with whatever patterns I chose to show them. And then it occurred to me that it might be worth trying a dry fly. It was a token of my desperation, because I now despised the dry fly just as thoroughly as I had once thought it the one and only way to catch trout. The olive upright, anyway, drove me to desperate measures and, drawing out my dry fly-box from its long unvisited pocket in my fishing bag, I inspected its contents with curious disdain. There were Blue Quills and Pheasant Tails and Imperials and dry Greenwells, there were Black Gnats and Knotted Midges and at least twenty other standard patterns, but for some reason my eye was drawn by a compartment in the box stuffed full of flies that I could not name. They were whiskless, the body was of dirty yellow wool and the thick hackle was brownish yellow. I remembered that they had been given me by a friend in Bristol who had given up fishing. They had never since been used and I honestly have no idea what impulse now tied one to the end of my line and then cast it over a rising trout. He weighed 1lb 10oz. And the next one weighed one pound and a half.

I did not empty the river. I had to make do with the brace. I lost a big trout and I put one or two down and then the hatch failed. I went home with just a brace of trout but I went home a happy man with my attitude to the olive upright suddenly transformed from something like resentment into warm friendship: a feeling extended to the floating fly that had brought me those two olive-upright-eating trout. I suppose this fly was a sort of Rough Olive, but I called it the Yellow Thing and since that afternoon on the Eden it has caught me hundreds more trout. It has fooled trout eating all sorts of olives, from pale wateries to blue wings and it possesses a strange and surpassing virtue that I do not pretend to understand, for there are days when it wreaks havoc among smutting trout.

There are, of course, days when it puts every one of them down but there are other days when, although the Yellow Thing, thickly dressed on its 14 hook, is a monstrous giant beside the tiny insects that the trout are eating, they seize it with a passionate desire. Fishing the Yellow Thing, moreover, is a straightforward business, whereas your tiny black flies need nice management. There are days when I struggle with them, for it is very easy to miss rises and a tricky wind makes the whole process twice as difficult. Success is hard won and very satisfying but there are times when you get it all wrong, losing your temper and with it the ability to catch a single trout. Yellow Thing days are, by comparison, delightfully simple. You know exactly where your fly is, for there it goes, sailing obviously down part of the Eden or the Wharfe and there is a trout rising to suck it in, which makes timing the strike a straightforward affair. And fish that swallow the Yellow Thing are usually firmly hooked. It baffles me, why smutting trout are sometimes eager for a fly so unlike what they are eating, but I am happy to stay baffled and fill my bag.

The Yellow Thing changed my fishing life by bringing me back to the dry fly. I still fished the upstream wet for choice but, when circumstances suggested that a dry fly might be more effective, then I tied a dry fly, not necessarily the Yellow Thing, to my cast and often caught fish. I still do. Without the Eden's abundance of olive uprights I might never have given the Yellow Thing a chance to prove itself and might never have re-discovered the frequent efficacy of the dry fly. So it is that the olive upright has made me as near a complete angler as I am ever likely to be and for this I am profoundly thankful, both to the fly itself and to the river where it hatches in such teeming plenty. I think I have now said more than enough about flies and, for the time being at least, enough about the second river in my life.

CHAPTER EIGHT

The Ribble, the Wenning, The Wharfe and the Eden: these are the rivers that have mattered to me, although two of them I fish no more. The two that remain are more than enough to keep a fisher happy for a long lifetime. They keep this fisher very happy indeed. From time to time he does fish elsewhere, which makes returning to his two rivers feel like returning home. Feeling at home is very important to him, which may derive from that time when he no longer felt that he belonged on the banks of the Wharfe. He loves the familiarity of his two home rivers and is eager to deepen the sense of intimacy that he feels when fishing them. Just sometimes he regrets this tendency in himself: to delve into what he already knows in search of a still deeper acquaintance, for he has spent happy days on other waters and his books have taken him to rivers where, if he went there himself, he would surely find fulfilment and delight. He knows that it would be good for him to fish more widely, especially since he has already acknowledged that it is sometimes refreshing to leave all those memories behind. But, before going on, he had better struggle out of the third person, to which he is increasingly prone when thinking about himself; in other words he had better turn he back into me.

I love my two rivers so much that I find it difficult to leave them and fish in other places. When I make the wrench and fish elsewhere, I usually feel better for it, I feel enriched. I have just mentioned those rivers that flow brightly through my imagination: literary rivers where the writers I most admire caught great baskets of trout. If only I put my mind to it and made the effort, I could fish at least some of them.

I should like to fish the upper Test and the Bourne, where Plunket Greene found such delight before the First World War. I should like to fish the Itchen at Abbots Barton and sense the shade of Skues along the banks, telling me to fish a nymph and watch for the subtle signs of taking trout. It is, I suppose, unlikely that I shall ever follow in the footsteps of either Skues or Plunket Greene, but I could most certainly fish the rivers of Devon, where Farson drank peace as a tonic to wash away the ravages of a disordered life. And little more than an hour from my door flow the border streams where Stewart crept and crawled and perhaps sometimes cursed his way along the banks well over a hundred years ago: Teviot, Lauder, Ettrick and Yarrow, all still fine trout streams and readily accessible to the visiting fisher.

Show me a map and I look at the blue lines on it, wondering if trout live in them. I should do more than wonder; I should search out facts, make contacts, book accommodation and take myself fishing to new places. It is foolish that I so rarely do this because, as a school-master, I am blessed with at least eight consecutive weeks of holiday each summer and have more opportunities than most fishers to broaden my horizons. The Wharfe and the Eden have too strong a hold on my affections. If only I could break free and explore new places, I should probably find that separation would in fact deepen my devotion to the two rivers that bind me. In recent years I have been just a little more enterprising; I have taken my rods to Scotland and elsewhere, although I must acknowledge that the initiative and the arrangements have usually come from someone else.

I have spent a week on South Uist, staying in a house where rats lived under the kitchen sink, climbing Hecla on a wild day of wind and lashing rain, with brief bursts of racing sunshine that seemed, as I looked down from those high places on the Atlantic fringe, to reveal a shining infinity of silver light. Wherever I walked on the island I stumbled over dumps of empty whisky bottles. I went to Mass and listened to a choir of girls singing in the Gaelic; it sounded like a song of youth and innocence from the early days of the world. I saw eagles soaring over the cliffs, I watched gannets plunging into the ocean while seals sunned themselves on the rocks. There were merlins hunting the moorland and harriers quartering the marsh. I enjoyed myself enormously; I went fishing, I tried reasonably hard and I caught two trout in the course of the whole week.

I have trekked miles through the Sutherland wilderness to remote lochs and lochans, I have drifted under sunshine over topaz blue sheets of water where red (or were they black)-throated divers were my only company, divers and the savage lineaments of Foinavon. There have been Sutherland days of a more frequent type, days when the rain came in endlessly malevolent torrents, days when the wind blew with a cheerless Presbyterian fervour and the shrouded landscape seemed to exhale a grim, Celtic hatred of any intruder upon its sodden despair. And such days revise your theology, for they convince you that heaven is a hot fire and that hell, whatever else it might be, is wet all over. I have caught trout on both sorts of Sutherland day. Just a few of the rare and sunny sort make ample recompense for the horrors of the common sort. I have caught a few trout from Sutherland's lochs and found pleasure in their capture, but the truth is that I am in love with rivers rather than still waters and will never bring to loch fishing the intensity of purpose that informs my efforts to catch trout from running water. I confess that, when fishing from a boat, I prefer flat calm and a blue sky, with the mountains mirrored and motionless in the lake, to those more boisterous days of wind and choppy water which are what real loch-fishers welcome. I am nervous in a boat, unhealthily aware of my mortality whereas, if I fish still waters from the bank, I feel certain that the fish will rise beyond the reach of my flies, which they almost always do. I am temperamentally and technically unsuited to loch fishing. I can enjoy a few days of it, if the sun shines, but it is more a sort of diversion than an activity belonging to the very serious business of catching trout.

Each summer I go to Speyside. I take some of my rods but I am drawn there much more by the pull of friendship and high places than by hopes of fish. It is true that I have spent a day at Tulchan, with salmon showing all round me and with the Spey gurgling somewhere just beneath my armpits. It is also true that I caught nothing, was little bothered by this and felt enormously relieved to find myself safe again on the bank. The Spey is a prolific and noble river, but it is the mountains that look down on her, the Cairngorms, the Monadhliath and the Drumochter hills, it is these mountains that bring me back, year after year, to the valley through which she flows. They are not the spectacular peaks of the West, thrusting jagged silhouettes defiantly into the sky. They are massive shapes, rising with calm assurance in great sweeps of brown heather, lifting themselves patiently in long and flowing lines, raising their vast bulk to the sky with the huge authority of sufficient strength. They gaze over Strathspey with a proprietorial air and, each summer, I share the view with them, standing on broad summits with unmanageable names and surrounded on all sides by a limitless prospect of mountains.

It is a fine thing to pant and sweat your way up slopes that seem to grow ever longer and steeper, extending themselves indefinitely so that you almost despair of the summit, wondering if your vision of it, what seems like several hours ago, was a piece of trickery, an illusion conjured up by the fickle Celtic air. It is a fine thing to despair of the summit and then to find that it exists after all, that you are in fact now lying on it with your friends, lying there in the middle of a wild symmetry of mountains, with the bright sun above you, with heart beating strongly and blood coursing vigorously, with a sense of health and wholeness so complete that you have forgotten ever feeling different from how you feel now; it is like climbing into a new world, like rising above mortality. And the taste of beer, even Scottish beer, and of whisky, especially malt whisky, is so wonderful after a long day in the Speyside hills that you swallow your beer and then sip your whisky with a profoundly reverent gratitude. And finally you go to bed in a warm glow of contented weariness, falling very soon into a warm and contented sleep.

I go to Speyside for mountains rather than for fish, but at least some of my rods go with me and there usually comes a day or two, or perhaps a few evenings, when I get round to using them. Sometimes I take them to the Spey herself in search, not of salmon, but of the big trout that swim there: more recently I have preferred to fish one of her tributaries, a river called the Truim that tumbles down from the hills above Dalwhinnie and flows into the Spey a mile or two above

Newtonmore. There is a book all about the Truim, written by John Inglis Hall; it is called *Fishing A Highland Stream*; is subtitled *Love Affair with a River* and is an altogether delightful book. It follows the Truim upstream from confluence to source and breathes a deep affection on every page. I read it long before I ever thought of fishing the river that is its theme, finding in Hall's relationship with the Truim something of my own devotion to the Wharfe. I often thought that it would be good to spend a day there, but I was slow to act, as I always am when contemplating some new venture in my fishing life. I thought about it and decided that next year would be soon enough; and then next year would pass without a visit to the Truim until finally, three or four years ago, a day too damp and cold and cloudy for the hills persuaded me to see if I could discover whether Hall's river deserved all the praise that he had lavished on it.

I started two or three miles upstream at Crubenmore bridge and the whole experience was a deep disappointment. There was a full water that would certainly have been classified as a fly water on the Eden or the Wharfe, although the peat stain was darker than the amber glow of my own rivers when they are flowing eagerly but not in spate. It was a dark but not a thick or muddy water; there was a trickle of olives and there were fish rising to eat them. I had read of two and even three pounders and I caught nothing that weighed more than two or three ounces. Most of my fish were unmistakeably parr. I tried dry flies and wet flies and none of them brought anything but midgets. I fished for a couple of hours on either side of noon and then decided that I had fished enough. I knew that it would be grossly unfair to question Hall's account of the Truim on the evidence of a single visit of about four hours, but I still felt disillusioned and I never really thought to repeat my unhappy experiment. I came to Scotland, after all, mainly to climb mountains.

But the next summer brought drought. My spring and early summer fishing had been very demanding; even the upstream worm, which I could now fish with something not too far removed from competence, had caught me far fewer trout than I had come to expect. I came to Scotland to climb mountains, but the unconscious mind was still hungry for trout and I can remember driving down from

Drumochter, driving down the valley of the Truim in blazing sunshine; I can remember the line of the river shining brightly not far below me, very obviously low but looking like a wild torrent of water compared with the slimy trickles I had left behind in England. Immediately I thought of worms, for here apparently was a river with enough flow to show a lively, well-scoured worm to good effect. I thought of worms and decided at once that I must give the Truim a second chance, to see if the upstream worm could catch me a few trout worthy of all the creeping and crawling and all the sweat that would doubtless form a necessary part of their capture.

It took a day or two to find a dung heap and a few days for the worms to scour in moss; the sun beat down and I sought coolness in the mountains. Then there came a day of rest which I decided to turn into a day of hard labour on the banks of the Truim. I had felt my worms and proclaimed them ready for the hook. I chose a ten and a half foot sea trout rod, which had never caught me a sea trout; it was perhaps a shade stiff for worming but I thought that it would serve. With this rod went a fly reel and an old fly line, a spool of three pound nylon, a net and a few home-made Pennell tackles; and there were, of course, my worms, transported from the old game bag in which they had been quartered to the more cramped conditions of my cotton peg bag. I thought about seventy worms would be enough and set off with them for the Truim. I was fishing by half past ten.

You are often advised to fish the upstream worm in the cool of the dawn. I can never bring myself to get out of bed in time to greet the rising sun and there are plenty of days, with rivers on their bones and the sun merciless, when the trout will eat worms greedily for their lunch. This day was such a one and it is days of this sort that have softened my hatred of drought and endless sunshine. It was a very hot day, the sort of day that, as soon as you start fishing, brings a smarting line of sweat to your forehead along its contact with your cap, but the glare from above is so relentless and so hostile that your cap must stay in place, although you may well regret that, on such a day, your cap was not rejected in favour of a floppy cotton hat. It was the sort of day when, even in the first few minutes of sport, the flash and dazzle from broken water makes your eyes dazed and weary, a day when sensible fishers – I am not one of them – put on Polaroid glasses and turn the whole world dull. It was the sort of day when only madmen and fishers would choose to be elsewhere than in shade. It was, in short, a day for the upstream worm.

I intend to devote the whole of the next chapter to the business of summer worming and so will now spare you lengthy details of method, saying merely that when I came to the Truim for this second time I had learned, with a longish rod, to throw a worm a few yards ahead of me, a worm attached, in the old-fashioned style, to a six-foot cast and a fly line. And by this time I could, with my home-made Pennell tackles, hook at least some of the trout that seized my worms. There were still too many that I felt and then lost but I could set the barb in the mouths of enough trout to make it all seem worthwhile.

It was one of the hottest days of an outstandingly hot summer. Fishing the upstream worm is an exhausting activity, for if fished in the traditional manner – rather than with running nylon attached to a fixed-spool reel – it demands a close approach combined with the effort essential to achieve concealment. You must kneel and creep and crawl and bend, melting into the shadows, lurking behind rocks or beneath leaning trees, making certain not to show yourself above the line of the bank. The Truim, moreover, at any rate the length I was fishing above Glentruim bridge, is perhaps the most strenuous river that I have ever fished. The banks are heavily wooded and where the trees withdraw there are huge slabs of sloping rock standing in the way of your upstream progress. The banks are difficult and the riverbed is worse, with slippery shelves and sudden holes and boulders everywhere, all inviting immersion or injury with every step. It is impossible to fish the Truim for more than a few hours without almost falling in at least a dozen times, and, of course, the slime that coats rocks in time of drought only makes matters worse.

Compared with the Truim the rivers of my own North Country are like manicured streams running through a pleasure garden. They are no less lovely but they are certainly less wild, and fishing them calls for the expense of much less labour, for you do not so often have to squirm through a scratching tangle of branches, or need so frequently to heave yourself over impassable barriers of rock; you do not twist your ankle with alternate steps along the bed of the river, or sit down so often and so unexpectedly and so uncomfortably in the middle of running water.

It was hot, sweaty and aching work. I slipped and stumbled and sat down without meaning to; sometimes I sat down on purpose in order to compose myself, panting, blinking, breathless in the midday sun, which assaulted me from the sky, flashed up at me from the water and struck into my face from those great glaring slabs of rock. Worms flew off the hooks or snagged the bottom or went to cover among the leaves. Time and again I took off my cap, to wipe my smarting brow, or pulled out my handkerchief and dipped it in the river and bathed my stinging eyes. It was, hot, sweaty and aching work, but it was as exciting as any fishing that I have known for, in the white water of the pool heads and in the narrow rush between close-set boulders, in rapid glides round steep shelves of rock, in long stretches of stony, broken water, in thin runs and riffles and in holes beneath the banks, there were trout waiting; there were twitches and pulls, there were sudden lunges; there were fish darting out visibly from their lairs to seize their prey; there were unseen attacks on the worm, which chewed half of it away or stripped it from the hook or, just occasionally, brought a trout splashing over the net. There were pounders and half pounders and trout in between. Once or twice much larger fish grabbed the bait and spat it out before I managed to set the hook, departing with a single swipe from a broad tail; and, late in the afternoon, something monstrous, which may have been a huge trout or may just have been a salmon, rolled in the water and pulled at the line and was gone.

I fished until about five o'clock, following the river through gloomy stands of pine where buzzards mewed, through gorges where the rock shone hard and hot. In places heather came down to the water's edge, alive with buzzing and biting things. There were fallen trees rotting in marshy hollows where damsel flies hawked for prey; there were gyrating clouds of smut over the river and every shadow was filled with the droning of myriads of flies. Everywhere there was a riot of life and a proliferation of decay. There was a railway not more than ten minutes' slog over the rough ground and, over the railway, ran the line of the main road; but it seemed, in spite of this, more like a wilderness river, flowing through a country without sheep or cattle, without influence of man, a forgotten tract of land where a wild water roamed and where wild trout seized a swimming worm with a greed born of primal innocence. I missed scores of them, returned at least twenty and killed seven. By six o'clock, when I had struggled my way back to Glentruim bridge, I was burned, bruised, scratched and very weary. I had also revised my opinion of Hall's river; I now approved. I was not sure that Hall himself would approve of my method of fishing the Truim but, whether or not this was so, I now recognised it as a river that deserved both praise and affection; and, ever since that day, whenever I have been to Speyside I have spent at least one day on the Truim. I have always fished the worm and I have caught good trout, but I have never found them as greedy for the worm as they were on that blazing day when I first fished it there.

Most of my fishing away from home has been in Scotland, although perhaps the best of it has been in a landscape different in almost every respect from the wild valley of the Truim and the rocky and sodden wastes of Sutherland, a place moreover where fishing a worm would be a sacrilege and a sin that cried out to heaven for vengeance. For each summer, some time after my fortnight in Speyside, there comes a day when I drive north only for a few miles before heading more towards the east. My way lies through Hawes and sometimes I have to remind myself not to turn right there, through Gayle and then over Cam Houses and so down to the Wharfe. I drive straight through Hawes and down Wensleydale, through Bainbridge and Aysgarth and Middleham. And every summer the same glimpses of the Ure make me wonder why I have never bothered to fish so inviting a river.

I cross the Ure in Masham, where the Ure is now so big that I find it less tempting, and drive over the Swale on my way to Thirsk. Then it is over Sutton Bank to the high open spaces beyond. Formerly this was sheep country, but now most of it has gone under the plough, to grow wheat and barley and oil seed rape. I regret this arable encroachment but the skies are very beautiful and the villages, built from stone of soft yellow limestone, with their neat squares and their high spires and their duck ponds, are delightful and unspoiled. It is all, of course, part of Yorkshire but, to my eyes at least, there is an air of elegant and easy living that makes it seem almost a landscape of the South.

Just before Helmsley I turn south for Malton and, from Malton, it is over the Wolds to Driffield. And it is, of course, Driffield that has drawn me, Driffield and its beck: the chalkstream of the North, where trout of four and five pounds hide among the weeds, where fat trout lie like golden shadows over the white bed of the stream and rise with a leisurely and contented air to sip olives from the surface of the beck. The kindness of friends has brought me to Driffield for more than ten years. To begin with I fished for just a day, now I usually spend two days there and, if things go well, these days are high points of the fishing year.

The Driffield Angling Club is the second oldest in England, founded in 1832 a whole 8 years before my own club at Kilnsey. Only the Houghton Club on the Test can boast a longer history; but I doubt if any fishing club in the country can boast a finer club house. There may be grander club houses, there may even be palatial club houses, clubhouses where members stay the night and lie between sheets of silk after eating fine food and drinking fine wines and savouring ancient brandy. I grant that there are probably much larger and more opulent club houses than that of the Driffield Anglers, but I cannot believe that there is a club house anywhere in England that so tastefully belongs to its surroundings and so powerfully breathes out the distinctive spirit of place and the very special spirit of the sport to which both it and its members are dedicated in their own ways.

The club house of the Driffield Anglers is built of warm red brick, with a red-tiled roof and with overhanging eaves where martins nest; it is surrounded by neat gravel paths and by well-tended lawns sloping down to the stream. There are waving lines of willows along the edge of the water, with tall poplars rising on the far side of the beck. Inside there is a light and airy room with bow-fronted windows affording the view that I have just inadequately described. There are stuffed trout hanging on the walls and they are big trout. There is a long polished table where a tying vice is always at the ready and where leather bound volumes wait for members and their guests to enter their beats before fishing and their catch at the end of the day. There are boards recording the names of club officials through the long years. There are maps of the beats and photographs of the water. There are glass cases full of flies and of club memorabilia. In the hall that you pass through on your way to this room there is a list of the members and a small table with scales and weights for the ritual weighing of trout.

There is much in all this that reminds me of the club room at Kilnsey, which in turn reminds me that I never told you of a shameful sacrilege, a barbarism beyond belief; I never told you that our club room has been destroyed, that its walls have been torn down, that most of its contents have been removed and that it is now desecrated space: no more than a secular extension of the pub from which it was once set apart in hallowed seclusion. And what was the purpose of this outrage, this monstrous offence against tradition and decency? Profit was its purpose, so that the proprietors of the *Tennant Arms* could serve more meals, so that people could eat scampi and chips where Kilnsey Anglers once sat and talked about their day's sport. I suppose I have never mentioned all this before because I preferred not to think about it and I also suppose that the destruction of the Kilnsey club room deepens for me the attraction of the club house at Driffield and the sense of history that I inhale there. Anyway, my point, before I lost it, was that the club house of the Driffield Anglers is more spacious and more elegant than our headquarters at Kilnsey ever were; it is also bright and comfortable and one of its virtues is the kind welcome it extends to its guests.

There is no sense of urgency about going fishing at Driffield. You turn up some time before ten o'clock, you book your beat and chat to the keeper and to any members who are there to fish. It is a leisurely beginning to what may yet turn into an exhausting day; it is a ritual, a sort of prelude and it is all part of the pleasure of fishing at Driffield. You ask about the season so far and the state of the water and the condition of the weed and whether the dry fly or the nymph has been more effective. All this may take up a full half hour or even a little more, but at last it is time to go and do what you have come to do by trying to catch a few trout.

The Driffield Beck is a true chalkstream, which means that yesterday's or last week's rainfall has virtually no influence on your sport; there may have been a downpour overnight but the Driffield Beck will refuse to acknowledge this in any obvious way. I am told that it takes at least three months for water to percolate through the springs and find its way into the stream. What matters most of all is last winter: whether it rained enough to fill the great reservoirs in the chalk, to burst the winterbournes and so feed the beck with pure water through the coming months. If, like me, you are a fisher of rain-fed rivers, you will always be surprised by the strange behaviour of chalkstreams, the way they disdain the influence of immediate events and flow with the gathered richness of the past. For me this is all part of the difference and the charm of fishing at Driffield, where I sometimes feel that the smooth and limpid water carrying my fly is another element altogether than the rougher, more troubled and frequently more coloured liquid that hurries down the currents of the Wharfe.

The first time I fished at Driffield found me almost afraid, for I had never before cast a fly over the trout of a chalkstream; I was convinced that they would be far too clever for me and that I should go home fishless and humiliated. I was given a beat where the beck splits round a marshy island and I went to it in a mood of mingled reverence and apprehension, imagining that the ghosts of the chalkstream masters were gathered and watching and ready to laugh. I knew that Hills had fished at Driffield and that C.F. Walker, a more recent writer and fisher, had been a guest there, describing the beck and its surroundings as 'almost pure Hampshire'. Both of them, incidentally, had found Driffield trout free-rising but unusually difficult to hook, a consideration that tended to increase my feelings of inadequacy, for, however free-rising they might be, I still doubted my ability to bring any of them up to my clumsily presented flies. And, even should I be lucky enough to chance upon a particularly greedy or incautious trout, it now seemed inevitable that I should be unable to set the hook firmly in his jaw.

I knew that Hills and Walker had both been to Driffield. I was not aware that either Halford or Skues had ever fished there, but I still imagined them among the spirits of the watchers waiting to mock my hopeless endeavours to catch chalkstream trout. And whenever, on my way to the bottom of my beat, I looked at the water, immediately I felt even more powerfully that I was out of my element, because the beck was very obviously so different from the rivers that I knew. There were no turbulent runs, there was no broken water; there was a relentless glide, with veins and creases of flow; there were waving beds of weed and huge trout hanging without motion between them, hanging over the chalk as though set in crystal. I could not believe that my rough skills, which might be adequate for tumbling upland streams, would be able to deceive these poised aristocrats of the chalk, hanging there in the pure water with, it seemed to me, an air of indifferent contempt for my presence on the bank.

I was daunted. I felt almost unwilling to start, knowing that nothing but humiliation and failure lay ahead of me, and so I walked the tended bank for a time, walked the mown path behind a screen of long grass and meadowsweet and willow herb, peering through this screen at the sliding water and the shapes of trout and telling myself that I was marking down fish for later attention. I sat on a bench and smoked, acknowledging the secluded beauty of my surroundings; for here was a place set apart from the world beyond between tall lines of poplars and willows, a place of green shadows and bright water, of rocking weed and motionless trout. At the bottom of the beat there was a busy mill; at its top a railway crossed the beck, but they possessed no intrusive force, no power to penetrate this timeless world where I fancied that I might find Halford and Marryatt, tempting trout with some floating pattern that they had just devised; or perhaps I should bump into Skues, lurking in the shadows, hiding from the dry fly men and experimenting with the nymph. As I sat there by the Driffield Beck my mind was full of Hampshire ghosts.

It was with a nymph, though a nymph after the fashion of Sawyer rather than of Skues, that I eventually covered a trout apparently fast asleep in a pocket of water between two beds of weed. The nymph was a weighted Pheasant Tail; it was seized as soon as it was seen and the trout that seized it weighed almost two pounds. I never changed my fly. I had caught my limit of three brace by three o'clock and I drove home in high good humour, with a revised opinion of the cunning of chalkstream trout and with a suddenly inflated opinion of my own cunning as a fisherman. I fished a day at Driffield, on the same Island Beat, in each of the two following summers and did not catch a single fish. I almost hoped, after the second of these trips, that I should never be invited there again, but my hosts were too generous to forget me and so it was that, on a bright morning in August, I came for the first time to the Hunting Bridge.

I think that, on every river we fish, there are places or lengths of water that exert a special hold on us. When I think of the Eden I think of the stretch between Beckfoot and Quiet Corner. When my mind's eye looks at the Wharfe, it follows the river down from Yockenthwaite bridge; or, if it is high summer and the river is too low to think of fishing up near the source, it turns its gaze to Spout Dub or Knipe Dub or to the long run that flows into Two Barn Flats. And now there is a stretch of the Driffield Beck that flows through my dreams; it is the beat above the Hunting Bridge for, although my experience of chalkstream fishing is limited to two Yorkshire streams, it seems to me that, when the beck is flowing from full springs, this beat is everything that chalk water ought to be.

It is true that, for the first half mile or so above the bridge, there is a golf course along one bank but, for the most part there is a protecting shelter of trees and, where there is brief contact, the sight of people hitting white balls makes you thankful to be a fisher, even a fisher with an empty bag and, anyway, you leave the golf course behind once you have rounded the first corner, for now you follow the beck upstream between fields of wheat and rough pastures. As the beck becomes smaller it also becomes brighter and the chalk shines through more clearly, and everywhere there are trout poised over the white bed in pockets of open water between the weed. Along the edge of the bank there is a fringe of tall grasses and reeds; there are willows and hawthorns leaning out over the water. It is awkward fishing because the trout scare easily, and from time to time your fly goes to roost in the branches or hides itself somewhere in the bankside growth. Drag is a constant danger and will defeat you just as often as you manage a drag-free drift; it is very galling to see a trout rising through the clear water and opening its mouth with greedy relish, only to swerve aside at the last moment, warned of something unnatural by the sudden skating of your fly. It is awkward and tiring fishing; you spend half the day getting in and out of the water and scratching yourself on the brambles that twine through the grass; beneath the shelter of the bank you creep up to fish that go down before you ever cast over them; you curse yourself for losing a big fish in the weed. It is awkward fishing, but it is true chalkstream fishing for wild trout and, when it goes well, it is as rewarding as any fishing that I have known. I do not think that I should like to fish only, or chiefly for chalkstream trout; I should miss the wilder beauties of the Eden and the Wharfe, but the fact that I fish for them on just one or two days each season adds both tension and novelty to the occasion and makes success, when it comes, doubly sweet.

On my first visit to the Hunting Bridge, although I saw plenty of trout lying out in pockets between the weed, I did not interest a fish until I came to Golf Course Corner. The memory of two blank visits was alive and heavy within me; the prospect of a third fishless day, which had come with me to the water as a dark possibility and a lurking dread, seemed suddenly inevitable. After failure with nymphs I was fishing a dry fly but already I had lost confidence in the dry fly as well, for my particular dry fly, which was a Yellow Thing, had floated unmolested over at least half a dozen trout, as had an Adams before it. I was too dispirited to bother with another change of pattern or a change of tactics and so, when a fish rose, I flicked the Yellow Thing over him, and he took it and was hooked and was duly landed. He was nothing special for Driffield, weighing just four ounces over the pound, but for me, after those two blank days on my last two visits, he was a wonderful trout.

I remember how all at once I felt the warmth of the sun and the lively breath of the upstream breeze. As I walked on in search of my brace, which I was suddenly confident would soon be achieved, a covey of partridge clattered out of the cornfield on my left, gliding over the beck in front of me; young pheasants flapped from the wheat in clumsy attempts at flight; an enormous hare loped its way along the mown pathway; crimson stands of willow herb waved and rocked over the water and, with every step that I took, relief and exhilaration sang out in me, insisting that it was good to be alive, acknowledging at the same time that it would be even better when one trout had turned into two.

I spotted a rise under the far bank and my fly fell right with the first cast. Very slowly a dark shape raised itself through the water and sucked in the Yellow Thing. I watched, as though bewitched by the deliberation of it all, and some numbing force delayed my wrist until it must surely have been too late. But it was not and my trout felt big and angry. He raced downstream, then turned and shook his head and remembered weed. It was the first time in my life that I had been weeded by a trout. I had read all about it in Skues and Hills and Plunket Greene and seemed to remember that you were meant to release all pressure on your trout in the hope that he would swim free. This was what I thought you were supposed to do and I was incapable of doing it, because my fisher's instinct, developed over more than twenty years when a loose line had so often meant a lost fish, my fisher's instinct was telling me to hold tight. I was lucky; I now saw that my trout was at the edge and almost on top of the weed.

I prodded the waving mass with my long-handled landing net and out he came in a very bad temper, lashing his tail furiously in a few yards of open water. I knew that I had deserved to lose him and that, if he went to weed again, he would almost certainly stay there. I held him on the surface and held him hard and, at the first half chance, I shot the net under him. I was lucky for a second time and lifted him in splashing triumph from the water. He was a short fish but he was very deep, deeper than any trout that you will catch from the Eden or the Wharfe. He was, in fact, a fat fish and I guessed him at two pounds, but I was misled by his unfamiliar proportions and the spring balance pronounced him a full four ounces short. He was no more than an average sort of chalkstream trout but he made the brace for me and a brace, as every fisher knows, is so much better than a singleton, for a brace is somehow a token of competence whereas a single fish is little more than a stroke of good fortune and most certainly not enough. He was an average sort of trout but he made the brace and at the same time he laid the dark ghost of those two blank days.

By now a proper hatch had developed, a hatch of small dark olives or, in my language, summer duns. The trout were nymphing, just beneath the surface and I changed my fly to a pattern of my own devising: a body of pheasant tail fibres ribbed with yellow silk, a dark-centred hackle from the shoulder of a hen pheasant's wing, a size sixteen hook. It was a change that worked and a change that pleased me, for it brought a third trout to net: one which, although he was no bigger that the first of the day, owed its capture to some thought and observation on my part. Then there was a fourth trout of a similar size; he was returned to the water and was the end of a wonderful morning.

Lunch was sandwiches and a bottle of Sancerre with my host, Oliver. We sat on a bench by the side of the beck, resting in the shade of the large willows that rose behind us, eating and drinking and talking of the morning's sport. After finishing my sandwiches I lit my pipe to accompany the last glass and thought how delightful it was to be drinking wine with a friend while sitting in the shade on the bank of a chalkstream; and how comforting was the thought that there were three trout in my bag and how warm was the hope that the afternoon would bring more; and yet a blank afternoon would be no disaster, since those three trout were, after all, sufficient reward for a day's sport. These were easy and contented thoughts bred by success in the morning, by the comfort of shade after sunshine and by the soothing influence of lunchtime wine. It was good the bottle was now empty because any more would have been too much. We were both keen to be fishing again and I headed off upstream.

I felt in a mood to explore new water and did not look for rising trout until I had passed the point where I had turned back at the end of the morning. I killed another trout; I lost one in the weed and then I followed the beck through an untidy covert full of scurrying pheasant poults. I rounded a corner and came back out into the sunshine, and suddenly I felt that I had somehow wandered out of Yorkshire, and backwards in time, and that I had found my way into the pages of a book. I knew, of course, that it was a trick of the imagination but, in spite of this, the illusion was powerful and I gladly surrendered. For here was a little river flowing down to me through the bright afternoon, with water clear as crystal, with green weed rocking to the pressure of the stream and with a bed of white chalk shining through the water only inches below its surface. And there were golden trout basking in the shallows, with reeds and willow herb swaying above them and broad fields beyond.

Perhaps it was the warm influence of the morning's trout, perhaps it was the lingering influence of the wine, but I remember feeling that I was no longer walking along the Driffield Beck but had somehow moved to Hampshire and the river Bourne near Hurstbourne Priors. I had found my way to Hampshire and at the same time I had gone back through seventy or eighty years, so that I should scarcely have been surprised if Plunket Green had suddenly appeared round the corner, carrying a long rod and, in spite of the warm sun, encased in a tight-fitting Norfolk jacket; or if, coming up to me to pass the time of day and ask about my sport, he had told me to forget about nymphs and tie my trust instead to an Iron Blue Dun. I knew that it was no more than a fancy, but there in Yorkshire on the edge of the Driffield Beck, with the little river and the pure water and the weed and the golden trout, I felt for a time very close to the world so beautifully recreated in the pages of *Where The Bright Waters Meet*.

For five minutes or so I sat down and allowed the imagination free rein. And then it was time to stop dreaming and see if I could catch any of those golden trout. The water was barely more than ankle deep, with one or two rather deeper hollows under the banks. The fish were very quick to take fright, although I managed to bring two of them to my fly, but I only pricked them and, in so far as unpleasant thoughts could find any purchase in my mind, I felt annoyed by my incompetence. I came to the place where the beck splits into two still smaller streams, where their confluence makes a deep pool almost out of proportion to the small scale of things. The wind had dropped and a cloud lay across the sun. I was wading under the bank and could not see into the water, but I saw the rise of a trout and covered it with my small wet fly. It was taken immediately and, while I was shaking free a trout just below the pound, there was a second rise from another unseen fish. I cast again and again the fly was taken, very gently, and then suddenly I knew that I had hooked a monster.

He wallowed on the surface, momentarily bemused, not unlike the fisher who had just hooked him, and it was then, I think, before my monster made any show of strength, that I noticed the dim and menacing form of two stakes driven into the bed of the pool; immediately I recognised the danger, feeling certain that my fish would do his best to wrap my line round one of them. I knew that I must pull him away from these stakes, drawing him down towards me and for a few seconds he seemed willing to cooperate, still splashing on the surface, still confused and uncertain what had happened to him. Every moment he looked bigger. And then he pulled himself together; there was a sudden dive, a wild surge of irresistible force and all at once my line was trailing loosely in the water and there was no longer a fly, let alone a huge trout, on the end of it.

If I had fought that fish for whole minutes, for ten minutes or more, subduing him slowly and draining his spirit and his strength; if I had seen his runs grow shorter and less savage, his plunges less deep and less strong; if the relentless pressure of rod and line had eventually beaten and broken him, so that he was hanging in the water, exhausted and spent; and if then, in a last and feeble gesture of defiance, with a last and feeble flick of his tail, he had somehow managed to throw the hook, I should have been heartbroken; there would most certainly have been tears. But it was not like this.

It was so brief and so unequal an encounter that I never felt close to catching him and those stakes, as soon as I had seen them, had more or less persuaded me that he would never feel the net. I had come to terms with losing him almost as soon as he was hooked and so, when the moment came, it was much less painful than the loss of many smaller trout before him. I found my disappointment somehow balanced by my respect for his size and his strength; I felt that he had deserved his freedom and I hoped that, down there in the pool, he would manage to rub my hook from his jaw. I cannot guess his weight, except to say that he was much bigger than any other trout that has ever attached itself to the end of my line. I hooked him and he broke me and I sat on the edge of the beck, surprised by the restraint of my reaction, by my mood of gentle resignation, my feeling of mild regret. Yes, I should like to have caught him and find out whether he weighed five or seven or however many pounds, but he had been far too strong for me, the battle had been over before it had been properly joined and, anyway, there were already four trout in my bag, and four fat chalkstream trout were already more than enough for one day.

I have never been so untroubled by the loss of a big trout, but I recognised what had just happened as the climax and conclusion of my day; at any rate I did not want to fish any more. I wandered off downstream, safely back in Yorkshire by now; I said my farewell to Oliver, who was keen to fish on for an hour or so. I told him of the monster that had broken me. I told the keeper as well, and then I drove home contentedly, hoping that next summer would bring me back to the water above the Hunting Bridge.

I love my chalkstream fishing and more recently I have fished the Foston Beck as well as at Driffield; it is a much smaller stream and the top of the water is perhaps even lovelier than the Hunting Bridge beat. My fishing in Scotland, however enjoyable it might sometimes be, is peripheral to my purpose in going there. Fishing lies at the very centre of my visits to East Yorkshire and these chalkstream days are the only fishing days away from my home rivers that are really important to me. Fishing the bright waters of a chalkstream is intrinsically delightful, but it is the force of contrast that makes the experience so absorbing; above all it is the visibility of the trout.

There are times, of course, when you can see your trout on the Wharfe and the Eden; they are probably more frequent than we imagine but they are still an exception to the general order and they are usually partial or imperfect revelations. At Driffield and Foston you more often see your fish and it is fascinating to observe each phase of a trout's response to your fly as well as your own response to the sight of him and to his size. If he is big, then you, or at least I, will feel suddenly anxious that you will bungle things and send him shooting beneath the weed. If you manage not to frighten him and if you cast a delicate line, you must then watch tensely while your pattern is subjected to an often leisurely review, which might end in rejection or with its disappearance into an open mouth. Sometimes there is no reaction at all, sometimes the first fall of your fly sends your fish darting for cover, sometimes he lifts in the water and looks ready to take but then turns away and will not move again.

It is full of interest and excitement; it is so different from fishing the runs and pools of the Eden and the Wharfe with upstream flies, when you watch the progress of your line with hawk-like eyes, ready, at the first pause or twitch, to strike with the deadly speed of a heron's beak. Even with the dry fly on my home rivers you are more often too late to turn your wrist than too early with the strike. The patience that you must employ to hook chalkstream trout is a great challenge for us fishers of rough water; it is a challenge that often defeats me but there is great satisfaction when I manage to control myself and wait for the right moment to set the hook.

I love my days in East Yorkshire. Given the continuing generosity of my friends, I shall keep looking forward to chalkstream days as bright and special days in the course of each season, although my days during the last two summers have been less delightful than in the past. Dry winters and hot summers, combined with abstraction, have greatly diminished the flow of both becks and the water in them has been less pure and less bright than I have come to expect. Please God, send them rain, send them days of steady winter and spring rain, rain that will seep down into the great springs and fill them full, so that they in their turn will fill the becks and flow brightly over the white chalk. And may I come again to the Hunting Bridge to find the water full and clear, with the weed swaying to its pressure and with the wild trout of Driffield poised and golden over the chalk.

CHAPTER NINE

It is at last time for that chapter on the worm that I have so long been threatening, although I must confess at the outset that it is not going to be quite what I had intended. Twelve months ago, when I was busy with some earlier chapters and was at the same time looking forward to another season's sport, I felt confident that one more summer, with its opportunities for practice and experiment, would turn me into a master, entitled at last to expound all the finer points of fishing the worm and to pronounce with calm assurance on every detail of technical controversy.

It has not turned out as I wished. In fact I have found that, in spite of long periods when conditions seemed perfect for the upstream worm, with low water and hot sunshine for weeks on end, in spite of this and in spite of arduous days of aching perseverance, I killed very few trout with my long rod and my Pennell tackle and my worm wriggling seductively as it trundled down the shrunken streams. It was a bitter disappointment and it has taught me that it will be several seasons – perhaps as many as ten – before I can write with authority on fishing the upstream worm. I do not know why it was so ineffective last season, whether this was because I was fishing badly or because, for some reason beyond my knowledge, the trout felt no appetite for a bait that so often drives them wild with greed. There are mysteries to the upstream worm that I have yet to penetrate. I am still a novice rather than an expert and it will be years before I am ready for the definitive treatise on fishing the worm that may form the crowning achievement of my life as a writer and fisherman.

I cannot give you masterly advice on the upstream worm; you will have to wait for that and it may never come, but I can say why the upstream worm draws me and why I think it a sporting way of catching trout when the conditions justify its use. For the upstream worm does not belong to every season and to every state of water. It belongs to high summer and to rivers on their bones. Anyway, before returning to these matters, I had better say what precisely I mean by the upstream worm, because there are several methods of propelling a worm upstream and they are not all to be recommended or even allowed.

The worst, easiest and most common method is to use running nylon and a fixed spool reel, which is not what I mean when I talk of fishing the upstream worm. This, in my opinion, is a disreputable way to fish a trout stream. It takes only a short time to master, the worm can be cast long distances with little effort or skill and so the wormer no longer needs to imitate the heron in the stealthy cunning of his approach. It puts the whole water at his mercy; it is too easy, it is a degenerate practice and I shall waste no more time on it.

There is a less odious modern development of the upstream or clear water worm, which relies on a centre-pin or standard fly reel loaded with nylon; or you can tie thirty or forty yards of nylon to the end of your fly line and use this, together with a longish fly rod, as your worming gear. Falkus has much refined this method as a technique for sea trout; it is the method of some of my friends and it is the method with which I first caught trout on the worm in low water. It is an intelligent adaptation of tradition, exploiting the possibilities that arose with the appearance of nylon line. I suspect that Stewart and Nelson and Pritt would have turned to it with enthusiasm, abandoning their former ways without a moment's regret.

It takes art to throw the worm at once gently and a fair distance and there is still, because of the limit of your range, an urgent need of concealment. It is not a method to be despised; it is a method with much to recommend it, but it is a method that I never used without a prick of conscience and which I use no longer, ever since the fascination of the difficult bound me fast to the much more demanding practice of the wormers of old, a practice forced upon them by the limitations of gut, but one which the modern wormer should adopt in the noble aspiration to make of his calling an arduous vocation.

In fishing for trout with the worm we should, I think, conscious of the suspicion or outright disapproval in which this method of fishing is held, and admitting the fatal effectiveness of the worm on many occasions, renounce the more efficient techniques which the progress of science has made possible. We should quite deliberately make things difficult for ourselves, so that we can justify our practice by appeal both to its long tradition and its high challenge. This means a fly line and a six foot nylon cast on the end of it; it means flicking or rolling or casting or swinging the worm ahead of you, slowly gathering the skill to deliver your worm roughly where you want it; it means, because you will never coax your worm more than a few yards ahead of you, that you are almost on top of the trout you hope to catch, and so you must move as quietly as the grass grows if your hopes are not to be confounded. It demands sweat, labour and backache under a scorching sun; it calls for stealth and delicacy when the odds are stacked against you and it brings, when it goes well, a bag of trout and sore limbs and deep satisfaction.

I use an eleven foot rod for worming. You will read, in the old books on the art, that fifteen or sixteen feet makes the ideal rod for the upstream worm. With all respect for my predecessors, this seems to me to border on cheating; it attempts to surmount the problem of throwing the worm a suitable distance by using a rod of such inordinate length that it barely needs to be thrown at all. Doubtless the management of so long a rod calls for skills of its own, but it still strikes me as a clumsy and unattractive stratagem. The worm can be presented with a much shorter rod; we should learn to pitch a worm properly and limit ourselves, at the most, to twelve feet.

I have told you that I am no expert with the worm and here I am, laying down the law in unambiguous terms. I have enjoyed pronouncing on the one acceptable method of fishing the worm and so I shall continue to pontificate by telling when you may and when you may not catch trout with the upstream worm. It is not a method for the spring of the year, which almost always brings water suitable for the fly and the fly is always preferable when it brings a reasonable prospect of success.

Fly fishing is a much higher and more beautiful art than the upstream worm, which is only to be employed when daytime sport with the fly is unlikely to prove effective. This rarely happens in spring and, even in those rare years when the beginning of trouting coincides with a long period of dry and settled weather, even then the wormer should stay his hand and leave his worms in the compost heap. It is an undeniable drawback of fishing the worm that trout are often hooked deep in the throat, which means that they must be killed.

Now in spring trout are often too thin for the table and should be returned as gently as possible so that they can put on both flesh and fitness. In spring we should be careful to kill only well-conditioned trout; since the upstream worm is likely to deny you this choice it is not a suitable method for the start of the season. The wormer must wait through March and April and May. June is the finest month of the year for fishing the fly. It is in July and August that the wormer comes into his own and it is my belief that, whatever the conditions at other times of the year, the principled wormer should confine his activity to these two months, for this self-imposed restraint almost does away with the objection that we wormers are inspired by greed. And even in July and August we must only turn to the compost heap when rivers are more rock than water. In a wet summer the ethical wormer will never get as far as wetting a worm.

It was not trout-lust, it was not an insatiable appetite for dead trout that first drew me to the worm. It was the prospect of absorbing sport when rivers had shrunk to trickles and it was, above all, that same sense of history that almost twenty years earlier had finally turned me into a fisher of upstream flies. It was my longing to feel part, not only of the landscape where I fished but also of the traditions that belonged there. I find it a deep pleasure to fish a pool on the Kilnsey water, a pool where Cadman and Pritt fished more than a century past, and think to myself that I have fished it more or less as they would have done, with a Snipe and Purple or a Dark Watchet when the iron blues are coming down the water at the end of May or, in time of August drought, with a well-scoured worm flicked up into the remains of fast water at the head of the pool.

It need not be oppressive, this feeling for history and this reverence for tradition, it does not exclude either evolution or innovation. I do not fish with greenheart rods and I have abandoned silk lines. I am happy to catch fish on the floating fly, a method which Pritt was wrong to dismiss as unsuitable for rivers like the Eden and the Wharfe. There are many days in the course of a season when the dry fly is the best, the most efficient way of catching trout. I think it is a less subtle method than the upstream wet but it is still a delight to catch trout on a fly that floats and it is better to be master of two methods than one. I do not feel bound exclusively to the practice of the old masters, any more than I feel obliged to resort to all their strategies. I am not, in a narrow sense, a Prittite, a hidebound champion of the past, but to fish where Pritt once fished with his friends, and to fish approximately in their fashion and to find, on a given day, that the old ways are still best, that the old traditions are still sound and sensible, this is for me both a delight and an enrichment. It is a chief part of the pleasure of the worm.

But these pleasures are many and they begin in the compost heap – unless it is a dung heap – which you explore with a fork, collecting the wriggling worms that are exposed by your excavation. It is almost a sport in itself, though admittedly a more primitive one than the sport it serves. There are times of frustration, when all the worms seem to have migrated beyond the reach of your prongs; there are times when you wonder if you are exploring a wormless compost heap, or one inhabited by no worms more than half an inch long; but there are times of plenty, when almost every turn exposes half a dozen of just the sort of worms you prize, slipping away from the unwelcome light or knotted together in humid embrace. Sometimes you seize the retreating extremity of a worm and, with gentle but steady pressure draw the whole creature from its damp home; but often, caught in this crisis, the worm sacrifices half of itself to preserve its hidden and perhaps better half. It is easy to become greedy when times are good, for there are no limit bags to enforce moderation. You wander down the garden in search of a score of worms, but the writhing bounty of decay leads you on and you are still busy with your fork long after twice forty worms have been slipped into your pot. The thrush and the robin realise what is happening, hopping nearer and nearer, and you reward their trust with an occasional gift. Meanwhile the rich smell of decay fills your nose and the sun climbs higher or sinks lower in the sky. Worm hunting is a real and earthy pleasure, a pleasure that carries within itself the seeds of addiction.

When at last you have torn yourself away from the compost heap there comes the ritual of moss, which is performed in the shadowed gloom of the potting shed. The moss itself, of course, has already been gathered, washed and wrung so that it is barely damp, and then pressed into a roomy earthenware pot. You must wash the worms as well, which will have wrapped themselves into a seething bundle of pale flesh, and then drop them on top of the moss. They will wriggle down through the strands and fibres before twining together again to form an intimate and writhing ball, for once out of the ground worms seek security in numbers. Cover the pot, to prevent escape, and remember each day to break their confederacy, separating them and returning them to the surface of their new home, so that repeated journeys in search of safety and soil will scour and harden them, making them bright and lively and tough enough to withstand their future service on the hook.

The wormers of old often ran two or three pots at once, for they took their sport very seriously. One is enough for me and the easy trouble of its maintenance – keeping the moss damp, turning the worms each day, removing sickly specimens and periodically replacing the whole stock – all this forms part of the high summer round. And the potting shed, with its musty smells and its clutter of old tools, with its mouldering nests high up there in the gloom of the rafters, with its shards, its cool stone slab, its cobwebs and its dusty peace, is a fine place to escape the sun and other people: a place for a pipeful of tobacco while you assess the condition of your worms and dream of the great trout they will catch for you when other fishers have abandoned all hope of sport. I have read that the progressive wormer now stores his worms in damp newspaper. I do not propose to imitate him, partly in blind allegiance to the old ways and partly because there is a sort of organic pleasure in the touch and texture of moss, something that you will never experience while tearing up back numbers of *The Times*; but I remain faithful to moss mainly because it seems to do the job perfectly well. I think my worms look almost seductive when it has scoured and cleaned them for a week or perhaps ten days. My worms will continue to toughen themselves in moss.

Read Stewart on worms, for in his eagerness to classify them by length and colour, by the presence or absence of a band, by the type of ground they frequent and almost, one might say, by disposition, also in the massive assurance with which he dismisses or recommends a particular type of worm as useless or just what the efficient wormer most prizes, he is highly entertaining. Do not take him too seriously. Trout are less selective in their choice of worms than he claims. I think he was driven by the desire to invest the wormer's art with a degree of science that it does not possess. There was an appealing perversity in his nature that made him scoff at careful fly selection and yet insist that exactly the right worm, and none other, was crucial to filling a fisher's creel. Read Pritt, mark his preference for a green worm and then try to find one. I believe that trout treat one sort of worm much like another sort, except that they are sometimes frightened by too large a worm; but then there come days when the bigger the better seems to be the rule, when they will seize a giant of a worm without a moment's hesitation. Bright and lively and about two and a half inches seems sound advice, but you should always fish as large a worm as the trout have stomach for, because a biggish worm makes casting much easier.

The literature on the worm is much less extensive and less attractive than is the case with fly fishing. Sidney Spencer wrote a whole book on the upstream worm some time in the fifties; to my admittedly deficient knowledge it is the only modern contribution to its use, although writers on sea trout, notably Falkus, have written extensively on the topic. Almost everything you read about the clear water worm, in Stewart, Cadman, Pritt, Edmonds and Lee, Mackie and others, will be old fashioned and arguably out of date; but herein lies much of its charm, for it breathes the spirit of an earlier age, before fishers had learned to feel guilty about killing a few fish, when the trout season started with the artificial fly, moving to the creeper and the stonefly in May, to the worm in low summer water together with the drop minnow as rivers fell back from summer spates, reverting in between times and throughout

September to the fly, which was, of course, unanimously proclaimed to be the summit of the fisherman's art. In reading of the upstream worm you turn the pages of a lost epoch of angling, in fishing the upstream worm, as it should be fished, you bind yourself to a tradition that has almost died and now counts you, and a few arthritic fishers decaying quietly in remote northern dales, among its last exponents.

According to my code, the wormer, whatever other qualities he might exhibit, must possess that traditional attribute of the fisher, namely patience. This is because, according to my code, he refuses to impale a worm upon a hook until July comes along, and then only when rivers have fallen very low and clear. It is, of course, true – especially with modern tackle – that even in time of drought, and even under the midday sun, you can catch trout on the fly, searching for them in the remains of rough water and in the shadows beneath the trees. Even in the lowest of waters you may find trout, and big ones too, feasting on smut and the sport this produces is fascinating and very difficult, full of satisfaction on the rare days when it goes well. There are no days that do not offer at least the possibility of catching trout with the fly, but there are just a few days when even the most ardent fisher of flies admits himself defeated and seeks refuge in the shade of the nearest tree or in the cool of the nearest pub. He would do better to get out his worms.

In such conditions, of course, the fly fisher can hope for something like sport in the evening, especially on the very edge of dark. The evening rise is not dependable and, even when it happens, it is often difficult and frustrating, except for that short period when the near darkness seems to rob the trout of their caution and swings the balance briefly in favour of the fisher. Even in the lowest of waters there may come twenty minutes right at the end of the day, before the blanket of the dark takes away the last light, when the fly fisher can hope for exciting sport; but I do not think he is doing something more delicate or demanding than the midday fisher of the upstream worm. The late evening fisher of flies basks in the approval of his fellows, but when a fisher, with his river on its dry and dusty bones, with the sun high and relentless and burning hot, with the fish skittish and shy, calls the worm to his assistance and then creeps and crawls his way along the banks and catches a trout or two, he will, at least by some of his fellow fishers, be condemned as little better than a poacher or a setter of night lines. 'Hear, hear' some of you will cry. 'Nonsense,' say I, 'It was the wormer who had the harder time of it, however few or many trout he caught. For he fished under the hot and revealing eye of the sun, he fished when the trout were wary and very quick to take alarm, when every careless shadow or movement told them that there was danger stalking the banks. He came upon his fish with the silent stealth of the heron, he flicked his worm into the shrunken runs, into still turbulent pockets of water between the stones, into all the lingering remnants of troubled water, flicking it with a sure and gentle touch just where he wanted it to go. And then, as the worm was carried back to him, he deciphered the coded messages that it transmitted to him along the cast and the line, translating the strange language of the trundling worm with the knowledge and accuracy of long experience, so that he knew when it had brushed against a rock or was rolling along the pebbles or when it had caught a sudden and stronger current and was swimming more eagerly on its way.

'All this he could interpret and all this he could distinguish from the signals for which he was waiting: those sudden pulls and twitches that would tell him that a trout was toying with his bait, the steady draw announcing that a fish had seized the worm without feeling the iron and was ready to be hooked. He understood all the nuances of this strange code and he exploited his knowledge by turning it into defeated trout. To most of his victims he showed mercy; some few of them were killed and when at six in the evening, he stopped fishing with two brace in his bag and left the river in search of beer, he felt that he had achieved more than when last he had fished the same beat on a day a month earlier when the river had been falling back from spate, when the fish had been moving freely and been eager for food, when, fishing a team of wet flies upstream, he had caught trout from every run and pool and glide of the river. Wait until the conditions are right, try the upstream worm yourself and I shall be surprised if you are slow to agree with him. It is a fine way to catch a trout from a thin river beneath an unblinking sun.'

I cannot claim the expertise of the imagined wormer who has just fished his way through the last page or so, but I am keen to learn and to draw just a little closer to his knowledge and his skill. It is March as I write these words; the Eden will be open for trouting in less than a week and the Wharfe will follow ten days later. I am looking forward to the fishing of early spring and it will, of course, be done with the fly, but I am also looking forward to July and August and I am hoping for low water and bright sun, hoping to find the trout eager for the worm, hoping above all that in those two months to which I have confined the season of the upstream worm I shall be able to make satisfying progress in a method of angling that Stewart, along with most of the old masters, reckoned second only to the fly.

PART II

Chapter Ten

And there, something like twenty five years ago, I left it with my thoughts on fishing the upstream worm. I left it because I could see no way forward and recognised what I had written as incomplete. I waited for some sort of continuation or conclusion to present itself but none appeared. I gave my mind to other books and other interests and only rarely revisited the unfinished story of my fishing life, except that I plundered some of its material to make articles for magazines. I never forgot that I had written half a book, although it often seemed to me that it was destined always to remain unfinished and unknown; until now at last, and unexpectedly, the experience of recent years is telling me that there is more to say, suggesting at the same time that the process of saying it will be good for me and may even, for others, be worth the trouble of reading it.

As soon as I decided to resume this story I was faced with a decision: whether to refashion the existing chapters in the light of later experience or to leave them unrevised, preserving the thoughts and feelings of a fisher in his early forties. It was only partly indolence that persuaded me to leave well alone, for it seemed to me that a fishing life in two halves, written from two widely separated perspectives, might be more interesting than one that looked back over almost half a century from the same point of view. It also seemed to me, and I may of course have been wrong, that there was a freshness to what I had already written – especially in those chapters dealing with my earliest fishing experiences – that could only be damaged by interference. For better or worse I have left the preceding chapters as they were when I finished with them in my early forties; what follows is a new beginning and I am not entirely certain how to gather up the threads before making a fresh start.

In the context of this book it is, I suppose, an admissible, perhaps even an appropriate cliché to observe that, since the writing of the preceding chapters, much water, ranging from the weary trickle of drought to the raging abundance of spate, has flowed under the graceful bridges that span both the Eden and the Wharfe.

When I think of bridges, by the way, my mind often turns to Conistone bridge on the Wharfe and the deep pool in its downstream shadow where I have never managed to catch a decent trout although I am, of course, still trying. And then most likely my thoughts will hurry over the three bridges at Kettlewell, Buckden and Hubberholme, racing upstream to stand on Yockenthwaite bridge where, in summer after a week or more of hot and settled weather, there is no water at all beneath the bridge's single arch but only a dry basin of dusty limestone more likely to fry a fish than to keep him alive. But this is not what the mind's eye sees; when my mind's eye goes to Yockenthwaite bridge it sees a river falling back from spate and a pool glowing with the promise of trout, a pool where, in spite of its habit of disappearing, I have caught dozens of fish over the years. If my imagination is on the Eden rather than the Wharfe then it will probably go first to Warcop Old Bridge, narrow, high and elegant, where good trout and grayling haunt the wide runs that I can see on both sides of the bridge, and then it might move a mile or two upstream and look at the river from the bridge at Great Musgrave, looking for rising fish and looking upstream to the little sandstone church that stands on a high bank above the Eden. In spring it stands there in a yellow drift of wild daffodils and sometimes I am standing in the river below them, casting among the dark olives in the hope of trout.

We fishers have a special affinity with bridges but I had better leave them because I am meant to be picking up threads and tying up loose ends; perhaps I could start this process by telling you what I think of the young fisher that you met a few chapters ago and of the rather older fisher who remembered him and then wrote about the middle-aged fisher into which he had turned. After this it will be time to begin bringing you up to date. Anyway, at the risk of sounding unforgivably complacent, I find that I quite like my younger self. I can see many faults; some of them, and one in particular, have been acknowledged, others I shall leave obscure. I can see many imperfections, partly of course because I know more about myself than is revealed by my writing, but looking back at the young man who haunted the Wenning and the Wharfe and the Eden and seeing his progress as an angler, I like the idealism of his fishing, I like his strong and grateful attachment to rivers, especially to the Wharfe; I like his sense of history and tradition and I like his appreciation and his need of beauty. Perhaps most of all I like his conviction that to be a fisher is a profound blessing and I like that very personal conviction that an angler must make himself worthy of his calling which is, of course, all part of the idealism that I have already mentioned, as too is his closely connected belief that sin and fishing do not belong together. I like all of this in him because it seems to point to a degree of thoughtfulness and, dare I say it, of sensitivity. And I like it because now, at the age of sixty five, I still go fishing with something like the same heart and the same feelings.

You cannot live through more than twenty years without change; you should not want to, but the essence of my fishing is distilled from the same elements that formed themselves all those years ago on the Ribble and the Wenning and during my early association with the Wharfe. If catching a big fish does not always bring the rapture that once belonged to it, then my reverence for the shining beauty of a wild trout is even deeper than it used to be; it sometimes seems to me, as I hold a trout and gaze at it before release or execution, that I am cradling in my hands the whole beauty of creation. If, moreover, there is less raw excitement in my experience of a fishing day, then the ending of such days often brings a fullness of contentment, an intensity of peace and, especially on the Wharfe, a deep sense of belonging that between them take me beyond the edge of tears.

There is, of course, a sharper sense of passing time, there is the knowledge that many more seasons lie behind me than wait for me to fish through them on my way to eternity or oblivion. And this recognition feeds the current of melancholy that has always flowed through me and flows stronger now, because the thought that I must later or sooner be separated from so much that I love fills me, in spite of my Catholic faith, with aching sadness. I cannot understand how so many of my friends, men without any hope beyond the grave, seem able to contemplate the prospect of their own extinction without pain. I suppose it is this preoccupation with mortality that now invests my fishing days with more affecting, more complex feelings than the strong and easy emotions of much earlier years. From the days of my early manhood I can think of only two occasions when I sat by a river and wept. The first of them was when I made my brief and complicated reacquaintance with the Wenning after a long day in the summer hills; the second came at the end of that terrible day by the Wharfe when I thought that my fishing life was prematurely at an end. I have just told you that riverside days now sometimes end with tears, but the truth is that they have become a commonplace of my presence on the Wharfe and I am often uncertain why they flow. If there are trout in my bag then they will most certainly be grateful tears, but there will be sadness mingling with the gratitude because of the knowledge that my days by this river that I so love are numbered, and because the beauty of the river and its landscape are such that I cannot bear the thought of losing them. But this sadness will in turn bring back the grateful tears, because to have known the Wharfe at all is a blessing, a thought which once more makes me deeply thankful that God made me a fisher. And this perception will probably turn me to prayer and then I shall probably wipe my eyes and, remembering my vocation, get to my feet and go fishing again.

After what I suppose has been a steady and a stable middle age I find, now that I am almost an old man, that I have become more volatile again; part of my purpose in writing the second part of this book is to explain why, although perhaps a more potent motivation is that I love writing about fishing just as much as I love fishing itself. The writing is harder work, but when it goes well, when I feel that I have captured in words something of the essence of a fishing day, so that those who read these words might feel something of the enrichment that the day has brought me, then my sense of satisfaction is profound.

The years separating this chapter from the preceding ones have been mostly happy years, full of fishing and shooting and writing. There have been four books and scores of articles and writing them has been the complement to the sport that has been their theme; and the writing has made the days themselves a deeper pleasure because I have gone about them in the knowledge that I shall try to recreate them in prose, which in turn has made me more alert to their special qualities, more thoughtful, more receptive. Through fishing and shooting I have found fulfilment as a writer in the attempt to recapture and retain experience, in the reflection, the gratitude and the praise. There are times, by the way, when I should like to read my published work but it is impossible; once I have written something and declared it finished, whether it is a short article for *Shooting Times* or a whole book, I do not dare ever to look at it again, because I know that I should be appalled by what I found: appalled, ashamed and desperate to write it all over again, doing it altogether differently. I cannot read what I have written once I can no longer fiddle with it which is, I suppose, because I am unwilling to confront its unavoidable imperfection. In spite of this inability, writing about shooting and fishing has been a rewarding challenge and a consistent delight and it has helped me, by the way, to see that, much as I enjoy shooting, my devotion to fishing is a much deeper and more complicated and more rewarding thing, which is why this is the story of a fishing life and not also the autobiography of a shooting man.

The place that I love most in the world is by Spout Dub on the Wharfe. It used to be somewhere else: about a mile upstream beneath the tall sycamore that shades Knipe Dub and it was only last year that I recognised my change of heart without fully understanding the reason why. I have written of Spout Dub elsewhere in this book, calling it a prince of pools and so it is. I was there yesterday (May 2015) and, during a prolonged mixed hatch in which iron blues were prominent, I caught three trout from the run into the pool, all three of them wild and two of them big. Spout Dub is often kind to me and you may remember that it was the chief contributor to my first real bagful of trout on a September day more than forty years ago. I have already described the main features of the place: the dripping and slightly concave wall of yellow limestone where ashes and sycamores find surprising purchase, where dippers nest and where, when the springs are full, a runnel of water splashes into the pool over a mossy ledge and sometimes splashes the head of this fisher as he wades the shallow water in the shadow of Spout Dub's cliff, a cliff which, together with the trees on either side of it and the plantation of larches over the river, hides away the presence of his favourite pool, making it a secret as well as a sacred place.

I have not told you that, immediately downstream from Spout Dub, there is a grassy shelf above the river, five or six feet wide. This too is a private place, because the ground rises sharply behind it; it is shaded by sycamores and looks across the water to the larches and it is the place where I now most like to rest at lunchtime, listening to the rustle of the breeze in those mossed and lichened sycamores, listening to the whisper of the leaves while looking up the whole length of Spout Dub and watching the trout rising there. At the downstream end of my shelf there is something like a tiny cave, a roughly shaped low arch of limestone with, beneath it, space for a sandwich box and a flask, for a small bottle of wine with a metal beaker to drink it from. If I come there at lunchtime with a brace or more of trout in my bag, then, as I eat my sandwich and drink the two beakers of wine that are my special treat on Wharfedale days, I am as happy as any man can reasonably expect to be in a world full of sorrow.

I love this place for its own sake, for the tight green buds of the sycamores in early spring, for the dry rustle of their shrunken and pock-marked leaves on September afternoons. Yesterday the sycamores were hung beneath the leaf with greenish yellow blossom that was sweet, almost sickly, on the air. I love this place for the sight and the sound of the water beneath me, for its gentle slide between the rocks and for the milky whiteness spread over the surface of Spout Dub, a whiteness often etched with the dark lines and circles of feeding trout. I love this place for the sight of the dippers with moss or insects in their beak, perching briefly on a rock by the edge of the stream, white-bibbed and beautiful and always earning their name before they dart up to their nest in some hole or hollow of Spout Dub's cliff. I love this place for the beauty of leaf and grass and running water, for the sight of birds and the sounds of each season but I love it still more because it seems somehow to possess the power to dissolve pain; it is a place full of the past and it is also a place where I am happy with the present; much more importantly, it is a place where I am able to be happy with myself and with my mortality. It is because of all this that Spout Dub is the place where I most often shed complicated but welcome tears. I suppose what I am saying is that, for me, Spout Dub is a numinous place, a place of the spirit, a place where I connect with something important and powerful beyond myself, a connection that brings peace.

Yesterday there was only one trout in my bag at lunchtime, which may explain why yesterday there were no tears. He was a trout of very nearly two pounds but he was not a brace and so I sat and listened to the river and sipped my wine in the knowledge that I needed another trout for satisfaction. Although the olives and the iron blues had not yet started to hatch I was fairly confident that the afternoon would bring me at least one more fish; in the event it brought five, but at lunchtime there was the sense of unfinished business which always hangs about me on a fishing day until I have caught my brace; beneath it however there was a deep sense of belonging which made the indisputable beauties of the place seem twice as beautiful as I sat there and thought my way back to the undergraduate who had first come there on an autumn day when the blue wings hatched as I have never since seen them on the Wharfe. I thought of my first coming to Spout Dub, and thought too of a more recent time, of three whole years when I never once saw this most precious place, when I barely fished at all and even the thought of the Wharfe inspired a sobbing sense of separation and loss.

Soon I shall take you to that unhappy time, to the one substantial rupture in the continuity of my fishing life. It happened five years ago and it will be good for me now, I think, to return there, but before doing this I shall go back much further, go back to the time immediately following the completion of the first half of this book, to that time when the writing of it seemed suddenly to have met a dead end. And the reason for this loss of vision, I now realise, was at least partly that for a whole season I went fishing in the company of fear: fear that a sport which for so long had meant so much to me, had seemed my vocation and my fulfilment, was losing its hold over me, was turning into an empty ritual with no power to satisfy or move. This was the time – mercifully it was brief – when, on the banks of the Wharfe or the Eden, I felt as the man must feel who has given his life to God and then realises that he no longer believes.

It happened during a summer of few fish; it was a summer of savage drought and, even with the worm, I struggled to catch trout when conditions seemed made for it. I struggled much more with the fly but it was not blank days or light baskets that bothered me. What haunted me was this dark fear that a ruling passion was dissolving into emptiness. It seemed like a loss of faith or a failure of vision; it seemed like a sin, for my instinct told me to blame myself rather than my rivers or the pursuit that I was meant to love. Whatever it seemed like it is undeniably true that for a whole season I found in fishing, instead of all the vital emotions of the past, feelings much nearer discontent and sorrow. And sometimes it was even worse; sometimes it felt like a bereavement, like the loss of an essential and sustaining part of me.

It was a season of few trout but the few there were brought bitter disappointment, even the big ones, because they did not bring with them the old surge of elation and the sudden conviction that the world had just turned into a better place. And, if a heavy fish threw the hook or broke the line, there was not the blank sense of loss that there had always been in the past. I remember forcing myself to go fishing even more than usual, hoping somehow to recapture the old intensity, but this made things even worse. And all the time I was trying to understand what was happening to me and getting nowhere, like a doctor observing symptoms of disease and unable to see their cause.

It was entirely unexpected and it was, of course, most painful at Kilnsey, where there was just a whiff of the desolation that had come over me when for a time I thought that I had made myself a lifelong exile from the Wharfe. There was not, it is true, the crushing burden of self-loathing that had overwhelmed me twenty years earlier, but there was still some sense of guilt; for I felt ungrateful and untrue to the Wharfe because I could no longer find on her banks or draw from her streams the thankful contentment that had so often been their gift to me in the past. Instead of contentment and communion there was a bitter sense of emptiness, as though something very precious had drained away and left a void. There were just a few days when all seemed unaccountably well and I seemed to have rediscovered my riverside happiness, but there were many more days when I seemed to be fishing my way through a bleak land of lost content in the vain hope of reviving something that was already dead.

I looked into myself in search of the reason why. I wondered whether it was simple boredom, whether I had fished too long and too often so that catching trout had become a commonplace thing that no longer mattered. I said this to myself and did not believe it even for a moment. I asked myself whether I had tried to make fishing into something that it was not and could never be, giving it an importance in my life that it did not deserve and could not sustain, which meant that for years I had been fishing a fraud, a fraud that had finally been exposed; perhaps I had loved my rivers as only people should be loved and perhaps I had finally discovered the obvious truth that mere things, even things as life-giving and lovely as rivers, cannot return love, so that love given to them must sooner or later acknowledge its own emptiness. Perhaps, by turning trout and rivers into a central part of my happiness, I had been trying to hide from my own heart the barren loneliness of a bachelor life. Whatever the reason, it hurt that when I went to places where for so long I had drunk in beauty and contentment I could no longer feel their healing touch. I felt deprived and diminished.

I also found it difficult to escape the pain of this lost communion; it hung about me like an unwept grief. When I chose not to go fishing and went walking in the hills instead, it was a burden that climbed into them with me. Up there in the Howgills above Sedbergh, walking the long ridges of those rounded hills, I felt guilty that I had not gone fishing in search of the old joy. If I came over the brow of a hill and looked down on the wandering line of a moorland stream, then the sight would bring a sharp pang of sorrow; for once I should have half-wished that I was carrying a rod, so that I could discover if this tumbling stream harboured a good store of small trout; but now there was no such feeling, scarcely even curiosity enough to peer into one or two of the little pools and follow the darting shapes of any startled fish that were swimming there.

The end of the season, which had always been filled with a bitter-sweet sadness, came as a welcome relief from the pain of going fishing. I put away my rods and got out my guns. In the course of the autumn and winter I often wondered how it would be by my rivers the next spring. I crouched by rushy ponds as the light died, waiting and listening for the pulse of wings in the darkening sky above me, wondering whether the expectancy then gripping me would ever again visit me through the handle of a split-cane rod. I prayed that it would and began to hope. I could not believe that something as precious and vital as my joy in fishing had been forever lost.

There were days after pheasants when I missed birds with demoralising consistency, when I shot at them wildly and they flew blithely on their way; there were days when they flung back their necks and fell like stones to the hard earth. The bad days were days of seething frustration and shame. Whatever the weather the good days were glorious. I remember driving back from Scotland through torrents of rain at the end of a December day when the wind had blown half a gale and the birds had flown like feathered bullets and collapsed from the sky at the bark of my gun. As the car splashed its way through the Borders I saw again the pheasants that I had shot, saw them stop in the sky and then plummet to earth. I saw it all again, I relived the day and I drove through the downpour in high good humour.

At the end of shooting days that had gone well, bringing the sense of fulfilled contentment and deep peace that for me has almost always followed successful sport, bringing too that sense of a sustaining communion with the world of field and stream, at the end of shooting days I often wondered whether I should ever again find the same feelings on the banks of the Wharfe, hoping with a passionate intensity that catching trout would once again matter as much to me as shooting pheasants and duck. In the past it had always mattered more.

In the course of the winter there were evenings when I sat smoking by the fire, sipping claret and at the same time recalling how I used to feel when tackling up at the start of a fishing day. I remembered how I was possessed by a deep longing for trout and how, for the whole course of the day, nothing else but catching trout was really important. I remembered the thump of excitement that came with the hooking of a big fish, I remembered the bright relief and the shining fulfilment that came over me when at last he was drawn over the net. I remembered the dumb agony of loss that took hold of me when a good trout threw the hook and I remembered the peace that had been mine at the end of days when I left the river with the spotted beauty of four or five or half a dozen trout in my bag. And, of course, remembering these feelings brought with it the aching desire that they could be recreated, which in turn provoked a repeated probing after the cause of their mysterious loss.

Again the idea came to me that I had fished too much and caught too many trout. I had repeatedly rejected this analysis during the season but now it returned. Perhaps it had all happened too often, so that repetition had blunted the impact of feelings that had once been so intense. Perhaps it was like a piece of music that had once seemed so profoundly beautiful that its power to move could never fade but which, heard through again and again, becomes at last no more than a succession of sounds without force or meaning, sounds that can inspire no response but a sense of impoverished disappointment and loss.

It was a dreadful thought, this fear that my love of fishing had turned into a memory. It was still with me when a new season brought me back to Kilnsey, to Spout Dub and Black Keld and Watersmeet. I went there poised uneasily between hope and fear, nervous and uncertain of the feelings that I might find waiting for me on the banks of the Wharfe; it was a soft morning in earliest spring and I very soon began to believe that all would be well; for in walking the river and fishing its pools and runs, in seeing the olives on the water with trout rising to eat them and in trying to catch some of those rising trout, I found the feelings that I wanted to find and found at the same time that all the previous season I had been looking for the wrong ones.

It was a gentle day under cloud with a breeze moving quietly upstream, with a clear and generous water flowing full but with no hint of excess, the sort of water that best expresses the limestone beauty of the upper Wharfe. The spring olives came thickly. The trout responded eagerly but they were not careless trout, happy to swallow whatever fly I chose to throw at them; they were difficult and discerning trout and it was very hard to deceive them. I fished the Waterhen and the Orange Partridge, the Greenwell and the Snipe Bloa; I switched to dry flies and tried the Imperial, the Rough Olive and the Grey Duster. I killed three fish, all on different flies, all well over the pound and in fine condition; I failed with many more. The trout I hooked fought angrily and I was very anxious not to lose them. On the bank, lying in the faded grass, they were very beautiful. The trout that I could not catch were frustrating and fascinating at the same time. I kept willing them to keep rising so that I could keep trying to tempt them with different flies. I was disappointed when the hatch failed and the fish went down and the river flowed with only the patterns and sounds of its own making. I remember, at the end of my day, sitting smoking by Knipe Dub, full of the very contentment that I thought I had lost, a contentment qualified only by the dark thought that the next day would take me to London and so keep me from my river and its trout for a whole long week.

The prospect of this enforced separation was painful, but beneath it there were much deeper feelings of gratitude and relief. After months of self-searching doubt and discontent, I now knew for certain that the Wharfe and the Eden would flow through however much of life remained to me. And this was because I had realised that, all through the previous season, I had been confused; I had been looking for the wrong feelings, for unevolved or undeveloped feelings, without seeing that my attachment to rivers and their fish had changed because it was more than twenty years since I had caught my first trout. I was forty-two, not nineteen or twenty, and could no longer expect to feel the emotions of a young fisher in the years of my middle age.

When you have already caught more than a thousand trout you can no longer expect to feel, on catching yet another one, quite the same exaltation that came with the catching of the first trout of all. When you have lost more trout than you care to remember you will no longer suffer as you did when, with few trout to your name, the loss of one, especially a big one, turned the world dark and haunted you for days. When you have walked the same riverbank for more than twenty years, the beauty of water and rock and of the surrounding fields and hills will no longer strike you with the impact of its first revelation all those years ago. But familiarity should not breed contempt or disenchantment; rather it should acknowledge a quieter response to events and places, a response that, although gentler and less demonstrative, is governed by deep attachment, deeper, once recognised for what it is, much deeper and stronger than the showier feelings of first experience.

Some of all this I saw at the time, although I was so relieved to find that I was once again a happy and fulfilled fisher that I felt disinclined to attempt searching analysis. I just wanted to enjoy feeling whole again. I remember thinking that intense relationships often, at some stage of their evolution, experience a serious crisis and that, if this is survived, they often emerge from it with a strengthened bond, with a deeper commitment. I remember applying this to my fishing life and thinking that, in passing through that sudden trauma of doubt, I had moved from the unstable affections of youth to the steadier, more dependable and, yes, more rewarding devotion of maturity. Looking back on that whole experience from a distance of almost twenty five years, I think this interpretation was more or less right. It was a process of difficult readjustment and I think that what made it especially difficult for me was that, as a fisher, I was for a long time much younger than my years.

I was, after all, a late convert; I was already nineteen when I caught my first trout and fell passionately in love with rivers and their fish; and I was still fishing with something like the mind of a boy when childish things should already have been laid aside. For a time in my mid-twenties this childishness proved impossible, because the dark reality that excess had made of my life beyond the riverbank was too heavy a burden to be pushed aside and forgotten whenever I pulled on a pair of waders. But when the darkness lifted and allowed me back to the Wharfe, immediately I plunged back into my fishing life with a joy that was truly child-like; it felt as though, rather than at last growing up, I had grown the wrong way and headed back, back towards boyhood;

the thrill of the take, the pulsing excitement of a rod brought to life by the power of a running fish, the flood of relief that came with a trout in the net and the blank agony of a lost fish: I felt all this at the age of twenty five and more with the passion of a boy who knows that, of all the important things in life, there is nothing half so important as catching trout.

And so it happened that, at the age of forty, I was still trying to go fishing with the feelings of a boy. And there was something else too; for I not only cultivated a deliberately childish approach to the events of a fishing day; I also, and much more deliberately, built a sort of mental barrier or fence to enclose and protect my fishing world from contamination by surrounding reality. It became an enchanted world and I thought of it as a world of changeless delight and contentment – a sort of paradise regained – and part of that changelessness was meant to be me. This was the falsehood that caused the second crisis of my fishing life when I thought that my love of fishing was spent, not realising that it was in fact trying to tell me that it had changed and matured. And the vision of maturity saw that the joy and beauty of fishing were much more marvellous once a fisher had seen that imperfection and pain belonged to the whole of life and could be excluded from no part of it. It is, after all, a most wonderful thing that, in a world full of sorrow and loss, a man can find important and healing pleasure with a fishing rod in his hand.

****

I saw this, some of it at least, on my first visit to Kilnsey at the beginning of another spring and what it tells me now is that it was twenty five years ago when, somewhat later than most, I finally grew up as an angler.

I have made brief mention of a third crisis. Soon I shall make myself tackle it: a crisis that kept me from my rivers for almost three seasons. It is over now, thank God, although there are times when I still live in its shadow. I shall tackle it very soon but, after making my retrospective way through one difficult experience, I feel a sudden need to move among easier concerns for a few pages, while I gather my strength and try to sharpen my insight in preparation for telling you of a much more difficult, much longer and much more painful period of my life. For just a few pages I want to write about purely practical fishing matters, about flies and rods and hooks and that sort of thing; it will seem to me like relaxation or therapy while the mind gathers itself for another bout of introspection; it will seem almost like a rest.

This book, of course, has no ambition to teach its readers how to fish, although it has told you at some length how its author chose or tried to fish at different stages of his evolution as a fisher; it has told you how I began my fishing as an ignorant dry fly purist, how I later embraced the northern tradition of the upstream wet and, with the convert's intolerance of his earlier ways, entirely renounced use of the floating fly. I have explained how dry flies found their way back onto the end of my line and I have written the brief history of my involvement with worms. Over the last twenty years my practice as a fisher has seen further change, partly in response to modern developments in fly fishing and partly because of my own changing attitude to the business of catching fish. I think I should begin with worms.

When I last wrote about the upstream worm I was an enthusiast for its use in high summer drought. In another book I have already explained how, long before I achieved the mastery for which I once longed, the worm fell out of my favour; in fact I rather think that, after writing in such glowing terms about the upstream worm, I never fished it again. There was no sudden revelation of the wickedness of the worm; there were no visions full of disgusting writhing things, there was no dramatic gesture of renunciation. I remember that on several days I went to the river with a supply of worms scoured and ready for service, but I cannot remember that I ever fished with them.

What happened was this: I found that, even with the Wharfe and the Eden on their bones, I could often still manage to catch a trout or two on the fly and I began to think that creatures as beautiful as trout deserved to be caught by the method that is far and away the most beautiful method of catching them. It was a matter of aesthetics rather than morality.

The upstream worm, anyway, fell out of my fishing repertoire. Its use is still permitted at Kilnsey – by members only – although it must be years since anyone exercised his member's right to catch trout with the worm. I think I was probably the Kilnsey Angling Club's last wormer and I also think that a member who now chose to fish the worm would not find himself universally popular. You may fish with worms on the Eden at Kirkby Stephen and there are those who do so without fearing for their reputation. I have never quite said to myself that I shall never fish the worm again and – who knows? – a savage drought this summer might persuade me to have another go. It could happen but I rather doubt it. You know how keen I am to put a brace of trout in my bag but, in spite of this, I think that I should now prefer to catch a single trout on the fly than a sackful with the worm. I have said it elsewhere and I now say it again; I think I have urged forward my last worm.

I still fish both the wet and the dry fly and I still think that, in a falling and clearing water with the fish in taking mood, the upstream wet is the most exciting and satisfying way of all the many ways there are to catch a trout. It is the twitch on the line or the gleam of a turning fish; it is those subtle signs telling a fisher to turn his wrist that still thrill me whenever, responding to them, I feel the sudden weight of a trout. I love the upstream wet and it still probably catches me most of my fish in the spring. But, except in the aftermath of spate, the dry fly now reigns more or less supreme during the summer; and even when rivers are falling back from flood, even then there are times when the dry fly is the better choice. This is partly the result of recent developments in fly dressing, the most important of which is probably the emergence, from the mind of Hans van Klinken, of the incomparable Klinkhamer.

The Klinkhamer, of course, was already in existence when I wrote the first part of this book. It came into being some time during 1984 and was doubtless soon being tied and used by progressive anglers in Britain. I am conservative by nature and it was years before the Klinkhamer entered my fishing life. I could probably search through my diaries and find exactly when it caught me my first trout but I cannot be bothered. It was sometime around the turn of the century when I discovered the potency of this marvellous fly. The original Klinkhamers were monstrous things designed for brawling Norwegian rivers; we now fish them in all sizes and there are seasons when they account for a significant proportion of my fish. They are one of the main reasons why so much of the season finds me fishing the dry fly.

But there is another reason, one which on reflection is perhaps even more important, and it will take me just a little time to explain. It concerns itself, initially at least, with the Wharfe and with the tendency of its trout to spend the whole summer feasting on smut, unless they are midges. At any rate they are black and very small and an infernal nuisance. Whatever they are, I used to fish for the trout eating them with flies that were small and black but never quite small enough. The pattern I liked best was called Spring Black, although I always thought of it as The August Black from the month of its best service. It was a Pritt tying: crow or magpie herl over purple silk with a shiny hackle from a starling's neck. I tied it on Veniard's fine wire 16s, which are more like most manufacturers' 18s. They are also no longer made. I did try much smaller hooks but I found that I could not consistently hook or hold big fish with them and I did not find that they rose significantly more trout. The August Black was and is a wet fly, although it is often damp rather than really wet; often it lies in the surface film rather than sinking just beneath it.

In the past there were times when, for weeks on end, I fished almost exclusively with the August Black and there were times when it caught me lots of trout. Fishing it in low water was a tricky and delicate business and success brought deep satisfaction. But there were other times when the trout would have none of it and there were even worse times when I bungled the few chances that came my way. Fishing the August Black, or any small wet fly, is particularly testing in an awkward wind, which means that you often do not know where your fly is and so miss rises and lose your composure and end up fishing like an idiot. At least this is what happens to me. It was on such a day that for no good reason, except that I was making a complete hash of things with the August Black, I tied a bushy sort of rough olive to my cast and immediately started to catch trout. I called this fly the Yellow Thing and I have already told you of its not infrequent efficacy with smutting trout. I have also told you how it was this same pattern that brought me back to the dry fly by catching trout eating olive uprights on the Eden. I have good reason to be very grateful to the Yellow Thing. In my present context what matters is that its mysterious appeal to trout stuffing themselves with microscopic black things meant that I spent less of each summer fishing small wet flies.

And now I am going to blow my own trumpet for a page or two. You will think that I have lost the thread of my argument but I am in fact still holding on to it (loosely) and, just to make clear what my thread actually is, I had better remind myself that I am explaining why the dry fly is now the staple of my summer fishing. Now that this is done it is time for the trumpet, although I shall blow it first in praise of someone else.

The best book by far on trout flies is the one by Courtney Williams. It is of course hopelessly out of date because it was written before modern fishers got to work and transformed the art of fly dressing. There are no Klinkhamers in its pages, no F flies or Sparkle Duns, no crippled or funnelduns; you will not find patterns that call for Antron or Lureflash or Z-lon, whatever that might be. Courtney Williams' *Dictionary of Trout Flies* is the record of a past age and it is a delight to read; it is pleasantly written, it is anecdotal and discursive, it takes its time, lingering over favourite flies and telling tales about the men who devised them and the men who fished them and the great bags that were caught with them. As a guide to trout flies it has been superseded by John Roberts' excellent reference book, but I still recommend it to you most warmly as a book to dip in and out of. Think of it as history; regard it as a record of ancient wisdom or a storehouse of curiosities with some continuing relevance for the anglers of today.

Anyway, you will find in Courtney Williams a fly called Simple Simon; it is a cross between a hackle Coachman and a Coch-y-bondhu and it is the invention of Williams himself. Over the years I have modified and I think improved it; I think my version of Simple Simon is a first rate wet fly to fish early in the season or in a coloured and falling water when the trout are not busy with a hatch but are on the look-out for food. I now tie it as follows:

Hook: 12

Thread: orange (instead of black)

Body: peacock herl ribbed with gold or silver wire with a turn or two of gold tinsel at the tail

Hackle: an iridescent dark green feather from a lapwing, in the unlikely event that you can lay your hands on one; otherwise a suitable substitute, if you can think of anything appropriate (I can't), or dark red or brown hen with a white hen hackle in front

I did not shoot my lapwing, by the way; it was found dead by a farming friend who thought that I might be able to make use of the feathers. I think the lapwing hackle makes Simple Simon a more killing fly and there must be a more readily available feather that would produce a similar effect. The orange thread is my other innovation. Anyway, Simple Simon, in both its original and particularly in its modified form, has caught me scores of trout from the Wharfe, although it has been less successful on the Eden. My point in mentioning this pattern is that some years ago I turned it into a dry fly, which I named Dry Simon. I have blown my trumpet in praise of Courtney Williams; now it is time to blow a triple fanfare for myself as the tyer of one of the deadliest dry flies that has ever floated enticingly down the currents of a trout stream. And it has just occurred to me that the glossy greenish black feather from a starling's throat would probably work well enough as an alternative to the lapwing hackle. I shall tie some Simple Simons with it this evening and see how they fish when next the conditions are right.

Getting back to Dry Simon I have found it a most wonderful fly; it catches trout in coloured water; it catches them when rivers are low and clear. It brings trout up when they are not rising, trout take it when they are eating flies that look nothing like it; they take it when they are gorging on blue wings or pale wateries or midges or smut. Dry Simon has filled my bag on the Wharfe; it has fooled trout repeatedly on the Eden. The trout of the Driffield Beck have seized it with fatal greed; the trout in nearby Foston Beck have found it irresistible. Teme trout love it; on the Rea Brook the trout cannot have enough of it. Wherever I have cast Dry Simon I have found trout eager to eat it in widely differing conditions. There are, of course, times when its magic fails but there are more times when it works. Only yesterday (15/6/15) I was on the Wharfe. The river was very low and very clear and the trout were very busy eating smut. Dry Simon caught me nine trout, six of them wild or overwintered fish, and it was a very happy fisher who drank his lunchtime wine on the grassy shelf by Spout Dub. Dry Simon is a great fly; I commend him to you and here is how to make him:

Hook: 12
Thread: orange
Tail: a dozen or so fibres of Krystal Flash trimmed short (about 5cms)
Body: peacock herl ribbed with gold or silver wire
Hackle: ginger or rusty dun cock wound through a white cock hackle

Now that I have blown my trumpet in praise of Courtney Williams and Simple Simon, in honour of myself and my creation, I can begin to pick up my thread, as long as I can remember it. It has to do with smutting trout and how I used to spend all summer long fishing damp little black things to them, until I discovered that there were times when, for some reason, the Yellow Thing proved very attractive to these smutting trout; a year or two later I found that Dry Simon was even better medicine and this does finally bring me back to my thread, which is to explain why my summer fishing now relies on the dry fly much more than it used to. The reason, of course, is that fishing a big, bright floating fly is a much easier business than fussing round with little black things. I still fish little black things, I fish them wet, damp and dry and I fish them when big, bright floating flies are having an off day. But when the fish are smutting and the sun is bright Dry Simon is always my first choice; I fish him mainly in broken water and glides and I do not expect him to attract every trout over which he is cast. When trout are smutting even little black things never manage to do this, and little black things, with their little hooks, bring the inevitable frustration of pricked and lost fish, whereas Dry Simon takes a firm hold of most of the trout that take a liking to him. You may think that a great big fancy fly is a crude stratagem to employ against smutting trout; you may think that we fishers should rise to the challenge of the minuscule and you may be right. As I fisher I am still troubled by a perhaps primitive longing to catch fish and, on the whole, Dry Simon does this more efficiently for me than little black things. I think this is a thread that I can now lay down in order to pick up a new one.

I have just told you that I still want to catch trout. A fishing day has never been for me a day in delightful surroundings, full of birdsong and flowers and the beauty of running water, a day that may bring the added pleasure of a trout or two but a day that will still have been well and pleasantly spent without this bonus of fish. A fishing day without fish has always and still is for me a day of gloom and failure. I still want to catch trout and you may be shocked to learn that I still want to kill some of them, although I now return many more fish than was my former practice. I do not intend to get entangled in the morality of fishing and field sports. I used to be strongly opposed to compulsory catch and release; I still think that it raises ethical problems because I think the case for fishing is somewhat undermined if it completely divorces itself from food. I am also uncertain whether, if we think that trout deserve mercy in the form of release after capture, they do not also deserve to be spared the suffering that comes with hooking and then playing them until they are exhausted and spent. It seems to me that they should not be tortured if they should not be killed, but I have argued all this elsewhere and I am not going to argue it all again.

In purely philosophical terms catch and release is, I think, ethically suspect, but I have come to accept that, as a measure of conservation, it has an important place. On the Eden I now return most of the trout that I catch, mainly because for more than ten years the Kirkby Stephen water has been a wild fishery; fishers are still allowed to take a brace of fish but the stock of trout would certainly suffer if this right was regularly exercised. Most anglers return all the fish they catch, others including me take a fish here and there; and this, it seems to me, is as it should be: not that other fishers put everything back while I continue to kill trout, but that we should be allowed, if the rare urge takes us, to remember the origins of our sport and take our dinner home with us.

On the Wharfe I behave differently. The Kilnsey water is generously stocked, too generously in my opinion although my loathing of stocked trout has softened over the years, mostly because I want to kill trout for the table. Given this desire or appetite, which is shared by a significant proportion of the members, the Wharfe's own store of trout needs help from our stew ponds, which means in turn that I can kill fish with an easy conscience. For the only argument against killing trout in any river is the danger of depleting the population of wild fish; when you kill stocked fish you are actually helping the wild trout by removing competition for food, although this might, I suppose, bring into question the wisdom or justification of stocking in the first place. Anyway, the Kilnsey water is stocked, I am glad that it is stocked although I should be happier if it were stocked with rather fewer and incidentally with smaller fish. I am glad that it is stocked because I want to kill fish and my general practice is to take stocked fish and to return wild fish under two pounds. Occasionally I break my own rule; almost always it is beauty that is to blame.

It happened yesterday with the last fish of the day. Dry Simon, in a low, very clear water, with the trout smutting insatiably, had caught me three stockies (killed without a second thought), two big overwintered trout in superb condition (killed after very brief hesitation) and I had returned four wild trout between eight and twelve inches, acts of mercy that had cost me no pain. In the afternoon I fished above Knipe Dub and the Stepping Stones for the first time this year. It is a beat that was formerly a favourite of mine.

For some reason I have neglected it of late, perhaps because it turns lunch by Spout Dub, which is almost a mile away, into something of an effort. Anyway, I was there yesterday afternoon, with a light upstream breeze, with sunshine through the leaves dappling the water and with trout making delicate marks in the river's surface as they helped themselves to the limitless bounty of smut. I was very glad to be there, because it made me realise all over again what lovely water it is for a fisher of flies, water with a swift succession of pool and run and glide, with an alternation of open water and water overshadowed by trees. And sometimes the water was flowing over pebbles and stones, sometimes it was shining over smooth shelves or hollowed basins of rock.

I caught and killed the third of my stock fish from Stepping Stones Pool; I returned a wild fish from the lip of the next glide. I fished a deep run where I expected to bring up a trout but where none came. And then I came to another glide, a long and lovely glide beneath the shadow of a high bank on my left. It was a glide full of memories, for it has given me many fish over the years and they have very often been notable fish because they have usually been big and they have often been difficult, demanding a stealthy approach and delicate casting in low water; they have been difficult to catch because they have been so easy to frighten and almost always they have been wild. It is also the glide where, on a still and cloudy afternoon in August all those years ago, with the river falling back from spate and with blue wings hatching all day long, I caught so many trout on the upstream wet that even the next day I could not remember just how many of them there had been.

Yesterday there were not scores of trout showing, but there was one sipping away at the bottom of the glide. Dry Simon put him down and I even thought of changing to something small and black. There was another trout showing half way up the glide, where the smooth flow along the bank turns just slightly against a slight outcrop of rock. This is the place where the big trout lie, here and in the faster water right at the top of the glide. This is the place where I have failed more often than I have managed to catch the trout that I have seen rising there.

Perhaps I should have changed flies yesterday, perhaps it was laziness but anyway Dry Simon fell lightly enough a foot or so above the ring of the rise and a moment later I was playing a heavy trout. He leapt and looked yellow all over so that I knew at once that he was most certainly a wild as well as a big fish. He weighed one ounce short of a pound and a half; his flanks and his belly were buttercup yellow, his spots were small, dark chain-mail spots with just a scattering of red; his fins and his tail were translucent, amber, perfect and delicate, and his head was shapely and small, a consideration which inclines me, by the way, to think that he was probably a she.

Whatever the sex of this trout my new rule tells me that as a wild trout short of two pounds he (or she) should have gone back to the glide from which he or she came; but I knew as soon as I saw him – I can't be bothered with the she any more – I knew as soon as I saw him in the net that I was incapable of obeying my own rule. It was, of course, his beauty that did it. He was a perfect trout and I knew that I could not surrender him. It may be childish, it may be primitive, it may well be wrong, but there are some trout that are so beautiful that I have to take them. I should be lying if I claimed that, when I kill such a trout, I am thinking mainly of food. The truth is that edibility is my justification for killing a fish like yesterday's last, but the motivation is beauty, beauty and the irresistible longing to possess it, to call it my own. Perhaps I should tell myself that a trout's beauty soon fades once it has been taken from the water; the sheen dims, the spots lose their lustre, the yellow turns pale. I do not need to tell myself any of this because I know it perfectly well. It fails to influence me because the immediate impact of all that beauty, shining in the mesh of my net, is more than I can resist. I am helplessly in its thrall.

So there is my current attitude to taking trout. I do not like catch and release as an inflexible rule although I can see its value to preserve fish stocks. I kill far fewer trout than I used to, especially wild trout, but I kill stocked trout with enthusiasm and tell myself that in doing so I am also doing good. And stocked trout, by the way, at least the Kilnsey version of them, taste absolutely delicious, although the wild trout of the Rea are the finest trout that I have ever eaten. I killed just a few of them recently when staying with Merlin and Karen Unwin; these I did kill with thoughts of food, though they were also very beautiful, with more red spots and redder fins than you find with the trout of the Eden and the Wharfe. They were fish between twelve ounces and a pound and we ate them for breakfast; the flesh was just pink, delicate, indescribable. I did, by the way, put back many more fish than I killed.

I am not sure what else I need to tell you before turning to the detailed story of more recent times. The nearer I come to this, the more unwilling I feel to begin. It will be good for me once I have started, it may even be good for you, but I am putting off the effort and, yes, the discomfort of getting down to it. Perhaps I could write about rods for a page or two, and then I could talk about hooks and, best of all, I could discuss literature, telling you which fishing books I have read during the last twenty years, although I now realise that I did this some time ago in a book of my own called *Once a Flyfisher*. What I can do is to proclaim my admiration for the writing of John Gierach.

It was in *Once a Flyfisher*, I think, that I wrote dismissively of *Trout Bum*. I cannot check this because, as you already know, I cannot read anything that I have written once it has achieved the dignity of print. And I cannot check whether it was in another book, this one called *That Strange Alchemy*, that I changed my mind and declared *Trout Bum* a minor masterpiece. This process, anyway, has happened somewhere in my writings and, since it happened, I think that I have read all Gierach's books. I also think that he has gotten (sic) better with time. In his earlier work you can tell that he is trying; in more recent books the writing seems effortless and reads like a sort of meditation on fishing, rivers, friends, landscape, conservation, American values and what matters to him in life. I have mentioned what matters in life deliberately because, except for a shared passion for fishing and a common love of the natural world, except for this and the urge to write about them, I am fairly certain that what most matters in life to me and to John Gierach are very different things. At the same time the ties that bind us are important bonds and I feel enormous sympathy for the picture he presents of a man who has built himself a fulfilled life as a writer and a fisherman. And he is consistently funny and he makes his world seem very attractive, very beautiful. And in reading his books you do more than read about fishing, you encounter an approach to living that is tolerant, generous and sane. I have read other American fishing books, books by Thomas McGuane and Nick Lyons and they are good books, but they are nothing like as good as the best of John Gierach; because in the best of John Gierach you do more than go fishing with him; in the best of John Gierach you inhabit a life and you find that it is a life worth inhabiting and that you have been enriched.

I thought that I should be able to write more about books but I find that, with the exception of Gierach, I have already read and written about the fishing books that have been important for me. And so, having run out of books, I shall now turn to rods and one of the minor sorrows of my fishing life, for I loved my rods of split-cane, my Sharpes and my Hardys, and it has hurt to acknowledge that they are outworn and outmoded, almost as much a part of history as rods of greenheart and lines of braided silk. There is a vogue for bamboo in the States – promoted partly by Gierach – and it may be that rods built by experts, and costing the earth, cast beautifully; and perhaps top-quality American rods – I am thinking partly of Skues' Leonard – have always been better than their English equivalents. Anyway my cane rods, my Hardy's Perfection, my Hardy's Halford Knockabout, my three Sharpes and my soft seven footer by Norman Goodwin of Skipton, my cane rods are clumsy and unresponsive sticks compared with the graphite rods that have replaced them. They are also much more beautiful than my dark grey or brown rods by Loomis and Sage, which are dull things in repose; but at work they are much more efficient and much easier to use than any of my cane rods; they come to life when loaded with a fly line and they make even my casting almost adequate; nothing will ever manage to make it elegant as well.

My first graphite rod was a nine foot Loomis, bought for me by a friend in the States. Immediately it replaced all my cane rods as my rod of choice and I seem to remember that it caught its first two pounder from the Wharfe only two days after it became mine. A year later the same friend bought me a more expensive Loomis, an eight and a half foot GLX, whatever that means, which promptly ousted the run-of-the-mill Loomis and has been my mainstay ever since. The GLX is just as powerful as my first Loomis and yet somehow more delicate, more precise in its action and even lighter to use. It carries a 4 line rather than a 5, as does the seven and a half foot Sage which Merlin and Karen Unwin brought back for me from Utah. The Sage has a lovely soft action; it coaxes out a line and is ideal for a day with an upstream breeze. I have another Sage, and I cannot remember which of my friends got it for me while on holiday somewhere in America. This, like the Loomis, is eight and a half feet long; it loads with a 5 line, is very powerful and I am not very fond of it, but it is still a useful rod because, even with my casting, it will throw something like a straight line into the face of an awkward wind.

These are the rods that now go fishing with me. I do not love them as I loved my cane rods. I never get them out of their cases just to look at them; I never put them together in the bedroom where they rest when not in use and then swish them to and fro. Somehow they are rods without character but they are so good at their job that it is years now since I went fishing with any of my cane rods, although I still occasionally get one or other of them out of its slip before putting it together, swishing it to and fro and thinking of times past. Sometimes I become sentimental about my cane rods, especially about the old Mitre Hardy that my parents bought for me, the rod that I once wanted to sell, the rod that, by catching me my first trout, made me a fisherman and was the first cause of such pleasure, such fulfilment, such joy.

Hooks are less evocative objects than rods. Hooks wake no memories, at least they wake none for me; hooks are dull and practical things and preferably sharp. I do not mention them because I intend to hold forth about the relative virtues of hooks by different makers. I am not going to compare Tiemco TMC 102 Ys with Kamasan B 405s. I mention hooks because I have broken a promise made at the end of my last book, where I swore solemnly that the next season would find me fishing with barbless hooks. It did not and nor did the next or the one that followed the next. Even today I still use hooks armed with wicked barbs and, in spite of that broken promise, I have no intention of mending my ways.

I can hear the howls of protest, I can hear you insisting that the welfare of trout demands the use of barbless hooks. I can hear all this and I concede that you have a point but I believe that I have a much better point, which is that, if you are genuinely concerned with the welfare of trout, you should not be fishing for them at all; you should be a warden of rivers rather than an angler: a man who cares for weed and water and spawning beds, for caddis and shrimp and nymphs of every kind, be they agile darters or laboured swimmers or the flat sort that inhabit the underside of stones. If your prime concern is the welfare of trout, then to contemplate a healthy river full of healthy trout will be fulfilment enough for you. If on the other hand you go fishing, even with barbless hooks and with the purpose of returning every trout that you catch, then you are acknowledging something that you reckon more important than the welfare of trout, namely your desire to catch them, to deceive them and hook them and then drag them through water until they are beaten and turn on their side. I grant that you are less primitive than I am; the absence of that barb and the release of all those trout both bear witness to this, but you are still a man of much cruder appetites than the man who finds his pleasure purely in the contemplation of running water and of the trout that swim there. You have no right to condemn me because in my desire to catch trout I use barbed hooks. I use them because I think they lose me fewer fish; I admit that they are more likely to damage trout although, with careful handling, this happens infrequently and, when it does, then I kill my trout, even if he is small.

Whatever sort of hooks you use, you should immediately renounce fishing if the thought of injuring trout unsettles or upsets you for, even with barbless hooks and even with tender care, there are trout that you will damage, there are some trout that will die as a result of your contact with them. There is this much of heartlessness in every fisher: that he puts his pleasure in catching fish above the discomfort, the pain, the fear, the damage that he may bring to fish in his pursuit of them. If I were John Gierach it is possible that I should now insert a single concluding word: period, which would proclaim that the argument was at an end. I am not John Gierach and, although I admire him as a writer, this particular habit is one that I abhor. I think that he may have grown out of it. I also think that I have said quite enough about hooks.

Is it a waistcoat or a vest? If it is the latter then it is not the sort that you wear under your shirt, which is a sort that I haven't pulled over my head for at least thirty years; you wear this sort of vest above your shirt and jumper, which inclines me to think of it as a waistcoat. It is definitely more like a waistcoat than a vest and it has about a thousand pockets. When I wrote the earlier part of this book I did not own such a waistcoat, or vest; I fished in a sports jacket or anorak, the pockets of which were stuffed with fly-boxes and reels of nylon and miscellaneous gear; what didn't fit into them went in my fishing bag and this arrangement seemed to work perfectly well. I bought a waistcoat, or vest, in Ludlow just over twenty years ago and I have gone fishing in one ever since. It would be wrong to declare them indispensable but they are certainly a good idea. Just occasionally I feel a vague longing for the old simplicities, for the battered jacket smelling of tobacco, with its sagging pockets crammed with a tin or two of flies and a few spare casts, pockets with holes in them made by sharp things or by a still smouldering pipe. But the waistcoat is an improvement and I now have a distinctly superior version which is, in fact, a vest because it comes from the States. It was given to me by a friend. Most fishers, including the friend who gave me the new Fish Pond waistcoat, or vest, have at least thirty bits of kit dangling down the outside of their vest or waistcoat. This is a practice that for some reason I have not adopted. I like my kit safely inside the many pockets and I do, as it happens, know where most of it lives.

I never fancied that, in employing these delaying tactics, designed to postpone getting down to some serious business, I should end up talking about waders and I cannot see that they will delay me very long. Perhaps the most remarkable fact about my waders, both pairs of them, is that at present neither of them leaks. Doubtless I am tempting fate by making this claim; I shall be fishing in the next day or so and I shall probably find a portion of the Eden or the Wharfe trickling down the inside of my right or my left leg. I have two pairs of waders because I have added chest waders to the thigh waders that served me adequately for forty years. Chest waders make fishing easier and also mean that you get wet less frequently. I should probably abandon thigh waders if I were not a Kilnsey member; as it is they are still essential because one of the rules of the Kilnsey Angling Club runs as follows:

'No member, guest or visitor shall fish in Salmon Trousers or waders the front of which reaches higher than the fork.'

There you have it and you may feel that you need an interpreter to penetrate this strange Kilnsey-speak, although you are probably clever enough to realise that Salmon Trousers means chest waders and that all that nonsense about the fork limits Kilnsey fishers to thigh waders. Okay, right, as Gierach might interject in this situation, although I am never certain what he means by it. Anyway, it is not a rule of which I altogether disapprove, because the Wharfe at Kilnsey is on the small side and chest waders would mean that we could stamp all over the river except through the deepest of the pools, whereas the fact that we are not allowed to wear Salmon Trousers means that we have to use whatever skill we possess with rod and line to cover fish rising in awkward places. If the Club decided that our waders could reach just a few inches above the fork, but no higher than the waist, I should be very happy indeed; it would not greatly increase the range of our wading, it would mean that we could sit down in wet grass without discomfort and it would do away with the sudden and unpleasant recognition that you are shipping water because your thigh waders have sagged. There is no prospect of this happening. The fork in front is destined to remain for years and years to come as the upper limit of our wading boots. Period.

I don't think that I can postpone the serious stuff much longer. At inordinate length I have told you that my attitude to fishing is something like it has always been, although I have fallen out of love with the upstream worm; I have explained why I fish the dry fly more than I used to and recommended a pattern of my own devising. I have talked about killing trout and about catch and release, I have praised the writing of John Gierach. I have held forth about rods and hooks and fishing waistcoats and I have even sunk as low as waders. I am not going to air my views on landing nets and fishing bags, except to say that I love my long handled net because it has a big hook on the end which can often rescue my flies when they have decided to perch somewhere up there in the trees. I love my net, especially its handle and hook, and this is more than I can say for my old fishing bag, which is not old enough to inspire affection, smells of last week's trout and is made of some sort of nylon rather than canvas. I have a large creel, which is very light and keeps fish much fresher than my bag. I like my creel but it needs a new strap and I have been meaning to get one for at least ten years. I am not going to write about fly lines and I think it is at last time to write about something worth the effort it costs to construct sentences, something that you might feel is worth the effort involved in reading it. Tomorrow, if not before, I shall make myself give it a go.

And I have just thought of something important and I shall try to be brief, because I have just thought of my rivers and how they have fared in the last twenty or so years. They matter much more than anything I have so far told you in the course of this chapter. How healthy are the Eden and the Wharfe? Well, they are much healthier than many rivers, although both have suffered in various ways. In the early years of the new century there was a sudden collapse in the trout population on the Eden, which has never been fully explained. People muttered about the disinfectant used during the outbreak of foot-and-mouth-disease in 2001, but I do not think this can have been the cause of the problem because the fishing was still productive in the two years immediately following the outbreak.

It was in 2004 that the Eden's trout seemed suddenly to have disappeared. I think there must have been a succession of poor spawning seasons, caused perhaps by floods or by drought at the wrong time. Anyway, the river has recovered. The whole river system now receives only fifty stock fish each year (on a short private stretch) and the Kirkby Stephen water now holds a good head of wild trout with lots of two-pounders and no shortage of much bigger fish. Fly life on the Eden is still fairly abundant; it still breeds all the ephemeropterans it used to, although the hatches of olive uprights and blue wings are perhaps less thick and less frequent than formerly. There are still plenty of sedges and the riverbed swarms with shrimp. All in all the Eden is in good heart.

On the Wharfe there was serious sheep-dip pollution something like twenty years ago with more than one incident. Sedges disappeared and hatches of the various olives were reduced to infrequent trickles. Recovery has been slow but sedges are now reappearing and upwinged flies are much more numerous than, say, ten years ago. Dairy farming, by the way, is now extinct in upper Wharfedale, which might have helped the increase in invertebrate populations. In recent seasons I have seen thick and prolonged hatches of spring olives and iron blues; they have not been common occurrences but the fact that they have occurred at all is encouraging and must give hope for the future. Blue wings are a concern; in the last twenty years I have fished through one big hatch; I come across a scattering of duns in places where once they hatched in teeming droves.

The Wharfe is one of many rivers that are now infested with signal crayfish, invaders from America that spell more or less instant doom for our native species. The effect on the fishing is less easy to assess. That trout feed on them very greedily, growing big and fat and pink-fleshed, is beyond doubt. I am not sure that these crayfish-eaters are noticeably less prone to eat flies. There was a time when many Kilnsey members thought that the crayfish had turned our trout into confirmed bottom feeders and there was a time when I was inclined to agree, but recent seasons have seen a river full of free-rising trout, both wild and stocked, both big and small. Recent seasons have also seen a river full of wild fish between six and twelve inches, which indicates successful spawning in three or four consecutive years and so suggests that, as yet at any rate, the crayfish have not impaired the river's capacity to breed trout. Whether crayfish damage invertebrate life is beyond my knowledge.

And there, very briefly, is my version of what went wrong with my rivers and how they have coped. It is now time, at somewhat greater length, to tell you what went wrong with me six years ago and find out how far I have recovered. My rivers have proved more resilient than I have sometimes feared. The fact that I am now fishing them again after an absence of three years gives me hope that I might share just a little of their strength.

CHAPTER ELEVEN

I am meant to be telling you about myself but find that I suddenly want to tell you yet more about Dry Simon and his talent as a catcher of trout. I fished the Wharfe last Wednesday (24/6/15); the weather was hot and bright, the river was at base flow, frighteningly thin and fearfully clean; of the four fish I caught three came to Dry Simon. Three of the four, it must be admitted, were stock fish but they were fish that had earlier refused my little black things, both damp and dry; they had ignored the Yellow Thing in two sizes; they had disdained Klinkhamers and all but one of them – he weighed 1lb 4oz – had been unimpressed by a fly that I call the Indescribable; they had rejected at least three other patterns. Then in the afternoon Dry Simon caught me a magnificent wild fish of 2lb 5oz, which made the brace and in doing so made the day. Perhaps the most remarkable aspect of this capture was that somehow I managed to put him back.

My rule, you may remember, allows me to kill wild fish over 2lb; it is a rule I made simply because I doubted my ability to show mercy when faced with such a prize. Last Wednesday I surprised myself; and then it was the turn of Dry Simon to surprise me as well, which he did by catching two more trout, both big stock fish that went in my bag. I should probably stop feeling surprised when Dry Simon keeps catching trout in difficult conditions because he does it almost all the time. Anyway, I fished again two days later. It was cloudy and cool, the river was marginally lower, just beginning to collect scum in slack water, and its brightness was just beginning to grow dim with the creeping spread of flannel weed and slime. It was a cheerless sort of day. Lunchtime found me by Spout Dub, sipping my wine with dry eyes and in sombre mood. I was not even half way to the brace. I had caught and returned four smallish wild trout and, as I sat there sipping claret, I reflected on the business of catching trout and its effect on me.

I first acknowledged that, unlike some of my friends, small trout do not satisfy me; some of my friends are almost as happy catching six and seven inchers as fish four and five times their size. I am different, although it is not that I want monsters; I would much rather catch five fish of one pound than one fish of five pounds. I am not in search of monsters but I am hoping for fish big enough to kill should I feel like killing them (which, lets face it, is usually). I also realised, as I sat there rather gloomily by Spout Dub, that the brace, always important, now means more to me than at any stage of my fishing life. It comes, when it does come – which at present, thank God, is much more often than not – it comes not as throbbing excitement, not with an electric thrill or with wild elation, but with a sense of deep relief and still deeper satisfaction. It comes with tears, very gentle tears, and it acts on both body and mind; tension dissolves, weariness fades away, disquiet and foreboding, so often my unwelcome companions, suddenly lose all purchase on my mind, leaving me happy with myself and with my situation; sanguine, relaxed and of course eager, unless I am drinking my wine, for trout number three. One of the best things about the brace is that I go searching for this third trout in the comforting knowledge that I have already caught two.

Catching a brace of trout now provokes in me a physical and mental reaction that baffles and delights me because, although the effect is profound, there is no excess, no violence to any of the feelings that belong to it. Those feelings are, in fact, profoundly peaceful, even though they usually bring tears; and, even though you are probably a fisherman, given that you are reading this book, even so you may wonder whether a man who attaches such central importance to a brace of trout, a man who often feels that his whole happiness depends upon it, may be a man in danger of losing his mind. If you are asking yourself this question then my answer to you is that I almost did.

On Friday my lunchtime by Spout Dub was unsatisfactory. The beauty of the place was somehow unable to penetrate. I felt weary, out of sorts and anxious and, although the wine was soothing, there was no celebration to drinking it because there was nothing to celebrate. There was not a brace of trout in my bag and I looked forward to the afternoon without much hope, because it seemed to me that the river, like the fisher sitting a few feet above it, was stale and tired, and that all its trout of any size had gone to sleep and would stay asleep for the rest of the day.

At last, with my wine drunk and my sandwich eaten, I dragged myself down to Watersmeet and started to fish again. Working my despondent way through two or three trickling runs and the remains of a pool or two I found nothing to change my conviction that I should almost certainly drive home braceless, drive home with an empty bag. And then I came to a place I call Middle Run and saw a rise in a pocket of calm water shaded by a willow tree. Dry Simon floated where the rise had been; there was a gentle swirl and I turned my wrist. Perhaps two minutes later I netted out a lively trout, a stock fish of about a pound which I promptly knocked on the head. I was very glad that I had caught him but there was, after all, only one of him. Before he came into my life there had been weary resignation; he changed this to a sort of nervous fear that the day would still end in disappointment because it would end with only him. I was weary no longer, but I was still on edge, still in search of the contentment that could only come to me with the capture of a second trout.

There was no response to Dry Simon from the Willow Run, which is where Wednesday's two pounder had come from and where the years have brought me dozens of big trout. The Willow Run was very thin, a trickle rather than a run and it convinced me that I should be very lucky indeed to catch another fish. Despondency was beginning to reassert its hold of me as, with each cast, the prospect of another trout seemed to slip further away. Above the Willow Run the river curves slightly and very slowly to the left of an upstream fisher. This is smooth water, a very gentle glide with the bed of the river shelving down to the roots of the sycamores that line the right bank. The trout lie and feed in the deeper water under the branches and, although most of them are stock fish, they can be difficult. On Friday there seemed to be no rising fish, until I saw a slight disturbance in the line of scum gathered close to the right bank. Dry Simon managed to avoid the branches and was taken just as soon as he fell. He caught a trout of similar weight to the afternoon's first, a fish of a few large spots, a fit fish but a grey fish with one of his pectoral fins misshapen, gnarled. He was not a beautiful fish but this mattered not a fig; what mattered was that he had brought the brace, bringing with it immediately both fulfilment and peace. There was no punching the air, there were no whoops of delight. I did not stamp over the shingle in the exuberance of my joy. I sat down, as soon as I had killed him and felt very glad that I had come fishing and very happy that I was alive. All weariness was gone, any anxious thoughts had disappeared. I felt a deep sense of wellbeing and an irresistible inclination towards tears. Five minutes later I dried my eyes and started fishing again.

The brace was enough for me, the brace was contentment, happiness, gratitude, peace. Dry Simon was less easily satisfied, Dry Simon wanted more and he made this plain to me when I cast him speculatively onto the almost imperceptible flow of the river under the trees; I cast him there and suddenly found that he had caught another trout. This one was four or five ounces heavier than the first two. Still hungry Dry Simon immediately put a fourth trout in the bag, a fish from the run just above the flats weighing 1lb 10oz. I felt nonplussed, almost bemused by this sudden turn of fortune, bemused and at the same time very thankful, although neither the third nor the fourth trout worked on me with the same gentle, the same deep and healing power of that unlovely second trout. They were simply additional reasons for happiness, as was the fifth trout from Mile House Dub, a rising fish that weighed almost two pounds. And then suddenly I knew that five trout was enough, because this fifth and last trout made me wonder whether it had all been too easy. I asked myself whether three trout in my bag might not have been the best result of all, because three trout would have pointed to skill and perseverance on a day of demanding conditions, of difficult sport, whereas five trout perhaps pointed to ill-educated stock fish bent on self-sacrifice. Perhaps three trout would have been better but I was, of course, very happy with five. More often than not, if the opportunity presents itself, I will gladly help myself to the sixth fish that club rules permit. Yesterday for some reason I chose to stop one short of my limit. I sat by Spout Dub for five minutes, drinking in the numinous beauty of the place that I love best in the whole world, and then I drove home.

Remember the conditions, a river on its bones, a thin and weary river barely creeping on its way, a general absence of rising fish and those few that were showing very easy to put down. Remember all this and then judge the achievement of Dry Simon with it all in mind. Remember too that he was able to bring fish up as well as draw rising trout to the hook. I grant that my five fish were all stock fish, but they had been in the river for more than ten weeks and were far from the bemused and witless creatures they had been when first tipped into the Wharfe. And I have not mentioned that, in the course of the day, Dry Simon caught six wild trout between 8 and 12 inches. I think you will concede that, since this sort of performance is for him in no way out of the ordinary, he is undoubtedly a great fly.

But my concern, of course, is not meant to be with Dry Simon at all. My concern is meant to be with me and, with myself in mind, and probing the evolution of my relationship with the fish that I catch, I think part of the transformative power that the brace now possesses for me has its origin in the time when a brace of trout seemed no more than a memory, a very painful memory, a time when the Eden and even the Wharfe seemed to have flowed out of my life for ever, carrying away with them a large part of my happiness. It is a long story and I am not altogether sure how to tell it. I think I shall break off from time to time in order to lighten the mood by telling you about some of this season's fishing days. Anyway, it is a story that cannot be told unless I make a start. It is time for me to begin.

****

Six years ago, in the summer of 2009, I retired after thirty years as Head of Classics at Sedbergh. They had been thirty years full of pleasure and satisfaction, full of friendship and laughter, full of Latin and Greek and a sport called Fives. I enjoyed teaching and thought that I was good at it; I enjoyed the company of the young (most of them) and the company of my colleagues (nearly all of them). I loved my Latin and Greek and the thought that I was passing the literature of the ancient world on to another generation. Sedbergh is set in wonderful countryside and I loved escaping from school into the loneliness of the Howgill Fells, as of course I loved to go fishing just as often as my work allowed. It was not all delight and satisfaction. Boarding schools bring their own pressures and problems and I was not exempt from them; there were some difficult times but they were times that passed; there were times of doubt and worry and there were academic and more personal failures. I was an imperfect being working in the middle of several hundred similarly imperfect beings but all in all we rubbed along fairly happily and I left Sedbergh feeling that in the course of thirty years I had done rather more good than harm. If that is a correct assessment then my career can be counted a success.

I retired because I was almost sixty and feeling very tired. Admittedly the holidays were long but the work during term was relentless and brought times of jaded exhaustion. I wanted to leave while I was still good at my job; I did not want what I had seen happen to just a few of my colleagues to happen to me; I did not want age and weariness to undermine my efficiency and my authority – there was just about enough of it – and my ability to communicate with the young. It is very easy, as an aging schoolmaster, to turn into an anachronism. I wanted to avoid this and, of course, I wanted more time to go fishing and shooting with the leisure and the mental energy to write about them as well. I thought there was at least one more book in me and I wanted to make it as good as it could possibly be.

Given that I was leaving the school I thought that it would be a good idea to leave Sedbergh altogether and move 20 miles away to Brough, an unpretentious village at the foot of the high Pennines where property was cheap and where I thought I should soon feel at home; where, moreover, I should be less than five minutes' drive from my little rough shoot at High Park. The prospect was very attractive: I would fish, I would shoot, I would write, I would walk, I would read Latin and Greek for the sheer pleasure of it, with no thought for what questions the examiners might ask, I would spend more time on my land. I would preserve contact with old friends in Sedbergh, I would make new friends in Brough, I would try to make some contribution to my local community so that my life would not seem entirely selfish. All in all I would settle into a busy and fulfilling retirement. It seemed a good plan and there seemed no reason why it should fail.

I bought a cottage right in the middle of Brough and moved there in July. You do not feel immediately at home, suddenly set down in a strange house in an unfamiliar place, especially when you have left a beautiful small town where you have been very happy and where you have put down roots. It was a wrench leaving Sedbergh; it hurt more than I was expecting and for a few weeks I wondered if I had made a mistake. But it was only for a few weeks. By the time a month had passed friends had visited me from Sedbergh, fishing friends had been to stay, I had begun to make friends with my neighbours (two of them, Ron and Marion, were keen fishers and had even read at least one of my books); I was reading better stuff myself, I was reading Vergil and Horace with deep pleasure, my pheasant poults had arrived and I was busy looking after them and busy congratulating myself that they were five minutes and not half an hour from my front door. When the Glorious Twelfth arrived I went flanking on the moors, where I already knew the keepers and now began to make friends with Reg and Ronnie and Graham and half a dozen more of the locals. I was occupied, I was often in company, I was settling into my new life and I was, incidentally, delighted that Brough's beck – it is called Swindale Beck and there are trout in it – flowed behind my cottage, so that I could drink my sherry before supper while listening to my favourite sound.

30 June 2015

This book is not a diary, it is a narrative but I simply have to break into the story of my retirement to tell you that Dry Simon has done it again, and this time he was obliging enough to do it before lunchtime, so that my half hour by Spout Dub, with my wine and my sandwiches and my tears and my thoughts, was like half an hour in paradise. In fact if paradise is a reality, and if I ever get there, and if I find my experience of it broadly similar to yesterday's half hour by Spout Dub, I shall tell God the Father – who is presumably in charge of the place, unless he has delegated control to one of his two other persons or perhaps to a particularly efficient angel – I shall tell him that I am more than satisfied.

I was in two minds whether to go fishing yesterday. I have been fishing low water since I returned from Scotland almost a month ago; I have given up to the Eden until it rains, for the Wharfe is a much better prospect in long spells of dry weather because its base flow is, I think, just a little livelier than the Eden's and, much more importantly, its trout are in all conditions of weather and water somewhat easier to catch. Even the wild trout of the Wharfe – of which there are plenty – are less choosy than the Eden trout and on the Wharfe there is, of course, the additional presence of numerous stock fish. Now these stock fish learn quickly. I keep insisting that they can be very difficult to catch and I do not think that I am telling you a lie, but there is no doubt in my mind that stocked fish, however well they adapt to life beyond the stew pond, are easier to catch than wild trout of the same water. This only applies to the first season of their introduction. Over-wintered fish, although their appearance is always slightly different from that of the natives, are in their behaviour indistinguishable from trout that have spent their whole lives from egg onwards in the same river.

I was in two minds about yesterday's fishing because, however easy or demanding stock fish may be, I could not believe that I did not have a day of failure in store for me and, since I started fishing again two years ago, I have found blank days very difficult to cope with. When I was unable to fish – for reasons that I shall begin to explain in the course of this chapter – I realised just how central a place fishing had filled in my life. Being deprived of it was a sort of bereavement. Now you might think that after winning back the ability to get out my rods and go to my rivers again I should be happy just to be standing in the water casting a line. It has not proved so. Failure now hurts abominably and one trout is not enough; it never has been, not at least since my earliest fishing days, but now I am desperate for the brace and now there is an intensity to this longing that I find difficult to explain. Anyway, I could not help feeling that yesterday was the day when I was likely to be denied the crucial brace. I felt that I had it coming to me after so many days when, in spite of low water, the trout of the Wharfe have continued to attach themselves to the fly on the end of my line. Yesterday I felt predestined to failure, I felt almost certain that I should get skunked.

I had to make myself go fishing; I told myself that I had not had a blank day on the Wharfe since the middle of April and that blank days were part of fishing and that I should have to learn once more how to cope with them. I put my tackle in the back of the Land Rover, left Brough soon after nine and was fishing by eleven. I started in Spout Dub, where the fast water at the poolhead often yields up a fish even in the lowest of waters. I fished through Spout Dub without any sign of a trout. The Wharfe was as low as I have ever seen her and, even at the start of my fishing day, the prospect of a blank seemed to be hanging ominously in the warm air and hovering darkly over the shrunken streams. I felt taut and anxious, weariness was already beginning to creep over me, I was half way to a headache and my steps, as I made my way to Black Keld, were heavy and slow.

Black Keld is a small tributary stream that flows into the river at a corner on your right as you head upstream. Trout often rise along the line of the inflow. Yesterday I saw none, but in the glide immediately above Black Keld, beneath the branches of a bankside sycamore, I spotted a head and tail rise, spotting too that there was plenty of tail. Dry Simon fell just right, there was a swirl and I snatched the strike and felt only the brief pull of a big fish. I cursed myself because it seemed certain to be a day of few chances and now I had just bungled the first of them. I fished on up into the fast water at the top of the glide; something told me to turn my wrist and this trout was firmly hooked; he leapt from

the water, he ran for the willows at the top of the run; I held him from
them, played him with shaking arms and netted out a beautiful over-
wintered stock fish of 1lb 10oz. I could tell he was not a native because
although the pectoral fins were long and straight there were subtle
imperfections that spoke unequivocally of his origins; and his spotting
lacked the dense pattern of the Wharfe's wild trout. I was glad that he
was an over-wintered stock fish because that meant I could kill him
without breaking my rule. Even as I did so I realised that I should have
done the same if he had been unambiguously wild, and I recognised
that my rule was in truth an aspiration rather than a fixed statute of the
mind. It was an ambition rather than an actuality and I might achieve it
in the end. Anyway I killed my trout and felt better because I was half
way to the brace. Less than five minutes later the brace arrived.

While cleaning my first fish – I gut them as soon as I catch
them on warm summer days – I saw that the trout I had missed was
rising again. He seized Dry Simon as though the earlier brief contact had
been inadequate, as though he had been waiting impatiently for Simon's
return. He fought like a stock fish: short tugging runs rather than that
strong and sudden plunge for home. He was two ounces heavier than my
first and better fish but he mattered much more. As soon as I had killed
him I sat down in tears and, even as I shed them, I wondered how it
could be that two trout could mean so much to a man of sixty five. And
again it was their effect as well as their meaning that was so powerful
and so strange. Where was that weariness? Where was the strain? I was
sitting down but I knew that I should rise with something like a spring
in my step and the heaviness had gone from my head and I was filled
with a sense of relieved and fulfilled gratitude. I had suddenly turned
from a frightened man, a man oppressed by nagging doubts and fears,
into a man who was almost careless, a man who was very happy indeed.

There were two more trout in my bag by the time I came to
Spout Dub, sat down on my grassy shelf with my beaker of wine and
listened to the murmur of the leaves and the slip of the river over the
stones. They were both very gentle sounds because the breeze was light
and the river was so low. I acknowledged a beauty of the place that
I have left unmentioned and perhaps unappreciated; it is a single tall

sycamore across the water at the top of the pool; its roots cling to the bankside, it has the domed shape of so many sycamores and it leans right out over the river, standing sentinel for Spout Dub. It leans over the river and its reflection stirs along the surface of the water so that, sitting there on your grassy shelf, there are the shapes of trees below you in the river as well as on your either side and over there on the far bank. You sit there in the green shade and see the ripple of green leaves in the movement of the water beneath.

Yesterday there was sunshine in the leaves and on the water and I felt so grateful for being there with four trout in my bag that I even thought of pouring a libation of *Côtes du Ventoux 2013* into the river as an offering to its spirit or its god. Almost immediately I thought better of it and kept every drop of wine for myself, but the numinosity – I think I have just coined this word specially for Spout Dub, which deserves a word all for itself as a tribute to its power – the numinosity of the place was on the air all round me and in every sound. There were, of course, memories but, sitting there, I felt no fear, no anxiety, no dread at the thought of what might lie ahead. There was complete contentment and there was that precious gift, the gift of the river and its trout and the spirit of Spout Dub, there was that gift we all crave but so rarely possess, a gift given to us in fleeting moments and then roughly snatched away. It was given to me yesterday as I sat there by Spout Dub, it was given and it stayed with me for the rest of the day; it was the gift of peace, a gift for which I have so often longed over the last five years; it was a gift and a best blessing, inhaled with every breath of Spout Dub's special air, mellowed by each swallow of wine, deepened by each soft sight and sound, peace unaccountably made possible by those trout in my bag; yes, above all there was peace, peace palpable and profound; and when peace seems to have flown away from me I shall think of Spout Dub and its cliff and its sycamores, I shall think of the hidden shelf where I sit and drink my wine; and though my heart beats heavily with dark forebodings, though fearful thought are chasing themselves through the mind, I shall know that I can go to Spout Dub and find peace again, which is exactly what I am thinking now.

My lunchtime thoughts yesterday were not all quasi-mystical. I thought of dear old Halford and how, I seemed to remember, he renounced use of the Gold Ribbed Hare's Ear because he did not know what it imitated. I thought of Dry Simon and told myself that he imitated nothing on earth or in water. I also told myself that my standards were less demanding than Halford's had been, because I had not the slightest intention of rejecting Dry Simon as a monstrous fantasy unworthy of a true fly fisher. My only fear was that Dry Simon was in danger of turning me into a one-fly man, which is a state of being that surely robs fly fishing of at least half its fascination. I toyed – I must confess that I only toyed – with the idea of fishing a different fly in the afternoon. Dry Simon stayed on the end of my line. I went down below Mile House Dub to the slow water under the trees, where I caught a stock fish of one and a half pounds; there was another from the fast water immediately upstream and, with a limit of six fish in my bag, I decided to call it a day. Dry Simon had done it again and I did not eat my supper until I had sat down and tied myself six more of him.

****

It is time to return to the story of my retirement and there is every chance that I might manage to make some progress, because the weather is now so oppressively hot that even the thought of fishing brings me out in a prickly sweat. But I had better warn you; in just under a fortnight I am off to fish the Yorkshire chalkstreams and I shall almost certainly want to tell you all about it. It is also very unlikely that I shall be able to keep away from the Wharfe for more than a few days, even without rain and even given the persistence of this equatorial heat. Anyway, before I broke off I had told you how I began to settle down in Brough, beginning to feel at home in my cottage, beginning to believe that I had made the right choice in coming here and starting to hope that I could look forward to an enjoyable, perhaps even a productive old age.

Even though I was getting used to new surroundings and circumstances I found July and August not hugely unlike my experience of them over the last thirty years, for they had always been months of holiday, full firstly with fishing and then with the care of pheasant poults. It was only in September, on a day in its first week, a day that would have been for me, if I had still been working, the beginning of a new term, it was only then that it finally struck me how completely my life had changed; for I did not spend that day in a classroom or, much worse, in a succession of uniformly tedious and utterly pointless meetings, I did not spend it thinking of all the work that lay ahead of me and postponing making a start because I felt worn out just at the thought of it. I have told you that I loved my life as a schoolmaster and I have told you the truth; but I always loathed the beginning of another term, particularly the beginning of the endless winter term, a beginning made even worse by the two months and more of freedom that had preceded it. In those long summer holidays there usually came a time when work seemed a distant memory somewhere in the past, seeming at the same time a still remote and untroubling prospect somewhere in the distant future. Then there would come a time in August when, acknowledging that the summer holidays did not last for ever, I would draw comfort from the thought that there were still at least two or three weeks of them to come. But September follows August and inevitably early September brought the black day when freedom was suddenly at an end, when it was time once more to become institutionalised – which is an ugly word for an unpleasant process – and there would follow at least a week of exhaustion, as body and mind accustomed themselves to the re-imposition of a demanding routine, and then I would realise that, in spite of everything, I was happy to be a schoolmaster. This adjustment took a little longer with the passing of each year, which was one of the factors influencing my decision to retire.

Anyway, on the day that would in the past have been the first day of a new school year, I went fishing on the Tees right at the head of the river below Cauldron Snout, where the outflow from Cow Green Reservoir plunges down a succession of rapids and falls, joins forces with a sizeable beck whose name I have forgotten and so makes the

Tees. I was fishing new water with an eye for the following season and I liked what I saw. I had enjoyed the drive over the purple moors from Brough, where the sun glowed on the heather while great cloud galleons sailed the blue sky. It was one of those September days when everything shone, when the land was bright with running water after rain during the night. And the heather was in bloom and the rowans were clustered with red berries; and the rim of the sky against the moors seemed almost to sparkle in the clear air. And the white farmsteads of upper Teesdale, surrounded by their green fields, looked neat and clean and bright.

I enjoyed the drive from Brough to Middleton, where I bought my ticket for the river, and I enjoyed the road up Teesdale that took me to Cow Green. I did not enjoy walking down to the river from the reservoir. It took almost an hour and it was weary work in wading boots. I should not have minded but for the thought that the walk back, at the end of a long fishing day, would be much worse. I knew there was easier access to the river and blamed myself for being too lazy to find my way to it. I told myself that by next season I should have made sure that I knew where the farm was, a mile or so downstream, where you could park and be by the river in no more than a few minutes.

The walk down to the beginning of the Tees was tiresome but the river itself immediately made it seem worthwhile. I should have preferred the water an inch or two lower and somewhat less coloured; it was a full water which, for a newcomer to the river, would make it difficult to read; it was a dark water but already it was beginning to shine. It flowed through rain-bright heather moorland and I walked downstream beneath a line of steep cliffs, evocatively called the Falcon Clints, cliffs of white limestone with clinging ashes and junipers, seamed and shining with erratic lines of running water. I stopped where the cliffs met the river, thinking that I had left myself enough water for at least five hours' sport on the way back to Cauldron Snout.

I fished wet and I fished fancy, because there was no obvious hatch and my experience on the Wharfe had taught me that a hackle Coachman with Simple Simon on the dropper would often take fish in a coloured and falling water. It worked high up there on the Tees and they were all wild fish and there were lots of them; they were mostly small trout of seven and eight inches; some were even smaller but two or three weighed about three quarters of a pound. I usually find small trout unsatisfying but, for some reason, these fish delighted me. They all went back, of course, together with the two or three that I might have kept. I never changed flies, there were trout wherever I fished for them, there were numerous sudden snatches and brief pulls – perhaps I should have changed flies – but there were firm takes as well and I caught at least twenty fish. And the sun shone and the heather glowed and the breeze was light and the river sang. And I fished on in the knowledge that I could fish again tomorrow, that I could fish every day in September if I decided to turn them all into fishing days. There was something intoxicating in all this; in the cool bright air and the clearing river with its red-spotted wild trout, in the white cliffs, in the belled and nodding heather where the grouse called and, above all, in the sense of limitless freedom. It filled me with such exhilaration that the long trudge back to the Land Rover was much less of a labour than I had been expecting.

I drove home to Brough giving thanks for the new life that had been given to me and thinking that I should probably spend the rest of September on my home waters, leaving the Tees as a bright prospect for next year. The Eden and the Wharfe were quite difficult in those last weeks of the season. It was a dry month, which meant that my young pheasants enjoyed themselves, but rivers were low and testing. I did not fish every day but I fished three or four days a week; I caught enough trout to keep me happy and I ended the season in high spirits, convinced that retirement was going to be kind to me.

3 August 2015

There really was a libation today; I had finished my wine and noticed that there was a dribble of redness in the bottom of the old vinegar bottle that brings my claret or my *Côtes du Ventoux* or today's *Pays d'Oc* over with me to the Wharfe. There was just a dribble in the bottom of the bottle and I was feeling so full of gratitude to the river that I solemnly poured this dribble of wine into the water on the edge of Spout Dub. It was more a drop than a dribble; it was a very niggardly libation, it was an entirely inadequate offering but it was given with a full heart.

When I woke this morning I felt almost as dark as I felt three and four years ago at that time when I could not fish. The difference, of course, was that today I did go fishing. It was not easy but the thought of how the day would unfold if I stayed at home, this thought had soon sent me on my way.

It was no better when I got to the Wharfe at half past ten. It was already hot, the river was, if possible, even lower than on Monday. The spring that gives Spout Dub its name had finally given up the struggle and disappeared; my head was tight, my guts were restless, my mind was strung like a bow, feeling ready to snap, and I saw almost no prospect of finding the comfort that I knew would come with a brace of trout. I told myself that it had been bound to happen, that there was bound to come the day when I should come to the Wharfe in search of healing and find even the Wharfe unable to help. There was fear in every step, unspecific but powerful, unfocussed but ominous, perhaps even more unsettling because it was not fixed on some particular object, some disturbing idea or possible event, unless it was the dread that I was slipping back into the crippled state of being that had robbed me of almost everything that gave my life its meaning and worth.

It was not a good start to a fishing day, but at least it was a fishing day and at least the breeze was light and blowing upstream, which meant that I was fishing with my lovely soft-actioned Sage and could draw some pleasure from its gentle ways. There was no sign of a fish in Spout Dub. There were no trout rising along the inflow of Black Keld and, although there was a fish rising under the branches in the glide above Black Keld, he went down as soon as Dry Simon floated over him. And then I did catch a trout, an eight incher from fast water. You know that small trout mean little to me – except for some reason on the Tees – and this one meant even less because he was foul-hooked under the belly. Fortunately the hook came out easily enough and he was very quickly returned.

I trudged on, coming to a place that I call Two Barn Flats, a name derived from the presence of a barn in the fields on either side of the river, although one of these barns, built almost on the river bank, is actually upstream of the feature for whose name it is half responsible. This has confused some of my friends, who think that Two Barn Flats refers to the long glide a little further on. Anyway, none of this is of any interest to anyone but my friends and me. I came to the place that I call Two Barn Flats. More specifically I climbed a stile over a wall, which brought me to the long run and the longer glide that flows down the far bank beneath the shade of tall sycamores until the current loses itself in the calm body of the flats, which is incidentally one of the few places where the upper Wharfe spreads itself and looks almost wide.

Yesterday, with the river so low, the glide was almost motionless and only the very top of the run really deserved the name. But much of this diminished glide and run was in the shadows of those sycamores and fish were rising there. In fact it is very rare to come to the top of Two Barn Flats without seeing rings and hearing sips or sometimes gulps from the glide and from the run above it. Spout Dub is my favourite place in the whole world and I think I have said that it has given me more trout than any other pool or glide or run on the Wharfe (or any other river). I now realise that this is untrue. The moving water at the head of Two Barn Flats has beyond doubt put more trout in my bag over the years than has Spout Dub, which is still, in spite of this, my favourite place in the whole wide world.

My usual tactic with Two Barn Flats is to fish Dry Simon through the faster water of the run. If this works I feel happy. If it fails I feel less happy; in either case it will be time to tackle the usually more demanding trout of the glide, which are less likely, especially in low water, to take a fancy fly. You often need tiny wet or dry flies for these trout and there are not infrequent times when nothing at all seems to work, although you generally have plenty of time to experiment. I am not sure how long the glide is – fifty or sixty yards? – but by the time you have fished your way to the top of it the trout at its lower end will have recovered from the shock of your presence and started to feed again.

Yesterday I sat down on the bank and drank some water and looked at what remained of the run, slipping and sliding against the far bank and washing the roots of the sycamores that rose above it. There were four or five trout sipping in the shadows and I watched them with the first feelings of something like hope. For here if anywhere, here in the cool shadows of those tall trees, here in what could still almost truthfully be called fast water, here where the experience of many seasons had taught me that trout are often fallible, here there was at least the chance of catching a fish, although the brace still seemed an impossible expectation. And I still, by the way, felt half way to feeling ill.

I am not sure how I felt while playing the heavy trout that absorbed Dry Simon very delicately and then jumped clean out of the water. I was surprised, I was delighted, at the same time I was taut with anxiety and fear. He was a great relief in the net and he weighed 1lb 10oz, a beautiful over-wintered fish with the red flesh that only came to the trout of the Wharfe with the coming of American crayfish more than twenty years ago. I know exactly how I felt while playing the trout that took Dry Simon a few feet further up the run. He also leapt when he felt iron in his mouth and I knew at once that he was a wild trout and at the same time foresaw the intensity of my anguish if he should break me or throw the hook; for here, almost beyond hope, I was within grasp of the precious and healing brace, and I was uncertain how I would cope should I suddenly be denied it. Thank God my second trout stayed for the net. He weighed 1lb 8oz, he was densely spotted and golden yellow and any idea of returning him seemed an absurdity, any thought of rules and aspirations possessed not the slightest influence; he had made the brace and I wanted tangible proof of it in the green bass inside my rather smelly bag. I caught a third trout on Dry Simon from the glide. He was a stock fish and I was happy to catch and kill him but I should have coped stoically enough with the shock of his sudden departure. Anyway, he made three against the odds and I strolled happily down to Spout Dub, untroubled by the midday ferocity of the sun, to celebrate the sudden arrival of health and happiness with tears and wine.

The vin de Pays d'Oc was not exceptional (*Cabalié '14*: too sweet, little structure) but it seemed, from setting and circumstance, to have won the fragrance and complexity of *Margaux* or *Latour* in their greatest years: a rather pretentious remark which makes me wonder if I have ever drunk either *Latour* or *Margaux* even from a duff year. Anyway, as I sipped my wine as slowly as I could manage, hoping to prolong the pleasure of lunchtime wine by Spout Dub on a hot summer's day, I tried – not too hard – to fathom the mystery of the brace. I should have been happy just to sit there and enjoy its influence but I knew that I should be happier still if I could understand something of the secret of its power.

I knew that this extraordinary power of the brace had its origins in that time when I could not fish at all and thought that I should never fish again. I shall, by the way, get round to telling you about it very soon. For now it will be enough to say that with understanding and expert help from two doctors, with patient love from my family and my friends, with patience on my own part and with much effort and no small pain, I have found my way back to fishing and found that I can again draw pleasure and fulfilment from the whole process of catching trout; and because I thought these were lost feelings they have come back to me with much greater intensity, with much greater power to move. Moreover there is a sense in which, by catching trout, I am reaching back over the void to re-establish contact with myself before the sudden rupture of illness. Catching trout makes me feel whole again.

When I had got this far in my investigation I probably took a sip of wine and decided that I might have explained, partially at least, why catching trout affected me so profoundly. It did not explain the special potency of the brace, and I wondered whether this was because I had always partly defined myself as a fisherman. I was a schoolmaster, a fisher, a writer, I was other things as well; I was, for example, a Roman Catholic, and still am one and this, I suppose, is in fact far the most important part of me but, if you had asked me ten years ago what I was, I should have replied that I was a fisher, a writer and a schoolmaster. And when I stopped being a schoolmaster the fisher and the writer became suddenly more important. And then I suddenly stopped being either a fisher or a writer and my life fell apart. And now that I am a fisher once more, which incidentally has re-awoken the writer in me – anyway, now that I am once more a fisher I need the brace more than ever to prove to myself and the world – which couldn't of course give a damn – that I really deserve to be called a fisher because I can manage to catch, not just a single careless trout, but a skilful brace.

That was about as far as I could be bothered to go and you probably feel relieved. I could not be bothered to delve deeper because I found that my metal beaker held no more wine; and it was now, seeing that the vinegar bottle still had a dribble in it, that I selflessly decided to pour this dribble or drop as a thanks-offering into the languid currents of the river Wharfe. I hid my bass with its three trout in cool water at the foot of Spout Dub's cliff and went fishing. When I caught a fourth trout – a stock fish of about a pound and a half – I knew at once that it was enough. The afternoon was very hot. I had come fishing in the belief that I should almost certainly return home blank and, against all expectation I had caught four trout. Four trout were definitely enough.

****

Apart from that day on the Tees the autumn fishing days at the beginning of my retirement have left no sharp memories. The winter that followed was a winter of savage cold and heavy snow and I spent it feeding pheasants and shooting them, feeding flight ponds and shooting duck (until the ponds froze solid), shooting my own ground and shooting on the syndicate shoot where I still had half a gun. I shot as a guest on some nearby shoots, I shot in the Borders with a friend. I drank sloe gin in company, I drank sloe gin alone on solitary rough shooting days. Sometimes I shot well, some times I shot badly. I remember my birthday shoot, four days before Christmas, which I should have cancelled. It snowed heavily the day before and it was snowing when I woke up in the morning. Two of my guests rang to say that they were blocked in. I should then have rung my other guests and told them to stay safe and warm at home, but I was very anxious to shoot and I went ahead. There ought to have been none of us. Instead of none there were five. Further heavy snow showers fell throughout the day; in between them there was the transforming beauty of sunshine over lying snow. There were lots of pheasants and we shot 25 of them, together with a rabbit and a French partridge and a woodcock. More importantly my friends all got home alive and unharmed.

For weeks there was a deep cover of snow. Feeding pheasants was much harder work than usual but, when the sun shone, there was such beauty that to be at High Park was to walk in a new world. There were fields wearing white instead of those drab and faded colours that winter usually brings to them; the fields were white and the snow had covered over their ridges and hollows and bumps and tufts; the fields spread out in smooth folds and flats and shining lines, in shining curves and smooth slopes and above them rose the white and the blue of the smooth and shining fells. The fields were white and smooth and they shone, but the beck was a black ribbon flowing through the white fields between icicled banks. There was the fierce contrast of red berries on hawthorns and hollies all ridged with snow and ice along their branches. There were the red breasts of robins hopping round the feeders. Spruce and fir, snow-laden and deeply green beneath their burden, seemed strong and vital and seemed somehow to belong to this new white world, seemed somehow its complement. Smooth and pointed holly leaves shone. I looked at all this with wonder; it felt as though the snow had somehow given me more seeing eyes and, of course, cold weather with lying snow is perfect for shooting.

For me it was a glorious winter. I revelled in my new freedom and began to write a book about shooting and retirement. It might have been a good book if I had been able to finish it. By the end of January the last of the snow had gone. I love January shooting, when pheasants are strong on the wing; in that first January of my retirement I loved it even more than usual. But I was not sad when the shooting finished because it meant that fishing was only six weeks away, for the Eden obligingly opens for trouting in the middle of March.

I cannot remember how I filled that month and a half between the end of shooting and my first day on the river. I probably worked on the shoot at High Park and tied flies and I remember now that I was busy with my book and busy reading Ovid for fun. I do remember the first fishing days of the new season. They brought cold spring sunshine and spring olives and a few spring trout. Above all they brought the wonderful prospect of more than six months when, if I so chose, every day could be a fishing day. I thought that I should try to exercise some restraint; I also thought that I need not try too hard, because I knew that it was almost impossible to go fishing too often.

I remember with startling clarity the Friday in late March when I fished the Eden in the morning and went to see my doctor in the afternoon. I caught a brace of good trout and planned, as long as the doctor gave me the all-clear, to celebrate fishing and health with a bottle of better-than-usual claret. It was the 25th of March which, as all the world should know, is the first day of trouting on the Wharfe. I would have been over there rather than on the Eden had it not been for my appointment. My plan was to fish the Wharfe the next day and I thought that the better-than-usual claret would bring an appropriate air of festival to the eve of my first spring outing on my favourite river. I was not worried by the thought of what the doctor might have to tell me. I had been in two minds whether to bother him or not but my guts – volatile for some years – had lately been unusually restless and, though disinclined to go anywhere near a doctor's surgery (I think I had made no more than three visits in the preceding thirty years!) I had decided that it would in these circumstances be wise to make sure that there was nothing much wrong with me. My appointment, I remember, was at half past five. I walked into the consulting room looking for reassurance, confident that I should receive it and looking forward to opening my first bottle of *Talbot '95*. Twenty minutes later I walked out of the same room a condemned man.

17 August 2015

I shall get back very soon to the aftermath of that fateful visit to the Upper Eden Medical Centre, but before this you need to know that Dry Simon was a flop on the Yorkshire chalkstreams. In the past he has often been deadly both at Driffield and Foston but over the last three days the trout have turned their noses up, unless it was down, at him; he has floated over them without exciting a flicker of interest or they have signalled their disapproval by diving promptly under weed. I am glad this has happened because I caught lots of trout without Dry Simon's assistance and, before his unexpected failure, I was beginning to wonder if I should ever need to tie any other fly to the end of my line. Solving problems brings half the pleasure of fly fishing and which fly to use is, of course, the biggest problem of all. Even if he catches scores of trout, the one-fly man misses the point, although the one-fly man will certainly catch fewer trout than the fisher who thinks about natural and artificial flies.

Not that I needed to think profoundly or solve demanding problems in order to catch a pleasing number of chalkstream trout: on the whole they wanted nymphs and were not too bothered whether it was a Hare's Ear Nymph or a Copper Wire Nymph or a nymph with red bits and sparkly bits and a name that has flown my mind. I refuse, by the way, to sink as low as goldheads and feel just slightly guilty about fishing fast-sinking nymphs at all. Undoubtedly the cream of fly fishing is found near the surface of the water. You will find no discussion of the finer points of Czech nymphing in the pages of this book. There is also something called French nymphing and I do not want to know anything about it.

I have reservations about the sinking nymph but I love fishing spiders: flies with the spare simplicity of great art, delicate and lovely flies that call for delicate fishing with those subtle signs of the take. I fished two days at Foston and the first of them brought some absorbing sport with the Orange Partridge and Stewart's Black Spider tied on a 16 hook. It was a lovely day for fishing, with no more than a faint stirring of air beneath a blue sky and with almost motionless white clouds. It was a day of high summer, with sunshine and meadowsweet and willow herb, but without that oppressive and stifling high summer heat.

By noon I had fished nymphs through a long, deep mill pool – you could spend all day there – and they had brought me five trout. The brace had worked its magic and chased away any traces of anxiety or discontent, for as soon as the second trout had come to net and been knocked on the head I sat down on the edge of the beck feeling happy and whole. It was now I realised that for me the brace possesses something like sacramental power; it is a source, not only of comfort, but of grace; it is God's gift to an unworthy fisher and he is very grateful indeed. We papists recognise seven sacraments. I say without any feeling of irreverence that this papist has been given, perhaps for himself alone, an additional and very precious eighth.

Anyway, as I sat there feeling happy and thinking arguably heretical thoughts, although to me they seemed more like prayerful and pious reflections on a great mystery, as I sat there, anyway, thinking whatever thoughts came to me, I noticed that olives were beginning to hatch and that a few fish were beginning to move to them. I took off the nymph, tied on an Orange Partridge and fished up a straight stretch of the beck where, here and there in runs or pockets of water between the weed, I could see fish feeding just below the surface of the water. I hooked and lost a fish, saw that he had immediately resumed his station and promptly hooked and lost him again. This all happened in less than five minutes and struck me as being fairly remarkable. I caught the next trout that I rose, but he was undersized; then I caught two well over the pound and put them back because there were already four trout in my bag. These victims of the Orange Partridge were all rising fish, they were all visible fish; there was a delicacy and a delight in flicking the spider a foot or so above them and then watching for those signs of the take, watching for a turn of the head or a movement of the body or for the white flash of an opening mouth. And when I lifted my rod and felt the weight of a trout it was so much more satisfying than the snatching, often savage take that comes to a sinking nymph. In the afternoon the trout turned to smut and the little Stewart Spider caught seven of them. All in all, with the blue sky and the sunshine and the slow clouds, with the bright water and the rocking weed and the shapes of trout moving to my flies, all in all it was a day that made me very happy to be a member of the Foston Fishing Club. I have fished as a guest at Foston for almost thirty years, but this is the first season of my membership; it can never mean what Kilnsey and the Wharfe have come to mean for me, but the beck is lovely, the fishing is full of interest and charm and it brings me into the company of old and precious friends.

The next day I fished at Driffield with just such a friend. At lunchtime I had caught one undersized troutling and was dissatisfied. Two glasses of Valpolicella eased the pain and in the afternoon I resorted to the nymph and caught a limit. That was on Wednesday. On Thursday it was back to Foston and, I admit it, back to the nymph, although I caught one lovely wild trout on the dry fly. On the way home I drove into a lamp-post in the middle of Thirsk and would have driven no further if I had not been driving a Land Rover. There was a tremendous thump but the damage, thank God, seemed limited to the lamp-post and the front bumper. When I got home I suddenly felt guilty and rang the police to confess my crime. They did not seem much concerned about a bruised lamp-post in the middle of Thirsk. After a late dinner I was moved by a sudden and rare urge to wipe my table mats and I remembered, after three days full of fishing and trout and deep delight, I remembered, as I looked at images of angling from the past, pictures of men fishing beneath silly hats and with long rods and in ridiculous shoes, I remembered how these scenes had for three years been almost my only contact with fishing and how their presence had sometimes brought me comfort but more often had called forth tears. But I could look at them now with real pleasure – my favourite is a representation of a day on the Dart and the angler enjoying it is in fact wearing an almost sensible hat and what look like thigh waders – because they reminded me of the last three days and of all the trout that I had caught and they made me feel grateful all over again.

****

The pain my fishing mats once caused me had its origins in that visit to the doctor one Friday afternoon. He had listened to my story of disturbed guts; he had said that he thought I was suffering from something called irritable bowel syndrome, which was tiresome but unthreatening; he had also said that he wanted to be absolutely sure there was nothing more sinister at work and would therefore make arrangements for a colonoscopy. And then, after a brief physical examination, he announced – if I remember things accurately – that there was an extraordinarily prominent pulse somewhere in the abdomen; again he thought that it was probably nothing to worry about, it was probably telling him that I was a thin rather than a fat man, but there was just the possibility of an aneurism and, just to make certain that this was not the case, he would make further arrangements for this to be checked by something called ultrasound.

I have already told you that I walked out of the surgery a condemned man, but this was not entirely true. I walked out a deeply worried man, half convinced that I had bowel cancer and half persuaded that my heart might at any moment explode, bringing to a sudden end the beginnings of a rather promising retirement. There was no celebratory claret, although there was sherry and red wine, more of it than usual instead of the better-than-usual stuff that I had been hoping to drink; there was whisky as well and the booze was good for me. The sense of doom retreated under its influence. I went to bed more or less sober and woke up without a hangover and determined to be positive. I told myself that there was probably nothing much wrong with me. It was simply a question of waiting to make sure. In the meantime far the best thing would be to go fishing as often as possible.

And to begin with it worked, although I did not go over to the Wharfe. I told myself that I should save the Wharfe until I had been given the all-clear, when there would, of course, be a huge celebration, although it would have to be a very private celebration because I had told no one among either my family or my friends about my forthcoming trial by colonoscopy and ultrasound. I think this was the first of my mistakes. Anyway, to begin with the fishing worked; there were days on the Eden and its tributary Scandal Beck when I forgot for a few hours that I should probably soon be dead. But the fear of illness was beginning to take hold of me; I was haunted by the spectre of disease, more and more convinced that there was something dreadful wrong with me; and this dark and terrible conviction began to poison the air of my fishing world. Of all days for it to happen, it was Easter Sunday when I finally realised that I could no longer find refuge or peace along the margins of running water. I decided that I would not go fishing again until doctors, surgeons and consultants had acquitted me or, much more likely, put on sympathetic voices to pronounce sentence of death.

There followed a strange and very lonely month. I saw virtually no one because I wanted to be alone. When my friends or my brother or my sister rang to say hello or to arrange a meeting I hid my fear from them and made excuses to avoid their company. Human contact was painful and even now I cannot tell you why, unless it was that in other men and women I saw health and happiness and found this contrast with my own condition very difficult to bear.

I put my rods away but I was frightened of the crushing fear and loneliness that laid hold of me in my house almost as soon as I woke every morning, and so each day, now that I could no longer fish, I fled to my land at High Park, spending as long as possible there occupied with both useful and entirely useless activity, although from one point of view all of it seemed useless because I felt certain that I should not live long enough to benefit from anything that I was doing. On the other hand it was all better than useful; it was essential because it helped me to push that dreadful sense of doom just a mental inch or two from the centre of my thought.

I dug, I dammed, I cut cover and I mended pheasant pens. I roamed the farm with my two spaniels. I lay in the sunshine and smoked my pipe. I said my prayers. The weather was glorious. Each day brought a blue sky with a light breeze and a slow drift of white clouds with broad shadows moving patiently beneath them. The morning air was tonic and sharp but by noon my little valley was basking in temperate April warmth and over it all lay the wonderful shimmer of spring: in the fields and the grass, in the branches and their swelling buds, in the violets and the primroses and the anemones and the celandines. The bright air and its shimmer seemed almost a living thing pulsing with birdsong, with the singing of blackbirds, thrushes, dunnocks, robins, chaffinches, willow warblers and croaking pheasants. Every day there was a woodpecker drumming in the Douglas firs and every day the sound of curlews floated through the clear sky. It was the April when Icelandic volcanoes cleared the sky of aircraft for a time and so the sounds of spring faced no competition from their roaring or their drone. As well as birdsong there was the splashing of the beck and the stirring of the breeze and the grating of my spade or my saw. Sometimes for just a few seconds there was almost silence.

It was a glorious spring and often there was comfort in this, often my mind was unable to resist the shining power of the season; there were times when I felt almost happy and I remember just one afternoon when the fear of disease and death left me altogether as I worked away along the sides of the beck with a deep sense of thankfulness and peace. Sometimes there was comfort in the spring glory but just as often it brought pain, because it seemed to me that I was saying farewell to all this beauty and this radiance; and the waking power of the season, spreading though the fields and along the branches and thrusting out of the earth beneath the trees, this life and this growth seemed only to emphasise my status as a creature on the edge of extinction. The beauty of the spring spoke to me differently on different days.

I spent as long as possible out on the farm each day. Then it was back home to feed the dogs and take a bath and try to rest. Sometimes I even managed to sleep for an hour or two, until it was time to get my dinner ready and then time for alcohol. I drank heavily each evening; it was controlled excess and it was a huge comfort. It sent me to bed ready for sleep and I woke the next morning feeling rested and without a hangover. It is undeniable that I woke in the morning feeling miserable but this would have happened without the booze. Without the booze I should have found sleep difficult to come by; I should have faced the morning feeling exhausted as well as miserable. With the help of alcohol sleep came easily and with it I could tell my morning misery that, even if it lasted all day, the early evening would bring *fino* sherry and the beginnings of comfort.

As soon as I had listened to the Archers I poured myself the first of two large glasses of *Tio Pepe.* There was often another half glass as well. I cared not a fig about units or their effect on the liver because I felt certain that some other essential part of me would stop working long before my liver gave up the unequal struggle. I took the sherry as slowly as possible, sipping it with something like sacramental reverence, and as sip followed sip, I could feel the strain and the fear surrendering to the influence of Spain's best gift to humanity. I listened to the radio while drinking my sherry, although I did not always pay it much attention. It was background noise, the accompaniment to the soothing ritual of *Tio Pepe,* and somehow it helped.

After the sherry came dinner without wine. I never lost my appetite or my pleasure in food; doubtless all that exercise out at High Park sent me home hungry. Anyway, dinner was without wine but always, after I had washed up and taken the dogs out, there was half a bottle of claret, drunk with lingering reverence in the company of a book or radio four. I started reading Trollope's Palliser novels and found them engrossing; together with the claret, and the sherry that had preceded it, they took me away from myself for a while. After the claret there was a small glass of malt whisky, which I drank while saying my prayers and planning what I should do on the farm in the morning. I think that I always resisted the temptation of a second glass. A single small one was enough. Then it was off to bed for half an hour's Wodehouse before I turned out the light and fell asleep. Without the sherry and the claret and the malt whisky I am not sure that I would have coped.

This routine continued for almost a month. After about three weeks I went to Kendal for ordeal by ultrasound, which revealed that my aorta was normal; the nurse also checked several other vital organs, including the liver, and declared them all in working order. This was, of course, a huge relief but there was a long week to wait for the horror of the colonoscopy; and my bowels were now so uncooperative that I was convinced almost beyond doubt that the camera would reveal a fatal growth. I knew that I had cancer, that it would kill me and I also knew that I was still in love with the beauty of creation, with fields and flowers and hills, with running water and spotted trout; I knew that I was not ready to die and face eternity.

I now told two close fishing friends and my brother John and my sister Elizabeth about my situation. I arranged to stay with Liz for a couple of nights on either side of the investigation. She lived only an hour or so from Brough and less than half an hour from Kendal; she would take me to the hospital and pick me up when the surgeon had taken off his black cap.

The day before the colonoscopy was terrible. I was allowed no alcohol and little food. I took an enema as soon as I woke up and spent the rest of the day dashing to the lavatory. In between these visits I read *The Eustace Diamonds* and gave up trying to relax. I went to bed early and barely slept. By seven next morning I was in hospital. For what seemed like an ice age I sat in a cubicle trying to distract myself with John Mortimer's Rumpole stories. Some time round noon I was wheeled into theatre feeling strangely calm. A very uncomfortable and undignified procedure followed, after which the surgeon pronounced that my bowels were healthy and that, after a short rest and a few slices of toast, I could go home.

24 August 2015

It was not as good as Spout Dub but it was good enough, and I have left the story of my illness to tell you about yesterday's fishing, when lunchtime did not bring me to my favourite place in the whole wide world because – for the first time this season – some inconsiderate member had booked the beat before I rang, so depriving me of eating my sandwich and, much more importantly, drinking my wine while surrounded by the numinosity of Spout Dub. Instead of sitting there on my grassy shelf I was sitting on the riverbank by the quiet pool above the falls that are the principle feature of our lowest beat on the Wharfe. They are dramatic and beautiful, even when the water is as low as it was yesterday. The river has cut itself two channels through the convex and confining lip of rock that holds up the river's progress and so forms the pool by which I was sitting; through these channels it plunges ten or fifteen feet in two foaming spouts that have delved deep pools in the riverbed beneath them: less impressive than Niagara perhaps but still a fine and stirring sight, and below the falls there are the rapids, where the Wharfe has carved smooth channels in the living rock, rushing along them through rougher holes and pots, constantly narrowing and then enlarging its flow, gushing over frothing steps and shelves and hurrying on its impatient way to reunite its divided streams and find calmer passage between the banks.

These rapids are perhaps a hundred yards long, perhaps a little longer. They were what had brought me to our bottom beat for, finding that I was denied Spout Dub, I thought that the broken water beneath the falls might be my best chance of a brace on what would almost certainly be my last visit to the Wharfe until September comes along and releases me from the tyranny of pheasant care. I am going to Wales next week with two friends. I went with them to the same place and the same cottage four years ago, when my health was even worse than I thought at the time; it will be interesting to see how I find it now that I am so much better. I remember it as one of the most beautiful places that I have ever been to and I also remember feeling that I was not well enough to draw nourishment from such beauty. I am hoping that next week will be different. Anyway, as soon as I return from Wales my pheasant poults arrive and I shall be too busy with them to go fishing on the Wharfe. The plan is to spend afternoons and evenings on the Eden and it is important that this happens. I have been avoiding the Eden and it is not because its trout are more demanding than the trout of the Wharfe (although they are); no, the challenge of difficult trout is a reason to try for them. The truth is that at present I feel lonely on the Eden. My favourite stretch is less than ten minutes' drive from my front door; I have fished it for more than thirty years and caught scores of big trout there and from Scandal Beck, which flows into the river at Beckfoot, a wide and deep dub where I have in the past so often begun a fishing day with high hopes and a light heart, heading upstream along the Eden or over the wooden bridge and on up the beck. Only this spring I caught a fish of 3lb 10oz from one of the beck's pools, the second biggest trout of my life, but even he could not quite chase away the loneliness.

And so there it is. On the Eden I feel lonely and disconnected from myself, whereas I fish the Wharfe in the company of kind ghosts, some of which are me. It is high time to go back to the Eden in search of big trout, in search of peace and at the same time looking for the person who fished there so often and so happily until things went wrong with his mind. I do not want to be the same as that person, which I recognise as an impossibility, acknowledging that change, even without the intervention of illness, is an inevitable element of being alive. I am hoping, not to find myself back in my old world, but to find some sort of continuity, which can coexist with change and which I have already re-established on the Wharfe. Part of the pain of mental illness is that it cuts you off from yourself and there is still this feeling of separation on the Eden. I think the problem may be that it was there on the Eden above Beckfoot, just over five years ago, that I suddenly realised I could no longer find happiness or fulfilment with a fishing rod in my hand.

Yesterday, anyway, I ate my lunch looking at the pool above the falls. It was not Spout Dub but it was lovely. Over the river the land rose above the bank in a sort of grassy knoll coloured by creamy meadowsweet and red foxgloves and the now-fading blue of cranesbill. There were hawthorns behind me, with just the beginnings of berries. The pool in front of me was pin-pricked with drops of rain; it was drizzle really rather than rain. The air was gentle and damp and the wetness was not enough for me even to think of a waterproof. It was one of those damp days by a river when the flowing water seems to have spread its influence beyond itself into the surrounding air. They are days that I love and yesterday I loved it even more because every drop of my claret tasted like the best wine in the world, a taste that had as much to do with the brace of trout in my bag as with the quality of the wine. Dry Simon had been their undoing and he had brought them onto the hook from the edge of those rushing channels and impatient rock pools below the falls. I have said enough about the importance of the brace. I shall not say too much more. I believe that it is a god-given gift to help me find my way back to health. I acknowledge that I shall never be the same, I recognise that my life has changed and that sadness has found in it a purchase that most likely it will never resign, but I can live with sorrow just as long as a brace of trout makes me know that I can be happy again. It sounds absurd but I know that it is true.

In the afternoon I fished a copper wire nymph through the two deep holes immediately beneath the falls; I was expecting a savage attack with every cast and was rather pleased when my nymph was unmolested. Then I drove upstream and fished the run into Two Barn Flats, where Dry Simon caught a big stock fish only an ounce or two short of two pounds. He also caught three small wild trout and I missed a rise or two before I decided that it was time to go home. And, by the way, I rather regret Dry Simon's name. I wanted it to bear witness to his origins from Courtney Williams' Simple Simon, but there is something arch or twee, there is something that smacks of attempted humour or cleverness in the name and it is, I suppose, a sad fisher who personifies one of his flies and starts talking about *he*. It is, of course, partly the fault of dear old Courtney Williams. If he had not called his fly Simple Simon then I should have called my fly something else and probably something better. The old fishers of the North, those men who first tied the Orange Partridge and the Snipe and Purple and the Waterhen Bloa, would have thought nothing of such affectation; they called their flies after the materials that made them, although there is in Pritt a fly called the Old Master (grey silk, heron herl body, hackled with a feather from the underside of a woodcock's wing). I am not sure of the Old Master's provenance or how he got his name. Dry Simon, anyway, is an unfortunate name for a fly; the best thing that you can say about it is that it is not alliterative and the other thing that I want to say is that, whatever the shortcomings of the name, it will remain Dry Simon. Catlow's Killer, for example, would be much worse.

Once I am launched into a digression I find it difficult to stop; I now find that I have more to say, for I suddenly need to tell you that the fibres of Krystal Flash from which I fashion Dry Simon's tail perhaps speak to the trout of some sort of shuck and so suggest an insect or beetle struggling to cast off its former self. Perhaps Dry Simon – the fly itself rather than the name – is not just as outlandish as I am inclined to think and what about Treacle Parkin (a rotten name) and Red Tag (plainer and much better), both of them flies with tufts of wool for tails; do these tufts turn them into what we now call emergers and so save then from the indignity of dismissal as unscientific and purely fancy flies?

I think I shall leave this question unanswered and return to the aftermath of my colonoscopy. It is an unhappy story, which is probably why I have been delaying my engagement with it by talking nonsense about flies.

****

You will remember that, immediately after my colonoscopy, I was told that all was well. Naturally enough I felt an enormous surge of relief. I can remember lying on the trolley that had wheeled me in and out of theatre, feeling suddenly very tired and at the same time very happy. The dark shadow of death had suddenly dissolved and there were, of course, celebratory glasses of wine that evening to welcome the brightness back into my life. There was no champagne because I am not particularly fond of it. Instead of champagne there was plenty of red wine and later, as I lay in bed mellowed by claret, I thought of all the fishing that lay ahead of me and decided to go to the Wharfe before the end of the week; it had been a dry spring and the water would be very low, but it would be a joy to reclaim the river that I loved beyond all other rivers and there was even the possibility of catching a trout. The darkness had lifted; I could look forward to the first full season of my retirement and I most certainly intended to make the most of it.

The next day I did not go fishing; I spent it with my sister and we went walking in the Duddon valley. I remember hearing a cuckoo; I remember it very clearly because it was the first of the year (and, I think, the last). I was still feeling relieved and happy, but along with this there was a wholly unexpected edge of disappointment and something like a residue of tension. I had expected, with the fear of cancer and death removed, that my insides would resume something like their normal function. This was not the case and it nagged at me, but then I told myself that I had been through a long period of anxiety and stress, and that it would take both mind and body some time to settle down. I enjoyed the day, a quiet spring day of gentle air and soft colours and tentative sunshine. I enjoyed the evening, although I noticed that the elation of the day before had disappeared. I had thought that it would last longer.

Only two days ago I had been condemned; now I had been acquitted, released; but the joy of this sudden and unexpected freedom had faded much faster than I thought it should have done. I tried to dismiss this as a sort of hangover, a leftover from those weeks of fear. I told myself that, with the passing of each day, I would breathe in reviving confidence, stability and peace. There was some comfort in this. My plan was to return to Brough the next morning, spend a day tidying up the house, which had been neglected while the fear of death lay heavy upon me, and then the next day I intended to go fishing on the Wharfe. It should have been a glorious prospect: the prospect of a life rescued from despair and restored to its former pleasures and pursuits, its former resilience. I would fish as often as I wanted, I would walk, I would write and, above all, I would rediscover and confirm my happiness. In spite of this prospect I went to bed feeling nervous, unsettled by a mood that was less buoyant than it ought to have been, a mood that was in fact bordering on dejection and looked forward to the morning with little enthusiasm.

I slept well but as soon as I woke I knew that returning to Brough was an impossibility. My guts were in turmoil, my mind was a chaos of wild thoughts and imaginings, telling me that either the colonoscopy had failed to see the cancer inside me or that there were tumours elsewhere, in my stomach or my liver or my lungs. I had, moreover, lost weight since my retirement, which proved beyond doubt that some hidden malignancy was eating away at me. I was not sure where the sickness had made its home but I knew that it was there and that it would be the end of me. Perhaps it was living in the pancreas or the kidneys and already beginning to enlarge its territory. In all this seething ferment of dread it never once occurred to me that my sickness was of the mind. I knew nothing of psychology and how the mind can affect the body; I knew virtually nothing of anatomy; all that I knew, with a dark and terrible certainty, was that my body was riddled with disease and that I could not go back to Brough and await death there in solitude. I did not have the strength to resume the sort of life I had been living for the last month. I wanted to go to hospital, where they would do all the necessary tests and might finally establish what was wrong with me. I suppose there was even the hope against hope that they might find a cure.

My sister was wonderful. She did not panic. She fixed me an emergency appointment with her doctor, who managed to calm me down just a little by suggesting that my present feelings were an understandable reaction to a prolonged period of solitary stress. I remember that he asked me if I might consider taking some antidepressant medication and I remember insisting that there was no need. After talking with the doctor I felt less agitated but more exhausted than I had ever felt before. In the evening I drank two or three glasses of wine, went to bed early and slept like a log.

The next morning Liz drove me to Brough, where I collected some books and some clothes. Then it was back to her house for as long as I needed to be there. The dogs were left with a friend. Within a couple of days I began to improve. I decided that I might not, after all, be dying. Each day I went for a long walk. I did some work in the garden. I read Trollope and rested. There were times when I felt almost normal and, after about ten days, I felt well enough to return to Brough, hoping gradually to rebuild a life that had so recently seemed approaching its end.

In the days that followed I did not go fishing, because I did not feel ready for it. I sometimes wonder what would have happened if I had made myself go to the Wharfe and if, having got there, I had been rewarded with a good day; it is possible that I should not now be writing this book. Anyway, I did not go fishing. It was early May; after a dry spring rivers were very low. I thought that I should almost certainly want to go fishing by the end of the month, especially if the Wharfe and the Eden were meanwhile refreshed by rain. Instead of going fishing I began to spend long days in the Howgill Fells, hills that I had loved since first coming to Sedbergh; now they became something close to a passion and I walked in them three, four even five times a week.

There is music in names, even if you do not know the places to which they belong. I did the Weasdale horseshoe, over Hooksey and Randygill Top and Green Bell. I went into Langdale – the Howgill Langdale not the famous one in the Lakes – I went into the Howgill Langdale, crossed the little hump-backed bridge over the beck and climbed Middleton and Simon's Seat. I climbed the Calf from Cautley, coming back over Calders and Great Dummacks. I climbed Fell Head from Fairmile. I climbed Yarlside and Kensgriff, Winder and Arant Haw, Crook and Knott and Sickers Fell. And, up along those long wide ridges, up on those bare rounded tops above those bare deep valleys, up there in the spring air with the pipits and the larks, up there in the Howgills I found something like peace and felt sure that I would soon be fishing again.

In the middle of June I did go fishing. I spent three or four days on the Eden, thinking that, once I had found pleasure there, I should be ready for the Wharfe. They were really parts of days rather than full fishing days; they were tentative, experimental and they rarely lasted more than a few hours. I was nervous of the feelings that I might find with a fishing rod in my hand; or rather I was fearful of the feelings I might fail to find. I dreaded the absence of the old delight and the old absorption, an absence telling me that I had lost my vocation as a fisher, that a source of fulfilment and joy had gone from my life. I cannot tell you the origin of this fear but it was there and it was real and it was why those three or four visits lasted for only a few hours. But at least I went to the river and I caught a few good trout and felt encouraged; I thought that slowly I was feeling my way back to something like my former fishing life; I was prepared to be patient. But then I woke up one morning, intending to go to the Eden, and realised that I could not go; those three or four brief visits had been a sort of rehearsal and, on waking that morning, I suddenly knew that I needed more time.

I find it difficult to recapture my state of mind that summer. Perhaps depression was hovering round the edges of my life but it had yet to take possession of the mind and root itself and spread its crippling tentacles. I did not wake up in the morning feeling sick with despair at the beginning of another day. There was anxiety, which kept wondering whether the ordinary aches and pains of a sixty-year-old body were symptoms of something worse; but it was an anxiety that somehow avoided leaping to the terrible certainties of the spring. I was able to tell myself that I was probably worrying about nothing. My guts were troublesome but I had learned to put up with them without interpreting their complaints as unambiguous tokens of malignancy. There was a feeling that things had changed and would take time to right themselves. There was some sense of diminished pleasure and capacity; there was some loss of confidence in the face of life. Sometimes there was peace, but it was never the deep peace that belongs to a fulfilled and contented life; it was a poor sort of peace, more like the absence of fear than the possession of real peace. Perhaps too there was something of passivity in my attitude; I was just waiting for my life to return to normal and rediscover its old resilience. Meanwhile I took to the hills as often as possible and frequently drove over to Grange to spend a night or two with my sister.

Up in the Howgills I climbed hills that I had already climbed three or four times in the past few months, finding as much comfort as I had found when I climbed Simon's Seat or Fell Head or whichever hill it happened to be for the first time back in May or June. The rhythm of toiling up steep slopes, the long ridges and the rounded hills, the deep secluded valleys, the larksong, the blue sky and the tonic air; in all this there was balm for a weary spirit, therapy for both body and mind, except that worries about my health began once more to push themselves forward to the front of my mind. The problem was my pipe. I had smoked a pipe with enormous pleasure for at least forty years. I had, of course, always known that it was bad for me but it had been so enjoyable that it felt like a risk worth taking; and I had often told myself that, although pipe-smoking was not exactly what a competent doctor would recommend, it was surely much less harmful than the cigarettes that I had smoked with such enthusiasm in my student days. I seemed, moreover, to climb Howgills as easily as men who had never sucked smoke into their throats and lungs; I also felt healthy and fit, apart from my bowels, although I woke every morning with a dry throat, when I also coughed a bit, and there were times when smoking gave me a sore tongue.

None of this was new, neither the effects of smoking nor the attempts at reassurance. What was new was that the reassurance now began to lose its potency and the dry throat, the cough and the sore tongue began to worry me all the time. Suddenly it seemed foolish to continue with a habit that was undeniably harmful and probably sinful as well; suddenly I began to think that I should give up my pipe, which was, of course, a perfectly sensible idea but the real reason for it at the time eluded me, because it never occurred to me that the spring's cancer scare, which had in fact been a scare mainly of my own imagining, had altered the set of my mind, making me alert for signs of sickness and disease, making me ever-fearful of the signs that my body was sending to me. I had been told that I was well, that I had nothing to fear, but the mind's eye had refused to refocus its gaze. I had become a hypochondriac.

I began to leave my pipe behind when I went into the hills, although I turned to it with nervous relish just as soon as I returned. Then one morning, when my throat and my tongue were doubtless unusually dry and sore, when my cough was perhaps rougher and more rasping than it was accustomed to be, one morning I decided to give up smoking altogether, a decision which led to a day and a half of tattered nerves and abject misery. I could not persevere. After a day and a half of twitching agitation it was clear that renunciation was impossible. Moderation was the answer: no tobacco before sherry time at seven in the evening and then no more than three pipefuls before bed. It was a regime that was occasionally observed.

August brought 250 pheasant poults to my shoot at High Park and with them the final acknowledgment that my state of mind was low, that I was living in a mood of more or less permanent despondency. August, which to myself I thought of as pheasant time, that month of the year devoted to the care of my poults, keeping them well fed and well watered and trying to keep them free from the unwelcome attention of predators, August had always, ever since I started releasing pheasants at High Park more than twenty years ago, been thought of as a special and richly rewarding time of year, especially if the weeks passed and the sun shone and my birds thrived, unharassed by owls and sparrow hawks, by foxes and stoats and buzzards and mink. It was good to see them growing day by day. It was good to spend time out on the land and under the sky, heaving drums of water up from the beck, carrying sacks of pellets or grain up to the pens, mending broken stiles or building new ones, hacking away at the gorse for an hour or two, taking the dogs for a run well away from the pens to a place where there was no danger of them coming across any poults, doing all this and more and then lying down in the shade to smoke and perhaps doze for half an hour in the late afternoon.

I had always loved pheasant time, even though some years had brought trouble with owls and hawks. I had always loved August but this time I found that my heart was not in it, that the looked-for pleasure and satisfaction were no longer there. There was some annoying predation by a sparrow hawk but losses were not great and it was not a difficult release. It was a dry and warm summer but the man who trudged up Pheasant Hill every morning trudged his way through a fog of dejection and thought of the tasks ahead of him as unwelcome chores. There was something more to this than the fear of disease, for I often caught myself wondering why I was bothering with all the trouble and expense of releasing birds when I felt a growing conviction that I should find no more pleasure in shooting than I had found in my unsatisfactory attempts to start fishing again. September was approaching but already I knew that, when September came, there would be no sudden longing to go to my rivers and catch some of the spotted trout that swam in them.

It was about this time that, on a sudden impulse, I went to the doctor and told him that I wanted to give up smoking. He put me in touch with whatever the service is called that helps people in Cumbria to renounce tobacco. I met a charming woman who measured the level of carbon monoxide in my breath – this was to frighten me – told me to fix a day for the great renunciation and gave me a supply of skin-coloured patches, which she told me would ease my craving for nicotine. We met on a Tuesday; I fixed on Friday as the day when the smoking would stop. On Wednesday and Thursday I smoked all day long; on Thursday evening, just before going to bed, I cleaned out my pipes and put them in the corner cupboard. I suppose that I should have broken their stems or thrown them in the dustbin. The truth was that I only half believed in my determination to go through with the ghastly business to which I had so rashly pledged myself.

On Friday the 27th of August 2010 I acknowledged, just as soon as I woke up, the monstrous significance of the day and immediately toyed with the idea of turning Friday the 27th of August 2010 into a day of no special significance at all by getting out one of my pipes, filling it with Players' Medium Navy Cut, putting a match to it and enjoying the first smoke of the day. Instead of this I put on one of those patches, shaved and dressed, threw my packet of Navy Cut – but not my pipes – into the dustbin, took out the dogs and embarked upon a life without tobacco. That was more than five years ago. My pipes are still in the corner cupboard but they have never been touched. In those early days of abstinence I often dreamt about smoking, although I found giving it up less appalling than I had been expecting and it doubtless helped that, to begin with, I allowed myself an extra glass of wine each evening. I frequently wondered how it would be if I ever managed to go fishing again, for my mind had formed an inseparable connection between fishing and tobacco. I had always smoked when I had finished tackling up; I had always sat on the bank and smoked before making my first cast. Without fail I had celebrated the capture of a good trout with pipe smoke; pipe smoke had tried to console me after a big fish broke me or threw the hook. And throughout every fishing day, whenever I felt puzzled by the behaviour of the trout, whenever I felt tired and in need of a rest, whenever I decided to change or dry or examine my fly, whenever any of these or half a dozen other situations arose, they had meant that I sat down on the bank and that, whatever else I did, I also lit my pipe.

In the event, when I did start fishing again, I scarcely missed tobacco at all. Occasionally there was mild regret and it would doubtless have been much worse if I had been fishing regularly when first I stopped. Nowadays it barely occurs to me, as I sit there on the riverbank between attempts to catch trout, that fishing days were once full of smoke. It is, in fact, since I began writing again that I have most missed tobacco, which is because, whenever in the past I was casting about for the right word or struggling with a difficult sentence or wondering what I ought to say next, I would shove a pipe in my mouth, light it, draw in a few lungfuls of smoke and wait for inspiration. Often it seemed to work. Anyway, it is in front of my laptop that I still occasionally feel pangs of longing for my pipe. If doctors and scientists suddenly changed their minds and declared that smoking is the best guarantee of a long and healthy life, much better for you than jogging or muesli or mindfulness, then I should start again immediately. And I am almost certain that, when the blow falls and I am diagnosed with a terminal illness, the pipes will come out of their cupboard and once more produce smoke; but, on the whole, I am glad that I have put them away. I am not sure that I feel much healthier but I feel less foolish and a little less frightened. Why I have spent so long writing about the end of my long affair with tobacco is not entirely clear to me. Giving up smoking was, of course, intimately connected with my hypochondria and was perhaps its only positive result. I believe too that, at a time when the range of my activities was diminishing and when I was beginning to fear that I was losing control of my thoughts and emotions, it gave me something on which to concentrate and made me feel that I was master of myself. It was also an excuse for drinking more wine and, by the way, at no stage of my illness was there any thought of giving up booze.

Anyway, I fed and watered my pheasants throughout September without any smoking breaks. I did not go fishing and I even stopped telling myself that I might feel like fishing next week. I told myself instead that next season would be soon enough. I did go flighting duck by myself and enjoyed it, but I was worried about the now looming pheasant season because my guts were unpredictable and often painful. I began to think that they would be unable to get me through a long pheasant day. Flighting was not a problem because it belonged to the evening, when things had usually settled down; and, anyway, I went flighting alone and the whole exercise lasted barely an hour. All this made it much less difficult for a man obsessed by the state of his bowels. By contrast organised pheasant shoots usually involved early rising, always involved company and went on for most of the day. I feared that my nerves and my guts would be unable to cope although, as I sipped my sherry in the evenings, I often found some sort of comfort in the prospect of solitary rough shooting with my own dogs on my own land and in my own company.

I never shot that season with my syndicate near Settle. I did organise a late October day with four old friends at High Park. Almost every moment of it was a misery because every moment I felt the cruel contrast between my present dejection and the exhilaration that I had always felt in past autumns at the start of another High Park season. At the end of that most wretched day I finally realised that I was suffering from depression and made an appointment to see my doctor, who agreed with my diagnosis and prescribed a low dose of an antidepressant called Citalopram. He also made arrangements for me to begin a course of something with an ugly name called cognitive behavioural therapy.

It was, I suppose, a reflection of my mood that I had little faith in either the pills or in the therapy. I gave up the pills after a week because they made me feel ill. I persevered with the therapy and found it useless, which was almost certainly my fault but, whatever the reason, the homework that I was given by my therapist, mental exercises designed to change the workings of my mind, to break my obsession with disease and its bodily signs, this homework did nothing to lift my mood or persuade me that I was not the victim of some fatal sickness. I worried in turn about lung cancer, bowel cancer, throat and oesophagal cancer, heart disease and at least half a dozen other conditions that I can no longer recall.

As it happened my mood did improve somewhat in January during the last month of the pheasant shooting. Perhaps the therapy was better for me than I was willing to admit, unless it was the influence of a drug called Olanzapine. Since that miserable day at High Park in late October I had been flighting twice and once I had worked the edges of my shoot with my two spaniels. That had been the extent of my shooting because I found, as with fishing, that all the pleasure had gone out of it. But I kept my birds fed and friends shot at High Park without my presence on Boxing Day. It came as a surprise – a welcome one – when the New Year brought with it the feeling that I was ready for some sport. I shot on half a dozen days in January, all on my own ground. I shot with just my dogs for company, generally I shot well and came home contented. For the last day of the season I invited two close friends to join me at High Park and I thoroughly enjoyed myself. Things seemed to be improving and I even dared to think that, when the coming of spring brought another fishing season, I might be able to return, firstly to the Eden and later to the Wharfe.

Meanwhile my doctor had made me an appointment with a psychiatrist in Penrith, who recommended that I should stay on a low dose of Olanzapine and add to it an antidepressant called Sertraline, which did not make me feel ill but, even after several weeks, had worked no significant improvement in my mood. I was better than I had been; I had enjoyed the end of the shooting and was still hoping to fish when the season came, but all the exuberance had gone from my life. Doing things was an effort and the fear of disease still lay over me like a black cloud. There was a new and more intensive bout of CBT with a different therapist. I tried to take it seriously because I was keen that it should work, but I had soon acknowledged that, however widely its effectiveness has been praised, this form of therapy was no good for me. I decided that I was stubborn and perverse; I forget how long it took me to realise this and stop wasting my therapist's time but she was still seeing me when the fishing season started and I made myself go to the Eden, hoping to catch a trout or two, hoping that catching them would move me as in the past and hoping that I would find in catching them a form of therapy more potent, more healing than endless talk and more suited to my perverse and stubborn mind.

It was a cold spring after a very cold winter and, on that first outing, I did not catch a fish. I spent at least part of my time by the river wondering if I had prostate cancer, which modified the pleasure of my return to the river. I went out twice more; on the second of those days I suddenly knew, shortly after I had started, that I should have to stop. I was on my favourite stretch of the Eden, between Beckfoot and Eastfield bridge. I had been fishing for perhaps an hour. I sat down to rest and immediately realised that I had to get away from the river, because the weight of previous experience, the gathered memories of so many days spent happily around the place where I was now sitting and trying to keep back my tears, this burden of past and now unattainable contentment was suddenly intolerable and sent me stumbling back to the Land Rover. And there in the driver's seat, when I was ready to leave, the tears did come, tears without comfort or relief, because I could see no prospect of finding anything but pain on the Eden and the Wharfe. I feared they would not see me for the rest of the season. It was a fear fulfilled. I had tried to start fishing again and the attempt had failed.

All through the early stages of my illness I had kept writing my monthly column for *Shooting Times*. I now gave it up and did no writing at all. I read less and less, spent more and more time lying on my bed although, whenever the weather was suitable and I did not feel too tired, I walked in the Howgills. It was this that kept me sane, for up in the hills, especially if the sun was shining, up there on those long ridges and rounded tops I found comfort and something close to hope. In July I managed to get down to Wales and join a group of friends for a week's fishing. We stayed in a cottage in a deep wooded valley. The sun shone and the evenings brought gin and red wine and whisky. I enjoyed the booze and managed not to have too much of it. I enjoyed the company of my friends and the beauty of the surroundings. The fishing was painless, because there were no memories and I went to it with no expectations. If it was painless it was also without serious involvement; most afternoons I would find a comfortable place to lie and doze my time away rather than trying to catch trout. I remember the last day of the week, which we spent almost at the top of the Wye. The river was very low and in the morning I had caught nothing but a few salmon parr. I had lost all interest in fishing and, after a sandwich and a bottle of beer, I lay in the grass and the warm air, listening to the faint murmur of the water, opening my eyes from time to time to watch the buzzards and the kites, and feeling more lazily contented than I had felt near a river for a long time. I felt convalescent; I felt at least half convinced that, when I got home, I should be able to continue my recovery by going fishing again. As soon as I got home I knew that I should find peace only in the hills.

And so it proved. I did not cause myself needless distress by thinking that I might want to fish, only to find that it was impossible. Instead of this I told myself that the pheasant season was months away and so there was hope that, when at last it came round, I should feel well enough to do some shooting. I put down my poults as usual but found their care even more depressing than I had found it the previous summer. There was no pleasure in the daily routine, and there was no real belief that all the effort of looking after 250 young pheasants was leading anywhere, because I did not really believe that late October would find me in the mood to go shooting. Late October found me knowing for certain that my guns would stay undisturbed in their cabinet. Throughout the winter I kept my birds fed; friends shot them a time or two and again the new year brought an unexpected lift of spirits and a few days' enjoyable sport, but there was no thought of going fishing when trouting started in March. I knew that I could not face the Eden or the Wharfe, because I knew that, if I went to them, memories of past happiness would redouble present misery.

It is difficult to write about depression because, if you are its victim, not much happens. Throughout the spring and summer I did spend as many days as possible high in the Howgills and continued to find comfort there. I think this was at least partly because I never made comparisons; I never set the way I was feeling against the way I had felt when climbing the same hill or walking the same ridge five or ten or twenty years ago. I went to the Howgills in an effort to escape from the listless misery that possessed me at home and I found that it often worked; and doubtless the vigorous exercise was good for me; moreover the undeniable beauties of height and colour and shape filled the mind with consoling images. The Howgills were important comfort but they held no healing power; they kept unhappiness at bay while I was among them. Away from them I passed whole days sunk in inactive and impenetrable gloom. I spent time with my sister and briefly felt better for it. From time to time my brother John came to stay and cheered me up. With his departure the cheerfulness always went away. Fishing friends, good and generous friends, spent time with me and I enjoyed their company. There was another fishing holiday in Wales but this time, although I had paid out the money, I did not go. I wrote nothing, I read very little and spent hours on end lying on my bed. There were days of unexpected cheerfulness but there were many more days of emptiness and there was a growing sense of general incapacity and enveloping hopelessness. In July I cancelled the order for my pheasant poults, telling myself that I would put out hoppers in September and have some winter sport with the wild birds that they drew onto my land. In the event I bought no wheat and never filled a single hopper or fired a single shot in the course of the whole season.

23 October 2015

I find writing about my depression very difficult. I thought it might be therapeutic, a sort of exorcism, but my efforts to re-inhabit the thoughts and feelings that were mine three years ago, these efforts work on me with almost opposite effect, bringing the fear that I might give new vitality to unhappy ghosts that have almost been laid to rest. And so I shall write briefly of present things, not on this occasion of fishing but of the progress of this season's young pheasants, which came to High Park – 250 of them – almost exactly three weeks ago. As I was feeding them this morning and feeling pleased that they looked so healthy and so big for birds of their age (about 12 weeks), I realised that I was enjoying myself, that August was something like it used to be, a time when the physical labour of feeding young pheasants and at the same time watching their progress brought, in the absence of disease or serious predation, its own pleasures and its own satisfaction. August is once again pheasant time in my life and today I felt very happy that pheasant time was properly back.

I have just said that it is something like it used to be but it is most certainly not the same. I live with a degree of anxiety that was unknown to me before I was ill; it goes fishing with me and temporarily departs once I have caught my brace. As well as joining me on the Wharfe it comes with me to High Park and my pheasant pens. It inclines me to weariness; it brings a feeling of strain and it plants worries, usually about illness or imminent death, worries that fix themselves on physical sensations and harry the mind. I am learning to live with this anxiety; it no longer rules my life and it helps that I no longer expect to feel as I felt before illness crippled me.

Illness has changed me; I accept the change and find pleasure in living again, in living with this anxiety recognised, at least for the time being, as a state of mind that has to be managed. Looking after my pheasant poults is, like going fishing, part of the treatment. Whether it will ever cure me completely is uncertain, but I have come to think that limited expectations are an essential element of recovery from depression. Don't look for rapture; look for a life just about worth living and you may find this just tolerable life much better than it sounds.

This is turning into a lecture. I shall get back to my poults and the pleasure they brought me this morning as I watched them pecking delicately at turkey pellets and sipping water like connoisseurs of fine wine. I watched them eating and drinking and at the same time listened to their high pitched, piping cheeps; they seemed nervous, anxious, vulnerable sounds and I wondered whether my birds were perhaps suffering from depression or low self-esteem. It was a fancy that passed; what remained was delight in the sight, yes, and the sound of my young birds and I could not help contrasting this with the time when the sight of a pheasant, like the thought of a trout, was a token of departed pleasure, of lost fulfilment and of foundered hope.

Later in the morning I was up on my high ground by the smallest of my three pens. The sun was hot, the air was humid but tempered by a strong wind. Here too my poults looked healthy and settled, which pleased me all over again. What pleased me in an entirely different way was the beauty of difference and the recognition that here too was something that, three years ago, had been smothered by the fog of depression that lay over me. I was on my high ground, looking down over the beck to the trees that covered the steep slope on its far side. And there, in the wind and the sunshine, I saw and responded to the beauty of difference. There was beauty in the different movement of tree and leaf; in the nervous shiver of the aspens, in the long sway of the ashes, in the exuberant flailing of the birches. These were trees that seemed to welcome the pressure of a strong wind in their branches; they were loose-limbed and supple, whereas the oaks moved slow and creaking boughs and the firs stood tall and stiff and unresponsive, acknowledging the wind with no more than an awkward and an unwilling stir. There was difference of movement and there was difference of colour too, for the ashes and the aspens were turning the underside of their leaves to the wind, waving silver as well as green, but the green of the oaks was darker and heavier and the green of the firs seemed almost black. And some of the trees were already browning towards autumn and just a few of them seemed somehow, even in late August, to have kept the fresher green of spring.

Four paragraphs have told me just how far I have come from the dark days about which I was writing; they have given me the strength to move on to the much darker days that were waiting for me in that coming winter, now three years behind me. I forgot to mention that in the course of the summer and autumn I had a third bout of CBT with a clinical psychologist. It was a disaster and usually started or ended with me in tears. I could see what I was meant to do; I understood that I needed to challenge those obsessive thoughts of disease that spawned and at the same time fed on a cycle of frightening mental and physical symptoms. I could see this with perfect clarity but my mind would not respond as it was meant to. Perhaps I was too tired to attempt change. Perhaps earlier failures with this sort of therapy inclined me to doubt its efficacy. Anyway, I knew that I could not engage with my therapist or her material, which filled me with frustration and churning discontent. Each session made my condition seem more hopeless. I forget how many of them I endured but, after the last of them, I felt much worse than before they had begun because I could see no release from misery beyond what once again seemed the inevitability of an untimely death. I had abandoned the Sertraline because several months of use had made no difference to my mood. I think I was still taking a small dose of Olanzapine but I am no longer sure and, if I was still taking it, any noticeable benefit had long since disappeared.

September came and with it came something like hope, because it brought an end to the dispiriting inactivity that now made up so great a part of my life. I have forgotten to mention that in the course of the summer I had been contacted by the Head of Classics at Sedbergh – an old pupil of mine – and asked if I might be interested in taking on some part-time teaching in the next school year: about eight hours a week spread over three days. I accepted the offer immediately, because I thought it might offer me an escape from the sense of hopeless isolation that was threatening to overwhelm me; of course it could not prevent my untimely death from one disease or another but at least it might divert my attention from it and, if by any chance I was not heading for an early grave and if I could make a success of this teaching, it might form an important first stage in rebuilding my life. It would take me away from myself, it would give me a sense of purpose, it would make me useful again. At the very least it would bring in some money – not that I was short of it – and give me something to do. I felt that I was being positive, that I was proposing to fight my depression with a more powerful weapon than whole years of intensive therapy could provide. Teaching, after all, was something that I was good at and it would also bring me among old friends. It was a cheering prospect and I spent August in better spirits, preparing lessons and walking in the hills.

September came along and the teaching started. I had expected some initial difficulty in re-establishing a routine and getting used to standing in front of a class again. I also expected that, after a few weeks, the whole thing would become much easier, that I should settle down and begin to enjoy the work and the whole business of finding myself part of a community again. It was, as I had expected, very difficult to begin with and, instead of getting easier, it got more difficult with each passing week, as I groped my way to admitting that a course of action designed to make me feel better was in fact making me much worse. Its effect was more like poison than medicine.

At the beginning of a teaching day I felt exhausted as soon as I got out of bed. At the end of the day I usually drove home in tears. I had been looking for a sense of belonging and found instead that, even in the presence of friends, I now felt excluded and alone. I was not part of a community; I was being paid to perform a limited function and that was all. And there were practical drawbacks to the whole scheme, particularly in that I no longer had a base in Sedbergh and there were long periods of the day when I had little to do and nowhere to go. And the three days at work left me so weary that I did almost nothing in the four days that followed. And my return to Sedbergh felt like a ghastly mockery of those thirty years when I had really belonged.

It was probably a foolish project and, even in different circumstances, it might have failed, but the reason for its collapse did not lie in the teaching, which was all sixth form, with small sets of polite, intelligent and motivated pupils; no, the teaching should have been stimulating and enjoyable. And the reason did not lie in the welcome I was given by my friends. The reason did not lie in the work

I was doing or in the spirit of the place where I was doing it. The reason lay in me and the fact that I was too ill for the task that I had undertaken. I think I knew this after three or four weeks but somehow I managed to keep going until half term, telling myself that all might yet be well, or at least tolerable. When term resumed I managed the first week and that was it. I woke the next Monday morning, realised that work was impossible, rang the second master – an old and dear friend – to say that I was ill and hoped to be better tomorrow. When tomorrow came I rang him again and again the next day. I never taught another lesson. I rang my friend to say that I could not see any prospect of a return and acknowledged to myself that I was the victim of a nervous breakdown. And now, having told you all this, I need to go fishing again.

31 August 2015

Sitting by Spout Dub at lunch time yesterday I acknowledged, while sipping my claret, yet another attribute of the place, for I realised that the spirit, the aura, the special air and atmosphere, I mean, of course, the numinosity of Spout Dub made it possible for me to think back over the dreadful winter that followed my failed return to teaching, to revisit it without feeling its shadow creeping out from a corner of the mind to darken my life again. Spout Dub belonged to the years before my illness. For three whole years I lost Spout Dub; now I have won it back again and somehow the lingering, yes the lasting and permanent influence of those three dark years has no power to taint the powerful and peace-charged air of Spout Dub.

But first things first, and the first thing to say is that, as I sat by Spout Dub, sipping my claret and realising that my favourite place in the world was an even better place than I had previously thought it, I was already in possession of the brace and its solid presence in my bag was all the sweeter because a single trout had only turned into twice as many in the last pool before lunch. I had been thinking that I should have to drink my wine without the sense of fulfilled contentment that comes over me with the possession of the day's second trout. The first of the day had come right at the start of my fishing and it had come from

Spout Dub itself. It was a very large stock fish and I confess that it fell to a copper wire nymph. I think I have already told you that I do not much like weighted nymphs and that I positively abhor bead-heads; I cannot help thinking that their use barely qualifies as fly-fishing, for they are no more flies than maggots are bluebottles, whereas patterns of the Skues style, which incidentally almost no one fishes these days – anyway, the patterns of Skues and our Northern spiders imitate nymphs that are already thinking of turning into flies or nymphs with the process half complete.

I am not sure that I am putting together much of an argument. After all I fish Dry Simon without having a clue what he represents; he is probably taken for some sort of beetle, which is as near as dammit a fly, but I am far from certain about this and if someone proved to me that trout ate Dry Simon in the belief that he was a corner of cheese I should nevertheless continue to fish him without so much as a prick of guilt, thinking all the while that I was doing something called fly fishing. And I fish fancy wet flies and they may well be taken for creatures that are nothing like flies – shrimps, for example – and this troubles me not a jot. I therefore abandon my ethical doubts about the Sawyer-style nymph, which now that I think about it is often taken for a nymph swimming to the surface of the river, that is for a nymph that now wants to turn into a fly, so that an angler fishing such a pattern might just about claim that he was doing something called fly fishing. I think I have lost my way in a tangled confusion of nonsense. I shall start all over again.

I dislike the weighted nymph for aesthetic rather than ethical reasons; artificial flies – I use the term loosely – made from bits of pheasant tail and strands of copper wire are much less lovely than those made from silk thread and the wings of the partridge and the waterhen, from heron and peacock herl and the feathers of hen and cockerel. I think this is indisputable. Dry Simon, I admit, is not a beautiful fly; he is too flashy to be beautiful but he certainly approaches beauty more closely than a Killer Bug or a copper wire nymph. Such things are less lovely than flies of fur and feather and the process of fishing them – unless they are very small – is often indelicate; you can feel them in the cast and they fall on the water with a plop and a little splash. The truth is that I do not much like weighted nymphs and fished for years without recourse to them; but it is also true that I like catching trout very much indeed and would far rather fish with a weighted nymph than not catch any trout. At Foston earlier in the summer, on a morning when I was failing to do what I had come for, I spotted some long-forgotten nymphs in a neglected compartment of my wet fly-box and almost immediately they put trout in my bag. More recently, in fact only two days ago, I was on the Wharfe in a big water; I had tried my usual patterns and they had failed to stir a fin. On an impulse I tied a weighted nymph to my cast and it caught fish for me at fairly regular intervals for the rest of the day. Simple Simon also caught some fish but I think he was helped by the weight of the nymph drawing him deeper in the water. Today the Wharfe was full and shining and very beautiful, clear but flowing coloured from the peat, like liquid amber shot with a darker glow. The recent effectiveness of the weighted nymph persuaded me to tie one to the end of my cast and try him though the run into Spout Dub. I was half way to the brace within the first few casts of the day.

In the run above Black Keld I pricked what felt like a good fish and caught an undersized trout. Under the sycamores in the run into Two Barn Flats I hooked a big fish and can remember thinking, as I felt the weight of him, that I was feeling the second half of my brace and that all was well. But then he ran for the roots and I had to hold him hard and he broke me. He was a bitter disappointment; telling myself that he was almost certainly a big stock fish – which is almost certainly true – brought little comfort. And then, half an hour later, I saw a rise in a seam of current running down a glide with no name. Dry Simon provoked a nudge and a splash and I knew that I should have changed flies before fishing to that rise, because I could see small olives – probably pale wateries – coming off the water, and I had seen that my rising trout was eating them. Thank God that Dry Simon had not put him down and that a small parachute olive put him in the net: a most beautiful wild trout of one and a half pounds that I killed with scarcely a second thought, acknowledging that my rule or aspiration or pipe-dream only applies – if it applies at all – to trout that come after the brace. I might as well be honest and admit that I have more or less abandoned my rule or ambition or protocol for the time being; I am, after all, making up for three seasons when I never killed a trout. Perhaps, now that I think about it, I should regard it as a long-term goal.

Anyway that second very beautiful wild trout made Spout Dub seem a wonderful place – which, of course, it is – and the first insight that came to me, as I sipped my claret and felt happy, was that my autumn fishing had begun. It might still be August but it was nevertheless already autumn. The long pasture above Spout Dub was full of downy thistles; there were the first signs of yellow on the leaves of the sycamores; along the banks meadowsweet stirred in the breeze on lanky stalks, more than half gone to seed and now a faded reminder of summer rather than its emblem; purple knapweed was turning brown at the heart of the bloom, grass was turning to pale straw, yellow ragwort stood in untidy clumps, rowans and hawthorns were beginning to show red and only that morning, as I had taken the dogs out before breakfast, I had noticed that the telephone wires were lined with chattering swallows. Back on the river the mallard were gathered in strong-flying parties of twenty or thirty and more.

These signs all told me that it was autumn, and then Spout Dub told me something else because I realised, while sitting there with a cup of claret in my hand and breathing in the soothing but potent air that hovers over the world's most sacred place, I realised that autumn is as much a mood as a season. Perhaps this applies to spring and summer and winter as well but I think it is especially true of autumn and of autumn fishing, when we suddenly find that, instead of looking forward to next week or next month, we are looking back to the cold beginnings of the season and wondering where all those intervening weeks have gone. Autumn fishing is often good; calm days of autumn sunshine are very beautiful but they are tinged with sadness and the stillness of an autumn day seems touchingly fragile, as though it is just waiting for wind and wetness to blow away the peace. And in autumn rivers flow with the powerful symbolism of passing time, and fishers – if they are at all like this fisher – are inclined to sit on the bank, watching the water with its cargo of floating leaves and giving themselves over to reflections on change and decay, on transience and mortality. It is bitter-sweet, it is conventional, it is self-indulgent. At the same time it is both affecting and inescapable and it is also true.

By Spout Dub today I felt just the beginnings of my autumn mood, but already I had noticed something much more surprising and important, for I have already told you that here by the Wharfe, by the side of the pool that somehow captures and reflects for me all the beauty of my river and all the experience that belongs to it, I have told you that here I can think of those three years of crippled existence without feeling any threat from them. But I now realised – and I mean this very seriously – that Spout Dub is also a place of healing and a place of revelation because, in thinking of my illness I realised that even in its darkest phase, although I was most deeply miserable, I had never stopped wanting to be me.

I think this might be important. I think perhaps the seeds of recovery lay inside me because I never looked at other people and wished that I were one or other of them. I envied other people their happiness but not their personality or their being. I wanted to be different, to be rid of the weight that was crushing me and of the darkness that enveloped me but I never stopped wanting to be Laurence Catlow. What I think I am trying to say is that I was almost at ease, underneath my misery and incidentally without conceit or self-satisfaction, with the sort of person that I was. I was very unhappy with what had happened to me, but I never blamed myself – or anyone else – for this and, even in the lowest depths of my depression, I did not fall victim to self-hatred or diminished self-esteem and I continued to find being me interesting. I felt wounded and broken and frightened. I felt bereaved, because I felt that I had lost myself and did not know where to start looking. Somehow I wanted to find the way but I lacked the strength or the insight to take any tentative first steps. Anyway, sitting by Spout Dub today with a beaker of wine in my hand and a brace of trout in my bag it seemed to me that, even in the black winter that followed my mental collapse, those aspects of personality that I have just mentioned were perhaps untypical in victims of depression and perhaps a hidden source of strength that helped me to avoid despair. I also saw that those thirty stable, happy and productive years before my illness must have been a help to me; for they meant that, even in the darkest phase of my depression, I was aware of the possibility of difference, because I knew that for most of my life I had indeed been different. It must be a much greater challenge for, say, a depressed adolescent to find a path to hope, because he will probably believe that the way he feels is all that life has to offer him, that his state of mind is a fixed and permanent aspect of his personality. The conclusion of my Spout-Dub-reflections was that there was in me a deep-down resilience, unrecognised and unconnected, by the way, with any virtue or innate goodness, there was a deep-seated and unacknowledged resilience which helped me to cling on to the hope that I might find healing.

It was a hope that for a time seemed all but extinguished. By early November I knew that I could never teach again. There was something like a week when, apart from taking the dogs out, I spent most of each day lying on my bed. It was a Saturday afternoon when, on a sudden impulse, I rang my friend Karen Unwin who, with her husband Merlin, has published my four books. I am uncertain why I rang her, except that I was lonely and desperate and hesitated to ring my brother or sister because I wanted to spare them pain and was unwilling to put pressure on them. Perhaps I thought that Karen would be less affected by learning that I was profoundly miserable and that I should be able to talk to her without making her feel that she had to do anything other than sympathise. I rang her to talk and, as soon as she answered the phone I burst into tears. Immediately she said that she was going to drive up from Ludlow the next day to give me whatever help she could. I did not try to dissuade her.

She came on the Sunday. On the Monday she arranged a meeting with my psychiatric nurse who in turn made an emergency appointment with the psychiatrist in Penrith. He put me back on Sertraline, recommending that I should build up gradually to double my previous dose. He also prescribed what I now realise was a very high dose of a particularly potent benzodiazepine called Clonazepam, developed to treat epilepsy and now widely (and perhaps unwisely) used to treat depression and anxiety. I knew nothing of this at the time; I knew that Sertraline and Clonazepam were pills; I had no faith whatsoever in their efficacy but I was willing to swallow them in the hope against hope that they might just possibly do me some good.

Karen now insisted that I should return with her to Ludlow. At first I was unwilling but only briefly, because I realised that I was frightened of being left alone and I also thought that, if increasing the dose of Sertraline produced initial side-effects, these would be better borne among friends. I was lonely, I was lost, I was fearful. Knowing all this I also knew that I needed company and needed love. Sitting by Spout Dub yesterday I acknowledged that human intervention, which seems a cold and heartless description of Karen's rescue and care, was twice as potent in preparing me for recovery as any medication. I needed love. I also needed for a time to have someone else in charge of me, because I was too weak to take proper charge of myself.

I spent about five weeks in Ludlow, building up gradually to the maximum dose of Sertraline, swallowing three pills of Clonazepam each day and drinking too much wine. You are not meant to combine benzodiazepines with large amounts of alcohol. In my case there seemed to be no obviously harmful consequences, although the booze might have impaired the effectiveness of the Sertraline. But the booze was something to look forward to, bringing both pleasure and comfort to a man who needed both. I never felt heavily sedated; I avoided drunkenness and I never once woke with a hangover.

Anyway, during those five weeks I was often in tears but there were times almost of happiness, times of near contentment and times of something not entirely unlike hope. I rose late, pottered into the office and read while Merlin and Karen, helped by Sue and Jo, got on with their work. Sometimes I made tea or coffee for the workers, sometimes I ran small errands into town. I drank half a bottle of wine at lunchtime, which was probably a mistake but at the time it seemed to help. Then I slept for an hour or two before returning to the office and telling myself that I had got through another day. The evenings were not a problem; they brought the comforting ritual of food; they were full of friendship; there was wine before, with and after dinner and then it was time for bed. Sleep was not a problem either; I was never troubled by insomnia at any stage of my illness, which is apparently unusual with victims of depression. Again I cannot help thinking that, whatever it might have been doing to my liver, the wine helped me to find the peace and refreshment of sleep. Sitting by Spout Dub yesterday I realised that student excess, leading to that terrible day when I thought I had lost the Wharfe forever, came to my assistance here, for my fear and hatred of uncontrolled indulgence was so intense that, although I knew that I was drinking too much, I felt at the same time that I was in charge of my drinking. I knew when to stop, because the prospect of waking up with a raging hangover or without knowing how I had got myself to bed, the prospect of this and the thought of the self-loathing that it would inspire, was too terrible to contemplate. I cannot recommend heavy drinking as a remedy for depression, but I am fairly certain that, in my case, it helped me to cope.

Ludlow was good for me. I felt fragile and my mood was volatile, with sudden lurches and falls, but on balance it most certainly improved. At the end of those five weeks I was feeling less uniformly hopeless, less drained and defeated than when first I arrived. About ten days before Christmas my brother came for me and I spent the next fortnight with John and his wife in Bury St. Edmunds. Again there were some happy times and some times of tearful misery. Again it felt good to be under the protection of people who loved me. Just before the new year they drove me back to Brough, spent three nights with me, after which they needed to return to their own lives, leaving me, for a few weeks at least, to face the future on my own.

Sitting by Spout Dub yesterday and able to look back over that crisis in my life without feeling any threat from it, I realised perhaps for the first time just how lucky I had been because I was able to surrender myself to the loving care of friends and family. Whatever else they were, those seven weeks away from home were a time of rest and I see now that they brought the beginnings of recuperation. I do not know what would have happened without them. I was very nervous when I said goodbye to John and Marilyn; I was fearful of my own company, fearful that the old hopelessness would reassert itself. But the period of rest, the period of reliance on others had strengthened me and brought buds of hope. Left alone in Brough at the new year of 2013 I felt nervous, vulnerable, fearful; I did not feel hopeless or desperate.

All this I saw as I sat by Spout Dub with a brace of trout and a metal beaker of wine. Before I stood up and went fishing again a question suddenly formed itself in my mind; it was a question that had asked me for an answer several times before and I had refused its request. Now it seemed somehow more pressing and I knew that I should have to respond; I also knew that I had looked back enough for one day, that I was suddenly weary of introspection and eager to catch more trout. I would ask myself the same question the next time I went fishing and see what answer came back, trying to discover where my Catholic faith had been in that time of desolation. I knew it had been somewhere but I was uncertain precisely where. It was, of course, a question of the utmost importance but, by the time I got round to it yesterday, I was already weary of self-analysis and ready for more trout. I fished up from Watersmeet and caught three more big stock fish, which meant that, with five trout in my bag, I drove home praising God for the goodness of his creation and praising Mary for her role in the redemption of man and her unceasing intercession on behalf of imperfect, impure and sinful humanity.

4 September 2015

I fished below Yockenthwaite yesterday, almost at the top of the Wharfe, and wondered why I have fished there so infrequently in the last two seasons. It might be the pull of Spout Dub. I am ashamed to admit that it could also be the absence of stock fish in the high river above Buckden and Deepdale; this should, of course, be a powerful motive for fishing there and I used to fish our unstocked beats as often as possible, because I found fishing for wild trout much more satisfying; something has changed in the last two seasons and it could just be that, in my inordinate longing for the brace, I am now drawn to the lower beats by the more gullible trout that swim there. Anyway, I drove away from Yockenthwaite yesterday afternoon determined to return just as soon as conditions were suitable again.

Yesterday conditions were almost perfect. I fed my pheasants in the morning and did not start fishing until half past one. There was no wine with my lunch; there was just a sandwich and a few mouthfuls of tea. The water was falling back from a recent rise, clear but peaty, lustrous and dark. It spoke to me as a water for wet flies and so I tied a hackle Coachman to the point and chose Simple Simon for the dropper. There was a robin singing its autumn song as I tackled up. I walked downstream past pock-marked butterbur leaves, past limp and dejected stalks of meadowsweet, past berried thorns and hipped briars. There were restless swallows in the grey sky and it was unquestionably autumn.

I started fishing where a dead tree stands sentinel over an otherwise open pool. It brought me a three-quarter-pounder and a few pulls. Above yesterday's first pool there came (unsurprisingly) another pool, this one a deep rock pool with a turbulent current down one bank; it is a pool where you might expect to hook one of the monsters of the high river, but it has never given me anything out of the ordinary, and yesterday I was not granted even a twitch or a pull. Beyond it is a long and very lovely glide, flowing down sixty or seventy yards from a miniature waterfall. It brought me a small trout of seven or eight inches and a fish perhaps two ounces heavier than the day's first. It brought me the brace, making me wish immediately that I had brought some wine, so that I should be able to sit on the bank under a soft and cloudy sky, sit there, drinking a toast to the high river and blessing the flowing water on its journey down the valley to Spout Dub. Without the wine I fished on contentedly enough, – it was a very peaceful afternoon – caught and returned four or five small trout and came after something like an hour to the long rock pool that greets a fisher on his way upstream just as soon as he climbs over a metal hurdle and returns to unenclosed land.

It is a very beautiful pool, shaped from the living limestone, and for me it has been bountiful as well. Yesterday there were four or five fish rising there. I tied on Dry Simon and the lowest of the fish splashed at it without taking. I returned the Coachman to the point and fished on. There followed a most wonderful half-hour. I am not certain what the fish were eating; a few small olives were hatching but they were too few to explain the frequency of the rises. There was black fly on the water, which may well have been the inspiration of those delicate circles and those sipping sounds. The trout may well have been feeding on tiny black flies but they were happy to help themselves to Simple Simon and there was nothing delicate about their response to discovering the fraud. They were good fish for the high river, fish over the pound but less than a pound and a half. They were good fish and they were slow to surrender and, like the pool from which they came, they were very, very beautiful.

From the rock pool I caught four such trout; I kept two of them and was overcome by the recognition of beauty upon beauty. I had already absorbed something of the beauty of the pool and of the trout that came from it. Now too I consciously inhaled the soft beauty of the afternoon, with the sliding water and the sloping fields and the damp air, with the singing robin and the autumn swallows, with the weathered buildings across the river and the brown fells rising above them; it was almost sombre, it was also soft and it was very beautiful; but the crowning beauty for this fisher yesterday was the beauty of catching trout on wet flies fished upstream.

It would have been an even greater beauty if my flies had been those lovely, sparse spiders of the North, the Orange Partridge and the Waterhen Bloa; probably they should have been, but even with two fancy flies it seemed surpassingly wonderful. There were the water-carvings of the rising trout; there was the gentle fall of the line onto the soft shine of the river; there was a slide, a twitch, there was some subtle signal from the line and suddenly there was a bent rod and a fighting trout.

It struck me as marvellous how a process so gentle could be so instantly transformed into a pulsing struggle and a beating heart. But there was more; for I have never felt the imaginative appeal of the old upstream method with greater force and I think I saw something of the reason; for it seemed to me, as I cast my flies over the rock pool and saw the line move against the current and felt the weight of a trout before I saw the shape and the gleam of him in the water, it seemed to me that this water had itself become sentient, had come alive with the strength to move and to pull. It was a strange and transient illusion but it was deeply felt.

I caught four from the rock pool, all to Simple Simon; from the run beneath the riverside cottage I caught another pounder and another trout perhaps six ounces heavier from the pool below Yockenthwaite bridge, the same pool that runs dry after a week of settled summer weather. Both took the Coachman, both were returned and then it was time for the adoration of the trout. Before gutting and cleaning the four fish that I had killed, I now laid them on the grass and feasted on their beauty: on the shape and the shine of them, on their rainbow sheen, on red spots edged with a halo of silver and blue, on dark chain-mail backs and yellow flanks and delicately ridged amber fins and those full slender-edged and perfect tails. I have never responded more deeply to the beauty of brown trout (why, incidentally, are they called brown, which they most certainly are not?) and now writing about then has renewed the tears that fell over them yesterday, because I have seen that the sense of grateful reverence that came over me as I gazed at those four trout, lying in the grass by the water just above Yockenthwaite bridge, this deep and thankful wonder would never have moved me as profoundly as it moved me yesterday had I not lived through three seasons without feeling its blessing as a presence in my life.

And I saw something else: a revelation that came to me without the prompting influence of Spout Dub's air or a beaker of wine. It was an insight inspired by the indescribable beauty of four trout, an insight which told me that I had been wrong, in an earlier book, to think of trout as treasure and so to think of fishing as a sort of treasure hunt. It is an analogy that does both the trout and the process of catching them an injustice, for treasure can be tawdry or vulgar or downright ugly, treasure can be a monument to the unhappy partnership of inordinate wealth and appallingly bad taste, treasure is often treasure merely in terms of its value in dollars or pound notes. But a brown trout is neither tawdry nor vulgar nor ugly, and his beauty is in perfect taste and quite beyond price. And I have been wrong to write of gloating over a catch of trout. Men gloat over guilty things with secret greed and there was nothing of this in yesterday's adoration, which was an act of pious thanksgiving rather than a private impulse of desire. Trout are not hidden treasure and fishers are not modern versions of Long John Silver or Captain Flint.

Trout are great art and the fisher who casts his flies to them employs art to catch art and responds like the man or woman who sees something infinitely precious in a Madonna and Child by Raphael or who hears the same in a Beethoven quartet or a symphony by Brahms.

I saw this yesterday by Yockenthwaite bridge and it still makes some sort of sense to me; and running through it all was the deep sense of joy in that I had won back the capacity to be moved by the great art that swims in trout streams. There was this joy and at the same time there was the acknowledgment of an imperfection in my response; for, as the collector of art is not happy merely to see and to marvel but longs to call great art his own, so there was in me this longing to possess, which meant that I was not content simply to contemplate beauty and then return it to its element untarnished and whole. But it is, of course, a complicated business, given that trout are edible as well as art and I often think that fishers who give back all their trout to the river are undervaluing them and have reduced fishing to a sort of game. This is also a train of thought that has run far enough and I am going to abandon it before it either reaches a dead end or curls itself in tortuous circles of infertile complexity.

Leaving Yockenthwaite yesterday was very difficult. I had found such beauty and fulfilment there, down there by the shining river between the sloping fields, that it seemed almost a sacrilege to break their hold and climb up to the Land Rover. I had fished for less than three hours and part of me felt that I should like to fish on indefinitely, fish on up to Deepdale bridge and then keep fishing right up to the first pool of the River Wharfe, but I also felt that only disappointment could follow the fishing that had led up to the adoration of the trout, which had been both a climax and a conclusion; and so I made the wrench and drove home.

It was while I was on the road that I remembered how, after my last visit to the Wharfe, I had promised on the next to probe the presence or absence of faith in my illness and recovery. I immediately said three Hail Marys and told the blessed virgin that I should look for her presence in my struggle with illness when next I found myself by Spout Dub. And then I realised something else that has nothing to do with fishing or with the BVM but much to do with the appreciation of beauty.

I have written of trout as art; I believe that art sustains and nourishes and you know that for three years I lost the power to draw strength from fishing and from trout. I have won it back and this is a profound joy to me. But there is something that I have not regained and the realisation of it brought a sudden sense of diminishment. For, as I drove home, I realised how rarely I listen to music these days and how, if I do play myself some favourite record, it almost always brings disappointment because it wakes such a feeble response. Music no longer moves me as in the past, when it formed an almost constant background to my life and often was much more than a background, was a central pleasure and preoccupation. Mozart, Beethoven, Brahms, Wagner, Bach, these and at least half a dozen other great composers brought me enlargement, elation, sublimity, piercing sadness and poignant joy and, as their art is wordless, so the emotions that it woke in me were often similarly beyond words; but now it is as though depression and anxiety have left a hangover: a sort of emotional deafness in my response to music; I hear the notes but hear nothing more. I am deaf to the beauty of great music and it is a great sadness to me.

While writing these paragraphs I played some Chopin Nocturnes on my record player. It is music of haunting delicacy but it moved me only with regret that I could no longer feel or respond to its beauty and its burden. I returned the record to its sleeve. I felt that it was speaking a language that I no longer understood. Some day it will probably return, my capacity to experience the power of music. In the meantime I am very thankful for fishing and for trout.

CHAPTER TWELVE

14 September 2015

I returned to Yockenthwaite yesterday; I had again spent the morning with my pheasants and so did not start fishing until half past two, intending to fish my way slowly upstream and deep into the autumn dusk. There was sunshine, just touched with gold, and a light breeze; the river was raised and running clear but shot with colour from the peat. There was a slide and a whisper to its motion. The robins were singing softly, the swallows were restless in a quiet and twittering sort of way, there were yellow leaves floating on the stream and drifting on the air. It was an afternoon for slow fishing with gentle thoughts but, after an hour with only one undersized trout brought to net, I felt rattled and tired, for the afternoon had turned almost hot and, although I could bring fish to my flies, I could not hook them and was beginning to think that I was heading towards a blank day ending with the bitter taste of failure.

I had started in the pool of the dead tree, which I noticed was in fact not quite dead; it is an old sycamore, stretching up to the sky a gaunt pattern of bare, blunt and mainly barkless branches; the delicate and vital complexity of the healthy organism has all gone; it looks like the skeleton of a tree, but just here and there hangs a lonely green leaf, barely clinging on to life. It is a dying rather than a dead tree and today it claimed one of my flies. It was, by the way, in the pool of the dying tree that I caught and returned my pygmy trout. In the long, lovely glide beyond the next pool there were two or three trout rising; it was these that came to my flies – three or four different patterns – but refused to take a firm hold; it was these fish that unsettled me with the growing fear of a troutless day. It was not quite panic; it was more a sort of childish dread; it was made worse by memories of my most recent day at Yockenthwaite; it shut out the sun and blocked the prospect of autumn peace as I fished my edgy way upstream.

I came to the rock pool, caught a midget and provoked a nudge from another small fish. In the lower of the two pools below Yockenthwaite bridge there were no rising trout; I fished the water with Dry Simon and was suddenly fighting a big fish. The spring balance weighed him in at exactly two pounds; he was a big and a beautiful trout but he was still one too few for happiness. The bridge pool was blank and I drove a few hundred yards upstream to fish the top of the water between the two bridges, water that I rarely fish because it is open to the road and is usually infested with motorists and their dogs. They do, of course, have every right to park by the side of the road and enjoy the matchless beauty to be found by running water, and I have more than enough river to fish where motorists and their dogs have no access, but it is good to find, at five o'clock on a September evening, that the motorists have all driven away, taking their dogs with them and so leaving me to fish those beautiful roadside pools in peace.

The river between Yockenthwaite and Deepdale bridge is lovely water, much of it over bedrock with carved channels and deep holes, with short pools and narrow, restless runs. And the rock shines through with different colours in different places, now white, now yellow, now darker, deep amber or brown with clinging growth, now dimly glimpsed beneath deeper flow. The rock shines through and the water shines with the promise of trout. Yesterday evening I was perhaps less receptive than I should have been to the beauty of the river because I was searching so anxiously for the brace. There were no trout showing but before long Dry Simon helped me out again by bringing one up in a glide where the road runs immediately above the river on the left of an upstream fisher. He was not a two pounder but he was only an ounce short of the pound and he made the brace and immediately he brought the gift of autumn peace to the fisher who had just caught him. For now I sat down on a narrow shelf of grass below the road and acknowledged the evening calm; I sat there with a blue evening sky above me, with the bright fields patterned by pockets and seams of evening shadow, shadows now stretching themselves in the slanting evening light, with no breath of wind in the evening stillness, with a high and distant radiance bathing the fells, a radiance that seemed to be shining from another world; the changing leaves were motionless on the trees, the bracken was tall and still and brown at the roots; there was almost no movement except for the running of the river below me and there was barely a sound apart from the sound of the water flowing beneath my feet.

And so I sat there, inhaling the peace, and, although I was miles from Spout Dub, I knew that it was the time and the place to say a Hail Mary and then, surrounded by all this beauty and filled with this peace and feeling the contentment that had come with this second smaller but more wonderful trout, it was time to ask her where she and her son had been in those dark winter weeks almost three years ago when I had most needed them. I told her she had about twenty minutes, because by then I should want to be fishing again before the light began to thicken and fade.

The easy, and perhaps the true answer was that Christ and his mother had been in all the people who helped me, working through the love and the care that I received from so many friends. They had done their work through Karen and Merlin and John and Marilyn. A few pages back I said that, on my return to Brough, I was left to face the future alone. This was not true. There was my sister barely an hour's drive away. There was my dear friend Helen, whom I have left shamefully unmentioned until now. Helen is a farmer's wife, Gerry is her husband and I have known them for years. Helen is very busy but, when I was in the depths, she found time to ring me every day and endure my tears. It made a difference; and then, twice if not three times she answered my desperate cry for help and drove over to Brough and spent most of the day with me. Helen also took charge of my spaniel Finn during the weeks of my absence and, although she is very busy with work and family, she has always seemed happy to make me a cup of tea, to sit down and talk when I have called round feeling low. Helen has been the best of friends and my debt to her is very great. Andrew Moss and Kelvin Whitfield have also been true friends; they belonged to my fishing life but they generously stepped out of it when I could fish no longer; they kept in touch and came to see me and spent time with me. They encouraged me to believe that one day I should fish again. Then there were Ron and Marion only two doors away – they are still there – always willing to interrupt whatever they were doing to speak comfort to a miserable and often tearful me.

I have been blessed by family and friends and I have been very fortunate in my GP. I went to see Dr. Tod soon after John and Marilyn left me that New Year. I admitted that the Sertraline had been forced to keep company with too many glasses of red wine. He did not tell me that I was a weak or foolish or sinful man. He said that it was very tempting for victims of depression to make a friend of alcohol and, although the booze might have interfered with the action of the Sertraline, he thought that after so long on a high dose without any very obvious improvement in my mood, it was unlikely to be much help in the future. It was time to think of something else. I remember saying that I thought no pills would be able to help me. He said that he would talk with the psychiatrist in Penrith, and after he had done this, I agreed to phase out the Sertraline and try a different antidepressant called Mirtazapine in combination with a sedative called Quetiapine. I was to keep taking the Clonazepam but cut down from three daily tablets to one. I had, by the way, imposed some restraint on my drinking; I was back to my normal intake of one glass of sherry before dinner with half a bottle of wine after the washing up. This seemed – and continues to seem – an essential and central condition of a civilised life. On very bad days there was sometimes a glass of wine with lunch but such days were rare; on at least nine days out of ten there was no alcohol until the Archers had finished at seven fifteen. Anyway, I was willing to try the new combination of drugs. I was more or less willing to try anything and the psychiatrist had persuaded Dr. Tod, who like me had been inclined to think that pills were unlikely to cure me, that mine was what is called a chemical depression and that some form of medication, although it would not in itself restore me to health and happiness, might help me along the way. I did as I was told. I took the pills, starting some time around the beginning of February, and they did not make me feel worse. Looking back I think they helped me to feel a little better: very fragile, very nervous, often sunk in darkness but at the same time beginning to hope. And I am not meant to be writing about medicine. I am meant to be writing about God.

I sat by the river yesterday evening, having got there, incidentally, without the help of Clonazepam or Quetiapine though with the assistance of 30 milligrams of Mirtazapine, I sat there and thought that God had been with me through the dark days in all the people who had taken the trouble to show me that they were willing to take much more than trouble on my behalf. In some ways it was a glib answer but it persuaded me. And then there was something I have already mentioned: the fact that I never began to hate myself or wish that I was someone else. I could not pray, I could not go to Mass but I still believed that, as God's creature, I was precious to him and that, though he seemed absent from my life, he was present in ways that I did not know. I am not sure that I articulated much of this at the time but it was a background of belief and of ideas and I think it gave me hidden strength. I do remember not infrequently thinking of my depression as a sort of dark night of the soul, a night that was lasting for what seemed an eternity but without quite excluding the hope that there would some day come light.

I never blamed God or decided that he did not exist. Sometimes I asked him why all this misery was happening to me and just once or twice I wondered whether it was part of a process leading towards a much greater happiness; it was a thought that came to me with an almost total absence of conviction but it was still there. I asked God a few questions and, very occasionally, I said a Hail Mary on a sudden impulse. This was as near as I got to prayer, which needs a sort of mental – unless it is a kind of spiritual – resilience. Prayer is an effort and it was an effort beyond my strength; I was far too weak for prayer and I could not go to Mass. Looking back I am not sure why. Perhaps there was an element of agoraphobia in my depression. I was certainly frightened that my bowels might let me down and there was an encompassing nervousness in the prospect of any situation from which there was not the availability of easy and unobtrusive flight. Whatever the reasons, for something like two months Mass was an impossibility.

It may have been the end of January, it may have been the beginning of February, it may have been the pills, it might have been the kind influence of those long weeks of willing dependence on others, it might just have been the invisible working of the Holy Spirit; whatever it was, there came a Saturday about five o'clock and I felt that I could cope with Saturday evening Mass, that the fears which had for so long kept me from it were really phantoms, that there was not much to unsettle or disturb me in the thought of a short drive to Appleby and the first Mass of Sunday (celebrated on Saturday evening). And so I got in the Land Rover and went there.

There was no sudden revelation of God's presence in my life, there was no sudden bursting of light into the darkness of my mind, but I was glad to be there and the priest was very glad to see me back. He had, by the way, visited me several times at home. I was glad to be at Mass; I could join tentatively in the worship, I could even manage a few private prayers and I remember very clearly how, after taking the sacrament, I sat there in silent thankfulness and suddenly thought that, if I could manage to get myself to Mass, I might even manage, when at last spring came along, to get myself to the Eden or the Wharfe. I remember praying that it might be so.

****

These were something like the thoughts that came to me yesterday evening as I sat by the Wharfe and felt the sudden chill of an autumn evening on the still air. It was time to go fishing again. I drove up above the iron bridge and above the wooden footbridge beyond it to fish the first half mile of the Wharfe, fishing my way up to the meeting of Greenfield Beck and Oughtershaw Beck at the hamlet of Beckermonds. Soon after starting again I hooked a good trout that leapt in a gleaming cloud of spray and shone in the level light. He threw the hook and I fished on.

The sun left the river and lay only on the fell tops, the sky turned silver and I fished on through the shadows and scarcely cared that the midges had come out to feast on me. I returned a few small trout and, though it was time to leave, I knew that I could not finish until I had fished the river's first pool. And that first pool, little more than a narrow basin, a mere bath tub of water made restless by the inflow of the two becks, that first pool gave me a trout of fourteen ounces and a still deeper peace. And then I drove home through shadows and falling darkness and the dim shapes of the surrounding hills.

17 September 2015

This book has almost turned into a diary, a literary form that seems particularly suited to my genius; perhaps it is because there is no need to build a structure, to research or to plan ahead: your research does itself by happening to you, your narrative structure – usually flimsy and loose – builds itself from the progress of the day and you can, of course, make no plans when you do not know what tomorrow will bring. A diary waits on events and in this way suits my indolence.

If this book has at last become a diary it is usually a day behind and it now wants to tell you that yesterday I came to Spout Dub at exactly one o'clock with a brace of trout in my bag. The brace had been hard won, for all morning there had been few fish showing. Dry Simon had failed. He had failed to bring up any trout and he had put down a couple of risers as well. Whenever this happens, whenever Dry Simon has an off day or a rotten morning, I respond with a mixture of disappointment and relief. I have come to depend upon him, so that I feel disappointed when he lets me down; at the same time there is relief that fly fishing has once again proved itself a slightly more complicated business than it sometimes seems when Dry Simon is catching trout after trout and has not been taken from the end of my leader at any moment during my last half dozen visits to the Wharfe.

There were few fish rising yesterday morning. I did not think smut responsible for the few that were and I also thought that these few were feeding just below the surface. I tried an Orange Partridge, which was ignored by the trout to which it was shown. For some reason, perhaps guided by my fisher's instinct, I forgot about sub-surface feeding and tied on a small floater that had suddenly caught my eye, something it must have failed to do for almost thirty years. I recognised it as the work of a former keeper of the Kilnsey Angling Club called Fred Tattersall, and for a few minutes my mind roamed back to the years of Fred's service and his morning presence in the *Tennant Arms*, where he held court for the members, chain-smoking Woodbines – unless they were Park Drive – through an endless stream of advice and anecdote and complicated jokes. As well as a great smoker and talker Fred was an expert fisherman, a first-rate shot and, among many other accomplishments, he tied beautiful flies.

The fly I was looking at was almost a Grey Duster, with a body of bluish rabbit fur and a hackle that was not quite badger. It was remarkable for two reasons, firstly because the sight of it brought back a whole period of my fishing life and a person who belonged to it, with his stories and jokes and cigarettes, with his flat Lancashire accent and his round fleshy face, his boundless good humour and his restless activity. Fred liked a drink and sometimes liked too much of it but it was the smoking that killed him. Yesterday, as I tied on his fly, I remembered him and at the same time acknowledged how, for us fishers, memories cling to old rods and wait for us in neglected corners of our fly-boxes; they even hover round nets and reels. We carry the past round with us and from time to time it re-emerges in sad or grateful recollection. It was good to think of Fred Tattersall yesterday and to say a prayer for the repose of his soul.

The second remarkable thing about his fly was that it caught the trout that had just refused my Orange Partridge: a wild trout of 1lb 4oz which, needless to say, went in the bag. I was fishing the beat above Watersmeet; there were no fish rising in Middle Run or the Willow Run and Fred's Fly, together with on or two other flies, failed to bring any up. I came to the long curving glide beneath the trees and to the run above it. By this time I had restored Dry Simon and a rising trout splashed at him without taking hold. 'Fool,' I said to myself before changing flies. But Dry Simon had not put him down and Fred's Fly put him in the net:

another wild trout two ounces lighter than the first. And so Fred's Fly brought the brace and brought a contented fisher to Spout Dub. With the first sip of claret I prayed for Fred once more, thanking him for the gift of his friendship and for his fly and hoping that, wherever he was in eternity, he would be provided with a limitless supply of Woodbines (or Park Drive).

Spout Dub was autumnal; the air was soft and still beneath an even cover of grey cloud. The water was sliding on its way, sliding and shining and thickly scattered with fallen leaves. I noticed a new feature of Spout Dub in the untidy spread of a clump of butterbur leaves on the edge of the far bank. Somehow I had missed their presence all through the spring and the summer. Now in September they were turning yellow and flecked with brown. And there was yellow on the sycamores and a hawthorn near to those butterbur leaves was laden red. The sandwich tasted like a pleasant sandwich; the claret tasted like the drink of angels and there, enfolded by Spout Dub's autumn peace, I thought my way back to the late winter that followed my return to Brough and how I prepared myself for the coming of spring.

I thought of February two years ago and tried to remember how I had spent it and how I had felt. I remembered that my brother John came early in the month and stayed for a few days. Andrew Moss had been for a night or two in late January and both these visits helped, giving me something to do and someone to talk to. Whenever the sun shone, and often when it was behind cloud, I went into the Howgills and found a fragile peace there. I ordered pheasants for the coming autumn and winter, determined to give shooting another go. I tried not to think about fishing but, of course, I tried in vain. I did think about fishing but I set myself no targets. I hoped that, when trouting started again, I should feel like going fishing but, if I had to wait, then I told myself that I should wait patiently. On Saturday evenings I went to Mass and most days I managed to spend at least a few minutes in prayer. And, by the way, I often looked at the fishing scenes on my dinner mats and more or less believed that they spoke to me about my future as well as about the past.

Looking back at that February, as I sat by Spout Dub yesterday lunchtime and listened to a dipper singing its water song, I realised that even then I was beginning to feel better. I remembered how, one day after a walk in the hills, I felt so happy that I also felt frightened, because I felt that it was too good to last. It did not last; the next day brought a grim reaction that was difficult to bear, but it was followed by further good days and I began to find that I could look through the bad days to the good ones that surely lay ahead.

I continued to see Dr. Tod every week. He was endlessly patient, sympathetic and reassuring, persuading me that my worries were not necessarily signs of terminal illness. He took tests to prove his point and, above all, he talked to me as a friend. The medication may have been helping but I am quite certain that he helped me more. Sitting by Spout Dub yesterday and looking back two years to February and its signs of my improvement, I realised how, in spite of this improvement, my mood was still unpredictable and often difficult to manage. There were still days when I woke up and wondered how on earth I was going to cope. There were still days when I felt convinced that my life was near its end. I acknowledged that even now, two years on, there were remnants of these feelings living in the mind and that, away from Spout Dub, they were still able to shape themselves into dark and fearful convictions that would probably never go away. And then, suddenly and unexpectedly, I grasped another way in which my faith had helped me, back in the dark days, to believe that life might once again be worth living, that it was in fact already worth living when it was also full of pain.

I have told you of my conviction that God was present to me throughout my illness in the people who helped and loved me. I have said that my faith, even in the darkest times, gave me some sort of self-belief. Yesterday I saw something else and I think it was the numinosity of Spout Dub that inspired this insight: namely that I never doubted the beauty and goodness of the created world. I felt unable to respond, I feared that death would take me away from it to I knew not where or what, but I still felt that they were there, both the beauty and the goodness, and this contained within itself the hope, however feeble, however distant, the hope that some day I might reconnect with them. By February two years ago, in spite of continuing dark days, this hope was beginning to turn into something more like belief. And up in the Howgills there were times when I looked at the small portion of the world revealed to me and saw that it was beautiful and good and capable of great comfort; at the same time I knew that only the sacramental power of running water and rising trout and eight feet of carbon fibre could restore full and vital contact with all that beauty and all that goodness and its capacity to heal.

And this was when I realised that my claret was finished. Spout Dub is a wonderful place but its magic cannot work without the help of wine. It was time to abandon self-examination and go fishing again. The afternoon was even quieter than the morning. Fred's Fly failed along with at least half a dozen wet and dry patterns. I ended my day in the pool above the stepping stones, where Dry Simon unexpectedly hooked something enormous and almost certainly wild, because it knew at once where it was going and set off with unstoppable force, taking Dry Simon along for a trip from which he never returned. I was disappointed by the departure of this undoubted monster but in a resigned sort of way; there was no anguished sense of loss, rather there was a feeling of frustrated curiosity because now I should never know just how big he had been. Perhaps he would have been my first ever four-pounder. But the brace was in my bag, which undoubtedly meant more to me than the loss of an enormous trout, and so I drove home over the quiet hills in grateful contentment. The world seemed both beautiful and good.

24 September 2015

I have been over in East Yorkshire. Yesterday, at about a quarter to four, I caught and killed one of the most comforting trout of the whole season. I had spent the day before on the Derwent with my friend, Oliver Todd. The day before that, like the day in question, belonged to the Foston beck and had given me three trout to copper wire nymphs. You know that I regard them as a last resort, although I must admit that yesterday I tied one to the end of my cast at the start of my fishing, caught and returned a couple of small trout before alarming two or three bigger fish. I tied on a spider of my own devising. I call it the Grouse and Goose and you dress it as follows:

> **Hook**: 14 or 12
> **Silk**: grey or brown
> **Body**: herl from the primaries of a Canada Goose
> ribbed with the silk
> **Hackle**: well-marked feather from the middle of a
> grouse's wing

Yesterday I was fishing the smaller version and the first fish that saw it liked the look of it and weighed one pound four ounces. I was delighted to have caught a trout, even more delighted to have caught him on a spider and not on a heavy nymph. This is neither a self-help book for depressed fishers nor a manual for catching trout, but I cannot resist telling chalkstream anglers that they should fish spiders, because chalkstream trout are often very eager to eat them. That is one piece of advice. My other recommendation, of course, is that all trout fishers, wherever they fish, should never be slow to try Dry Simon: two indisputably major tactics that might well catch a fisher many more trout; they might even promote his happiness, as they most certainly promote mine.

Anyway, persevering with my Grouse and Goose I promptly bungled two or three fish by striking too soon or not striking at all. The takes were firm takes and it was my fisher's response that was to blame. It was at least partly because I could see my fish and their response to my fly, which encouraged me either to snatch or to wait for an obvious turn. Then I managed to raise my wrist at the right time and was fighting a good trout until, in my impatience to get the brace in my bag, I went for the net too soon and the hook came free. It was a terrible moment as my trout, mine no longer, sank wearily out of sight and it was also time to meet Oliver in the local pub, which meant that there was no time to make amends. I had grouse for lunch and a pint of wonderful beer. I would rather have eaten a packet of mouldy pork scratchings washed down with a cup of cold tea, doing this in the comforting knowledge of two trout already in the bag. The grouse was delicious and I had almost forgotten just how good bitter beer can be, but my pleasure in meat and drink was tainted by the recurring thought that I had lost a fish and missed others and was still a trout short of happiness.

Sport was slow in the afternoon, although I did miss at least one more fish in my eagerness to feel his weight on the end of my line. And then I ran out of rising or visible trout and went searching upstream. I scanned bright pools below little wooden weirs, I peered into pockets of clear water between swaying beds of weed and nowhere saw what I was looking for, until I came to a pool that Oliver and I both call The Limpid Pool. It is a big feature for Foston, which is a miniature chalkstream, and it deserves the name that we have given it. It is a deep pool below one of those wooden weirs, with weed along its edges; yesterday, even late in September, there were yellow monkey flowers trailing in the water. We call this pool The Limpid Pool because of the startling clarity of the water and the sometimes almost dazzling shine of the chalk bed over which it flows. Yesterday afternoon the cloud had thickened and the morning sun had gone; Limpid Pool mirrored the milky whiteness of the sky, so that I could not look though the water right down to the chalk. A fish rose on the edge of the stream; I could not see him, which was perhaps as well given my performance in the morning. Anyway, the Grouse and Goose fell a foot or so above the rings of the rise and a moment later there was that wonderful draw on the line which has nothing to do with the current, but tells a fisher that his spider has been taken and that it is high time for him to turn his wrist.

He was hooked and he was landed and those earlier failures made his capture doubly sweet. I had waited for the brace almost to the end of my fishing and now, with a trout just over the pound, the brace was made and I sat there on the bank among the monkey flowers and wept. The brace was made, my fishing was over for the day and my contentment was complete, except that it was much more than contentment; it was a deep and grateful and unqualified happiness that possessed me as I sat there, wondering how it was possible for two trout to work so powerfully on the mind of a man of sixty five, a man who had already caught several thousand trout before he caught those two more. It was not a probing sort of wonder; I was not in the mood for analysis; I preferred just to sit and thank God for giving my fishing back to me and giving with it the inestimable blessing that now comes with the gift of two spotted and shining brown trout. Before too long I said my farewell to the Foston Beck until another spring returns me to The Limpid Pool. Then I walked back to the Land Rover.

It was as I drove home, without this time making contact with a lamp-post in the middle of Thirsk, that, filled with the fulfilment of the brace and the happiness that it had brought me, I looked back to the beginning of the process that had led up to it; I looked back to the day in March two and a half years ago when I returned to the Wharfe after a break of almost three years and took the first step towards reclaiming my fishing life and finding again some of the feelings that belonged to it. It was high on the river just below Yockenthwaite and I could remember that the sun was shining, that is was a bright day of restless yellow spring light with a lively upstream breeze. I could remember too that it was Andrew Moss who got me over the hills into Wharfedale. He was staying over there to start his season and for at least a week he had been encouraging me to join him, perhaps for just part of a day, perhaps just to walk the river without forcing myself to fish. I wanted to go and I wanted to fish but at the same time I was frightened of how I might find it, frightened that it might seem as empty and as painful as my last experience of the river, which had also been at Yockenthwaite and had ended in hopeless tears.

I was frightened of fishing but at the same time I wanted to go and by late March two years ago I was feeling a little stronger, feeling that fishing might bring me some pleasure again, feeling some stirrings of the old longing to catch myself a trout. And I told myself that if it did not work I should be patient and try again when the time seemed right. It was a Saturday and, over the phone the night before, I had promised Andrew to meet him at ten o'clock by Yockenthwaite bridge.

You would have thought that what was a momentous occasion would have left sharper memories. I knew that the day of my return to the Wharfe had been one of prime importance: important not so much in itself but because it made more fishing days possible; it was a new beginning or a resumption rather than a dead-end. You would have thought my mind would have stored away clear impressions of such a day but, as I drove through Hovingham and Thirsk, through Masham and Middleham and Hawes, I could recall little of what had belonged to it. There was the sunshine and the yellow light; I was fairly certain that the water was full and shining from the peat. I knew that, meeting Andrew in the morning, I had been on the edge of tears, not tears of misery but rather of uncertainty, nervous tears hovering somewhere between fear and rising hope. I knew too that I had caught a trout, a good trout, and that I had been glad to catch him without any sudden rapture or surging joy. I knew that I had met Andrew for lunch, eaten a Cornish pasty and then fished above Deepdale in the afternoon without catching another trout. And I knew that I had left the river feeling that I had enjoyed myself and knowing that I should return but uncertain when. I could also remember how I had been to Mass the same evening and how a deep conviction of God's presence in my life had come over me as I said my prayers after taking the sacrament.

When I got home from Foston I checked my diary and found that my trout had weighed one and a half pounds and that the day had not in fact belonged to March at all but had been almost three full weeks into April. And I had forgotten that, before that April day on the Wharfe, there had already been three days on the Eden. Once my diary had reminded me, I could recall two of them, both in the company of Andrew Moss and Kelvin Whitfield; the first had been cold and cloudy and cheerless, a spring day drained of colour, the sort of spring day that is still trying to be winter; none of us had caught a fish but I had been cheerful and very glad to be fishing again. It was in fact this day on the Eden that at last saw me with a fishing rod in my hand again, but my memory had told me that this honour belonged to the Wharfe at Yockenthwaite. The reason for this is clear to me; namely that my mind would only accept that I was truly fishing again when at last I had spent a day on the river that had claimed my fisher's heart.

It is, by the way, significant that in the spring of 2013 I was again keeping a diary. For well over thirty years I had kept a record of fishing and shooting days, never a daily journal, but this had lapsed with the onset of illness, mainly, I suppose, because there was no fishing or shooting to write about. Anyway, its resumption was itself a sign of reviving strength and confidence, although looking at the entry for that first day back on the Wharfe I find the following jottings: 'emotionally fragile', 'felt like an old man on the river', 'stumbling, weary, balance problems'. But I also find 'the possibility of joy' and 'the determination to return.' They were brittle days, those spring days two and a half years ago; leafing through the diary last night I came across entries that did not belong to days on the river and they were often full of pain. There were days spent lying on my bed, days when lunchtime wine dulled both the horror of being alive and the consuming fear of disease and death. There is an entry for Easter Sunday that reads 'hopeless and desolate; no hope of ever recovering.' But there are days that record a determination to defy the dark messages that my mind was sending me and begin to be well again. There are days of something like peace spent high in the Howgills and, scattered through all these days of different mood and experience, there are just a few fishing days. Before long I shall revisit one or two of them.

26 September 2015

Dry Simon was back on form yesterday. Before lunchtime he had caught me two wild fish from a quiet river. They weighed respectively five and two ounces over the pound and they brought me to Spout Dub in a mood of quiet contentment. I have been looking at my diary of two years ago and it was of this I thought as I drank my wine with the leaves still and yellowing above me and with the quiet sound of the river in my ears.

There are no entries for most of the days. It was clearly the bad ones, the unusually good ones and the fishing ones (not many of these) that inspired me to mark them with some sort of record. I have said that my mood back then was brittle. I had not realised just how dark many of those days were and it was, I suppose, a sign of recovery that I could get through them and go fishing from time to time. I think by then I was beginning to realise, when all hope seemed gone and death seemed just round the corner, that my body and my mind might both be telling me lies; and this, of course, made it easier to believe the message of the good days, drawing from them real hope and real pleasure.

Anyway, sitting by Spout Dub yesterday and looking back to those few fishing days two seasons ago and the often dark days that lay between them, I gratefully acknowledged just how much further progress I have made since then. There might still be anxiety; there might still be moods of deep despondency, especially in the morning, but now there are whole days of happiness and there are days when the shadow lifts and I look into the future with steady eyes. Sitting by Spout Dub yesterday it seemed to me that, if I could live the rest of my life as I had lived the last year, I should not die an unhappy man. And from where, I wondered, had this healing come? It had come from all those sources that I have mentioned several times before; it had come from friends and from family; it had come from an outstanding doctor and some of it had probably come from the pills; time had been a part of it, an important part; faith had been a still larger part; and not the least part of it had been the gift of flowing water and a fishing rod and the brown trout they put in my bag, reconnecting me with former happiness, former fulfilment and former peace.

At this stage of my Spout Dub reflections I filled my metal beaker with the rest of my wine and tried to remember the day of my return to the world's most beautiful place. I had seen the bare details in my diary, and so I knew that it came on my second visit to the Wharfe early in June. Again I had thought it had been earlier, that it had happened some time in May; I was surprised that so many weeks had passed before bringing me back. There had been days on the Eden and there had been some big fish but there had been no more fishing on the river that I so loved. I think that I was waiting for the company of friends to get me over there again; I was still nervous of what I might find on the banks of the Wharfe. It was with my friend, Oliver Todd, that I made this second visit to the Wharfe. We drove over from Brough on a sunny morning. Andrew and Kelvin were already there and we had arranged to meet them for lunch at Spout Dub. And, by the way, I had not then realised how Spout Dub surpassed all other pools and places on the Wharfe or any other river in the world. It was special to me as the pool that had given me my first ever bagful of trout more than forty years ago and I also thought that it was secluded and very beautiful. But I thought Knipe Dub was just as lovely and associated it more intimately with my presence on the Wharfe: as the place where I had bidden the river an agonised and guilty farewell and the place where I had rested and prayed when, six months later, I found that I was not an exile after all.

We arranged, anyway, to meet for lunch at Spout Dub and my beat in the morning was above Kettlewell. My diary tells me that I caught a two pounder on the Yellow Thing and that I returned three much smaller fish. It is strange that I cannot even remember the big one. I can remember almost nothing of the morning, except that it was bright and that, nervous to begin with – lest I should find pain or emptiness – I became absorbed by my fishing and enjoyed myself. You would have thought that the chief feature of the morning, in the form of a two-pound trout, would have left a deeper impression, but the truth is that it has left no lasting impression at all. I wonder if the Clonazepam might have made me less receptive of experience or impaired my memory in some way. Whatever the reason that morning above Kettlewell is lost to me except for my diary's insistence that I caught a big trout.

Lunch by Spout Dub, however, I can remember. I have no idea what I ate – probably some sort of sandwich and a packet of crisps – but I know that Andrew and Kelvin joined us and that we drank the champagne which Oliver had brought to celebrate my return to the main beats of the Kilnsey water. I remember drinking champagne and thinking that, with four of us doing the drinking, there was not enough of it. I remember that the sun was shining and that, in spite of an inadequate supply of booze, I felt very happy, sitting there above the Wharfe in the company of friends. And I remember the main event of the afternoon, which was the capture of a 14 ounce trout from the Middle Run on the beat above Watersmeet. I know too that by four o'clock I felt dead tired and ready to drive home; and I know that, while I was pulling off my waders, I suddenly burst into tears for the joy of it all: for the trout I had caught, for the river that had given them to me, for the friends who were helping me and, above all, for the return of fishing into a life that felt incomplete and unfulfilled without it. I was back on the Wharfe the next day, back at Spout Dub for lunch with Andrew and

Kelvin (Oliver had gone home). This time there was enough wine for two generous glasses and again I drove home with a brace of trout in my bag, beginning to believe that my repossession of the Wharfe had been achieved and would be permanent.

Yesterday I left Spout Dub when my claret was finished, fished for three hours without stirring a fin, then drove up to Deepdale where I fished the last hour of the light and killed a trout of exactly one pound. On the way home it occurred to me that I had just spent a very enjoyable and normal sort of fishing day, the sort that had been common before depression took charge of my life; it had been a day without tears of any sort; there had been the deep and usual satisfaction that came with the brace but there had been no sudden swings of feeling. I had not begun my fishing in fear and weariness and anxiety. I had begun my fishing feeling fit for a man of sixty five and feeling eager to catch some trout; and a few had come my way and their coming had brought both pleasure and peace. Now I was driving home, my mood tinged with sadness at the thought of the season's approaching end, but I felt happy and suddenly realised that I was looking forward to spending tomorrow morning feeding my young pheasants. It came as something of a revelation to realise that I was, in fact, feeling more or less normal and, as well as looking forward to tomorrow, was more immediately looking forward very much indeed to a glass of sherry almost as soon as I got home.

28 September 2015

There was no brace in my bag when I came to Spout Dub yesterday, but this was because I had not started fishing. It was two o'clock and once again I had driven over to the Wharfe after a morning of pheasant care. There was no brace but there was also no feeling of failure or disappointment and so I drank my wine contentedly, feeling almost normal again and thinking as it happens about tears, or rather how I was increasingly less prone to them.

I think tears are fashionable, especially for men. Once we were meant to bite our lips and fight them back, but now it seems that we are advised to get in touch with our feminine side, becoming touchy-feely and happy to blub, letting our emotions, our empathy, our tenderness all hang out for everyone to see and approve. I wondered yesterday whether my own tendency to tears, which is only now abating, had within itself some element of self-indulgence, whether it had perhaps been almost encouraged as evidence of sensitivity. I wondered if it might even be regarded as an affectation and decided that it was not so.

I wept convulsively when my parents died. Long before that I had burst into tears on that afternoon when I revisited the Wenning for the first time after leaving her. I cried bucketfuls when I thought forty years ago that I had lost the Wharfe forever. I am fairly certain that there were no tears when I returned to the river the following spring. There were definitely no tears when, in my early forties, I thought for a time that fishing had lost its power to bring me fulfilment and joy. In the past great music had the power to inspire tears and it is strange that it has now lost that same capacity. Anyway, before my illness I think that I was on the whole an unweepy sort of person, the heir of a particularly northern heritage in my belief that strong emotions were to be felt rather than displayed. Depression changed this, depression often drove me to tears as some form of physical release from what seemed like an agony of despair. When depression at last began to relax its hold on me, moments of sudden happiness often brought with them an irresistible impulse towards tears and for some reason I felt no inclination towards restraint. I looked upon them as a celebration and any feeling of embarrassment had disappeared. Sitting by Spout Dub yesterday I decided that depression had loosened me emotionally, loosened or perhaps de-stabilised me; at any rate it had frequently moistened my eyes.

I turned specifically to fishing tears and began with those that had come at the end of my second visit to the Wharfe two seasons ago, acknowledging what I have already told you: that they were tears of joyful return. Through the rest of that summer there were about a dozen more visits to the Wharfe and, as far as I could remember, they were uniformly tearless. I think this was because my fishing days were still nervous, almost apprehensive; otherwise there would have been many more of them. I was fearful lest the black cloud of depression would come down on me and blot out the sunshine that I was beginning to find along the banks of the Wharfe. I felt like a convalescent by the river, which is, I suppose, precisely what I was; my mood was in general too tentative to surprise me with a sudden and spontaneous outflow of tears. There were good days; there was the day when I first fished the Wharfe without the company of friends; I felt lonely, but then I caught a three-pounder that made the brace and cheered me up without quite chasing away the loneliness. There was the day up at Yockenthwaite and Deepdale that had begun slowly but then, after an hour or two, the river had come alive and between them Dry Simon and Simple Simon had filled my bag. I could remember how a feeling of very quiet happiness took possession of me as fish followed fish; I could also remember sitting on the bank and wondering if it could last. I was glad to be fishing again but my mood was almost always qualified by a shadow of doubt. And then there came my last visit of that season, a day towards the end of September when I fished the Wharfe with Andrew Moss.

We were fishing between Watersmeet and the Stepping Stones. It was a cheerless day beneath cloud, so much I remember from the morning but not much more. When we met for lunch at Spout Dub neither of us had caught a trout and for me things went no better in the afternoon. I met Andrew again at about four o'clock; he was driving home and so we said our farewells after he had announced that he had just caught four trout with as many casts. And then he left me and I sat down on the bank above Black Keld, sat there in the long limp faded grass among withered thistle stalks and bent stems of seeded meadowsweet; I sat there feeling very lonely and very incompetent and suddenly very tired. I thought about finishing and driving home, but decided that I would make a last attempt to catch a trout from the run into Two Barn Flats.

After tying Dry Simon to the end of my leader, I trudged disconsolately upstream and, when I had climbed the stile that brought me to the top of the Flats and the long run beneath the sycamores, I sat down again and looked for rising trout. There were none. I might have sat there for five minutes and I might just have wondered whether it was worth bothering. And then I did stand up and I did not walk away. I waded into the river and began to fish. There were no trout rising but Dry Simon suddenly disappeared. The fish that had swallowed him was not far short of two pounds; I netted him and killed him and two or three casts later Dry Simon vanished again. This trout was only an ounce lighter than the first and, even as I waded ashore with him safely in the net, the tears were already running down my cheek. Frustration had turned into fulfilment, loneliness had flown away as I sat down on the bank again beneath the cloud and wept for love of fishing and for trout and for the river that, when hope seemed extinguished, had just given me my brace. They were pious tears; they were healing tears and I let them flow.

That was the day when the transforming power of the brace was first fully acknowledged. It also marked the time when tears became a regular feature of my fishing life. And they came again the same evening before I drove home because, after I had stowed all my tackle in the Land Rover, I stood by the side of the road, leaning on the wall, and looked down over the line of the river, now just beginning to sink into the autumn dusk. I looked down to the dark forms of the sycamores above Two Barn Flats and I found that I could hear the voice of the river that I could now only dimly see; and, as I stood there listening, I suddenly knew that the Wharfe was whispering to me, welcoming me back to her streams and pools to catch some of her store of spotted trout and to find happiness along her banks. I knew this and at the same time I whispered back to the river that I loved her and that, whatever else happened in my life, she would be there at its heart. And then I think I dried my eyes and drove home.

Sitting by Spout Dub yesterday I recognised that day as the day when the healing power of fishing really began to work on me. I also wondered, as I have probably wondered before, whether such powerful feelings for a river were perhaps evidence of emotional poverty in my human relationships. I did not care a fig and I wondered something else: whether those riverside tears had almost run their course, because fishing was once again becoming part of my normal experience; and here I was at Spout Dub, happy to be there, looking forward to starting fishing very soon and very much hoping that I should catch at least a brace.

In the end I did catch a brace but it came deep into the evening; I got my first trout fairly soon after starting; Dry Simon caught him for me from the Willow Run and then I struggled. I finished at Spout Dub and I admit that I tied on a copper wire nymph; with what turned out to be my last cast of the day I hooked, landed and killed a trout of exactly a pound. He gleamed in the dark grass of the riverbank and made me relieved and happy at the same time. There were no tears. There were no tears when, after plodding back to the Land Rover and taking my tackle down, I stood by the road and looked down over the line of the river, thinking that in less than a week I should have parted from the Wharfe for almost six months. There was sadness in the thought, much deeper gratitude for the season now almost past. I drove home dry-eyed and contented and glad that within two days I should be back for what might be my last visit of the season to the river that has given me back my happiness.

30 September 2015

Yesterday I went fishing. I meant to go again today, to fish until darkness fell over the season's last day. On Monday I had the flu jab; yesterday I felt drained and achy on the river; today I felt worse and so I did not go fishing. It felt like an untidy end to a most marvellous six months. And this book is now heading for an untidy end as well; I had rather hoped that its last page would find me, at the end of the last day of September, sitting quietly by the river as the light thickened, sitting there with a brace of trout in my bag and my story finally told. Well, it has not turned out as I hoped; I have more to tell you and you will have to absorb it without the leaven of my fishing days.

I have not gone fishing today because I feel exhausted and off-colour, but I do feel well enough to sit in front of my laptop and remember yesterday. The weather was beautiful: September at its most serene with still air and golden light and that sad autumn sense of fragility. Lunch, would you believe it, was not at Spout Dub, because I had arranged to meet Kelvin and Andrew and Richard Dover, another good fishing friend, at Watersmeet. Again I did not fish in the morning and it was two o'clock when I got to Watersmeet with a bottle of wine. My friends were already there and we sat together in the sunshine, drinking *Côtes du Ventoux* and talking about fishing. I proposed a toast to my three friends, thanking them for the help they had all given me on my way to this day by this river with this feeling of peace. They seemed touched by my words and then we talked of fishing again and then, at about three o'clock, we stopped talking and went fishing instead.

I watched Kelvin catch a one and a half pounder from the Skirfare's last pool. Half an hour later I caught a one and a half pounder myself from the Willow Run, rejoicing to find myself now halfway to the brace. And then there was toil. Dry Simon had caught me this first trout; together with half a dozen other patterns he failed to catch anything else, not even one of those frustrating tiddlers. And the shadows stole out from the western fells and the sunlight withdrew to the high tops and a September chill crept onto the evening air. When I came to Spout Dub the river ahead was white and silver beneath the sky; the pool itself was dim in shadow and there was not the slightest stirring among the leaves. There was a stillness all round me, somehow deepened by the slip and slide of the river; I should have caught the mood and tied on a small spider with reverential fingers, perhaps a Snipe and Purple or better still a Partridge and Orange. It was a disgrace to intrude a copper wire nymph into the middle of such serenity, but I confess this is what I did and it fell onto the water once or twice with a vulgar plop and I am glad that it worked. On consecutive days it brought me the brace to the last cast of the day and again my second trout was exactly a pound and again the gleam of him from the shadowed grass filled my fisher's heart with happiness. Again I remained dry-eyed.

As I drove home the hills sank quietly into the night as the last brightness, which was rose and crimson and pink, drained from the sky. I wondered about today and whether to go fishing. It seemed almost a sin not to spend it on the Wharfe in pious thanksgiving for the countless blessings of the season, for all the beauty and all the trout and all the joy they had brought me, for the relief and the release they had given to an often still anxious heart. While driving home I thought that today would belong to the Wharfe. While drinking my sherry before supper I was not so sure because I felt so tired; there was also, I must admit, the nagging fear that on the season's last day I might fail to make the brace. Anyway, as soon as I woke up this morning I knew that I did not feel well enough to drive over to Wharfedale; I toyed with the idea of going to the Eden and in rejecting the idea at the same time acknowledged that my plan to re-establish warm contact with a great trout stream had failed; I had in fact fished the Eden much more two years ago when I was still only halfway to feeling well again. I promised myself that next season would be different, that next season I would find room in my fishing life for two rivers; I could not let the fear of failure and loneliness keep me from a river barely five minutes from my front door, a river moreover that had been so generous to me in the past; I had loved the Eden, less deeply than the Wharfe it is true, but I must learn to love her again.

And so my season has ended, cut ever so slightly short by an injection and here I am, sitting in front of my laptop rather than on my grassy shelf above Spout Dub, sitting here and wondering how to bring this book to an end. I think it is already long enough but I should like to touch on just a few of last year's fishing days; for this was the season when I truly reclaimed the Wharfe, when it became again almost a regular part of the rhythm of my life. Of course I fished the Wharfe two years ago, but you know already that there was a nervous quality about it all and there were nothing like as many days as there would have been if my mood had been more stable. Last year was different; when spring came round last year I not only believed that I was well enough to go fishing; I also felt certain that going fishing would help me to feel even better. By last spring, in other words, I had come to acknowledge the healing power of fishing days and the especially potent power of the brace. I shall start with my first visit to the Wharfe in the spring of 2014.

I remember that I was particularly keen to probe the difference in my response to Howgill hill-walking days and days by the river Wharfe, because already then I was thinking that I was well enough, not only to go fishing, but also to start writing again and already I knew that what I wanted to write was something about my depression and the part fishing was playing in my recovery. I have told you what a help walking in the hills was to me when fishing was an impossibility. Last spring, now that I was fishing again, I felt that, compared with a day in the hills, a day on the river involved an extra layer of emotion and experience. My diary for the year is full of reflections on this matter and some of them may just be worth exploring.

My first visit of last spring came on the second day of the season. I was to meet Andrew and Kelvin for lunch at Spout Dub and I fished up from Watersmeet. I remember that it was a day of light cloud with a downstream breeze not strong enough to be troublesome. I remember that it was quintessentially a day of earliest spring with a sharp edge to the breeze and a full, clear river flowing through still faded fields. It was a cold air but it was tonic and clean; the landscape seemed stripped, seemed bare but at the same time it seemed almost expectant, seemed to share the vitality of the season, a season that, in its own slow upland time, would bring leaves and lambs and growing grass and trout rising to hatching flies. I was, of course, hoping for just a few flies and a few rising trout before lunch.

I remember greeting all the incidental delights of a fishing day: the dippers, the grey wagtails, the curlews in the sky, the light in the water, the budded branches stirring in the breeze. I remember such things but there are stronger memories, of a few spring olives with dark wings in the grey light, of two hooked trout and the thumping excitement of playing them, this and the sense of achievement and peace that flooded over me with the capture of the second, a trout that brought the season's first tears. I think it was then that I realised something that I have already mentioned: that it was because I have always partly defined myself as a fisherman that I found my exile from fishing so painful; that in going fishing again and catching trout I was in fact reclaiming a part of myself, which was why the river Wharfe and its trout were more important to me than the Howgill Fells, for all their spare and lonely loveliness and for all the relief they had brought to me when they were one of the few places where I could go without pain. But now that I was well enough, the Wharfe could give me something that I could never find in the hills. I went to the Howgills in search of comfort; I went to the river in search of fulfilment and in search of myself. I remember sprawling in the pale grass above Spout Dub, unconcerned that it was damp, and talking to Andrew and Kelvin with a feeling of perfect health and contentment. And this was the day when Spout Dub ousted Knipe Dub, together with everywhere else on the Wharfe, as my favourite place in the whole world, because I recognised it as the place where the healing power of the river was distilled to an unequalled potency. And it was recognised as such because, sitting there and talking to my friends, I suddenly felt very close to the fisher of more than forty years ago , to the student who had come there in a hatch of blue wings and caught his first ever bagful of trout. Sitting there by Spout Dub on that cold spring morning I suddenly felt whole again. I think I knew that this feeling would not last; I also knew that it would be waiting for me to experience all over again when next I came to Spout Dub.

Three days later I fished at Yockenthwaite. My diary tells me that, when I woke up, I knew at once that I should have to ring the doctor or head for the hills or drive over to the Wharfe. Thank God I chose the Wharfe, which confirms that by last spring I was beginning to think of fishing, not just as something that I could enjoy again, but as something therapeutic, something more powerful in its effect on me than visits to the doctor or long walks in the hills. I had recognised that fishing was good for me, that the Howgills were like a sedative or an analgesic, whereas the Wharfe offered the possibility of a cure. Anyway, I went to Yockenthwaite and I can remember virtually nothing of the morning, not even the capture of a trout that my diary tells me weighed 1lb 2oz and ate Simple Simon. The morning is lost to me but, even without my diary I could recapture the events and the emotions of the afternoon.

I drove upstream above Deepdale to fish the beginnings of the Wharfe. I remember soft light beneath cloud and a gentle upstream breeze that had lost the sharp edge of a few days earlier. I remember a full water now on the fall and I know that I was fishing it with two fancy wet flies, with Simple Simon and a hackle Coachman. I cast them to all the places that experience had taught me were likely to hold trout and they all drew blank and I told myself that it was early in the season and that one trout was enough. I knew this was a lie. And then I came to a big rock pool; the river flows into it through a narrow limestone channel, with a run of fast and broken water down one bank and, to an upstream fisher's right, a sort of half-bowl of much calmer water, deep and brown from the peat. There were no trout rising and I searched for them along the edge of the turbulence and all at once the line was tight and I knew immediately that he was big enough to kill. He weighed just an ounce short of the pound and he brought a sudden sense of communion with the river and its landscape that I find almost impossible to articulate, a sense of intimacy as between two old friends so comfortable in each other's company that they have no need of words. Perhaps the most remarkable aspect of this feeling was its combination of quietness and intensity. All anxiety, all fear had lifted; a very gentle happiness somehow possessed me as I felt the presence of the hills and the steep pastures around me, conscious above all things of the river's proximity, of the river's beauty and her transforming gift of two trout. And then, five minutes later, I caught a third fish, almost exactly the same size, and I felt, if possible, even happier than I had felt five minutes before.

I think it was at this time that my fishing days began to extend their influence beyond themselves, bringing remembered light to dark and fearful days, making them little by little less dark and slowly less full of fear. There were lots of fishing days and now, unlike the previous season, they were always on the Wharfe and as often as possible on either side of Spout Dub. It was now too that lunchtime wine turned firstly into a regular feature and soon into an essential element of days on the Wharfe. Previously riverside booze had been an occasional indulgence almost always restricted to fishing days in the company of friends. And then I found that, if I woke up and wanted to go fishing but felt that I was too anxious or too tired or too fearful, I could manage to get myself to the river with the promise of two lunchtime glasses on my shelf above Spout Dub. It worked. Half my fishing days last year would probably never have happened if my wine-filled vinegar bottle had not gone with me to the Wharfe.

I got used to feeling ill on waking and telling myself that I should feel much better once I had got over to Kilnsey and fished for a couple of hours; and then, as long as the brace was already in my bag, there would come the bliss of those two glasses (they were beakers really) on the grassy shelf above Spout Dub. Almost always the brace was made and I came to associate that half hour of rest and the wine that belonged to it with a feeling of perfect health and peace. Often there were tears and I think they were always grateful. This, anyway, is how the wine became an institution and I am glad that it is so. I do not know how many fishing days remain to me but I do know that I shall never go to the Wharfe again without my small vinegar bottle filled with wine. Piety demands that the gift of the brace should be properly acknowledged. And I need comfort if the morning has passed without bringing me two trout.

And so last season passed with fishing firmly re-established as a central part of my life from which I drew something like healing. When this season opened I was on the Wharfe within two days and came home blank. A week later I killed three trout, the best well over two pounds, and wept for the joy of it. And then the season ran its course and you have been with me through at least half of it. Fishing has never meant more to me; perhaps it means too much. Perhaps it is wrong of me to have turned a pastime into a vocation, but it has given me a way back to peace and to happiness. It has helped me to reach an accommodation with fear and with mortality; for I can live with both of them, I can look at them with open eyes as I sit by Spout Dub with a brace of trout in my bag and a beaker of wine somewhere near my lips.

And I think at last that I have said enough.

Also published by Merlin Unwin Books

Once a Flyfisher Laurence Catlow £17.99

That Strange Alchemy – Pheasants, Trout and a Middle-aged Man
Laurence Catlow £17.99

Nymphing – the new way Jonathan White £20

Megan Boyd – The Story of a Flydressser
Derek Mills & Jimmy Younger £20

GT – a flyfisher's guide to Giant Trevally
Peter McLeod £30

Flycasting Skills John Symonds £9.99

Trout from a Boat Dennis Moss   £16

Pocket Guide to Matching the Hatch
Peter Lapsley and Cyril Bennett £7.99

Pocket Guide to Fishing Knots
Step-by-Step Coarse, Sea and Game Knots
Peter Owen £5.99

Beginner's Guide to Flytying
Chris Mann and Terry Griffiths £9.99

Complete Illustrated Directory of Salmon Flies
Chris Mann   £20

Trout in Dirty Places Theo Pike   £20

The Fisherman's Bedside Book BB   £18.95

Canal Fishing Dominic Garnett £20

Flyfishing for Coarse Fish Dominic Garnett   £20

Fishing with Harry Tony Baws £15.99

Fishing with Emma (how to coarse fish) David Overland   £9.99

Flies of Ireland Peter O'Reilly £20

full details: www.merlinuwnin.co.uk